HOW PSYCHOLOGY WORKS

HOW PSYCHOLOGY WORKS

THE FACTS visually explained

Consultant editor Jo Hemmings

Senior editor	Kathryn Hennessy
Senior art editor	Gadi Farfour
Editors	Anna Chiefetz, Jemima Dunne, Anna Fischel, Joanna Micklem, Victoria Pyke, Zoë Rutland
US Editors	Megan Douglass, Cheri Clark
Designers	Phil Gamble, Vanessa Hamilton, Renata Latipova
Managing editor	Gareth Jones
Senior managing art editor	Lee Griffiths
Publisher	Liz Wheeler
Publishing director	Jonathan Metcalf
Art director	Karen Self
Senior jacket designer	Mark Cavanagh
Jacket editor	Clare Gell
Jacket design development manager	Sophia MTT
Pre-production producer	Gillian Reid
Senior producer	Mandy Inness

First American Edition, 2018
Published in the United States by DK Publishing
1450 Broadway, Suite 801, New York, NY 10018

A catalog record for this book is
available from the Library of Congress.
ISBN 978-1-4654-6861-1

DK books are available at special discounts when
purchased in bulk for sales promotions, premiums,
fund-raising, or educational use. For details, contact:
DK Publishing Special Markets,
1450 Broadway, Suite 801, New York, NY 10018
SpecialSales@dk.com

Printed and bound in China

For the curious
www.dk.com

CONTENTS

Foreword 8

WHAT IS PSYCHOLOGY?

The development of
psychology 12
Psychoanalytical theory 14
Behaviorist approach 16
Humanism 18
Cognitive psychology 20
Biological psychology 22
How the brain works 24
How memory works 30
How emotions work 32

PSYCHOLOGICAL DISORDERS

Diagnosing disorders 36
Depression 38
Bipolar disorder 40
Perinatal mental illness 42
DMDD (disruptive mood
dysregulation disorder) 44
SAD (seasonal affective
disorder) 45
Panic disorder 46
Specific phobias 48
Agoraphobia 50
Claustrophobia 51
GAD (generalized anxiety
disorder) 52
Social anxiety disorder 53
Separation anxiety disorder 54
Selective mutism 55
OCD (obsessive compulsive
disorder) 56
Hoarding disorder 58
BDD (body dysmorphic
disorder) 59
Skin-picking and hair-pulling
disorders 60
Illness anxiety disorder 61
PTSD (post-traumatic stress
disorder) 62
ASR (acute stress reaction) 63
Adjustment disorder 64
Reactive attachment
disorder 65
ADHD (attention deficit
hyperactivity disorder) 66
ASD (autism spectrum
disorder) 68

Schizophrenia 70
Schizoaffective disorder 72
Catatonia 73
Delusional disorder 74
Dementia 76
CTE (chronic traumatic
encephalopathy) 78
Delirium (acute confusional
state) 79
Substance use disorder 80
Impulse-control and addiction 82
Gambling disorder 83
Kleptomania 84
Pyromania 85
DID (dissociative identity
disorder) 86
Depersonalization and
derealization 88
Dissociative amnesia 89
Anorexia nervosa 90
Bulimia nervosa 92
Binge-eating disorder 94
Pica 95
Communication disorders 96
Sleep disorders 98
Tic disorders 100
PD (personality disorders) 102
Other disorders 108

HEALING THERAPIES

Health and therapy 112
Physical and psychological
  health 114
The role of therapy 116

Psychodynamic therapies 118
Psychoanalysis 119
Jungian therapy 120
Self psychology and object
  relations 121
Transactional analysis 121

**Cognitive and behavioral
therapies** 122
Behavioral therapy 124
Cognitive therapy 124
CBT (cognitive behavioral
  therapy) 125
Third wave CBT 126
CPT (cognitive processing
  therapy) 127
REBT (rational emotive
  behavior therapy) 127
Methods used in CBTs 128
Mindfulness 129

Humanistic therapies 130
Person-centered therapy 132
Reality therapy 132
Existential therapy 133
Gestalt therapy 133
Emotion-focused therapy 134
Solution-focused brief therapy 134
Somatic therapies 135
EMDR (eye movement
  desensitization and
  reprocessing) 136
Hypnotherapy 136
Arts-based therapies 137
Animal-assisted therapy 137

Systemic therapies 138
Family systems therapy 139
Strategic family therapy 140
Dyadic developmental therapy 141
Contextual therapy 141

Biotherapies 142

PSYCHOLOGY IN THE REAL WORLD

Psychology of self-identity 146
Identity formation 148
Personality 150
Self-actualization 152

**The psychology of
relationships** 154
Psychology and attachment 156
The science of love 158
How dating works 160
Psychology and the stages
  of relationships 162

Psychology in education 166
Educational theories 168
The psychology of teaching 172
Assessing problems 174

Psychology in the workplace 176
Selecting the best candidate 178
Managing talent 180
Team development 182
Leadership 184
Organizational culture and
  change 186

HFE psychology	**188**	Changing consumer behavior	**228**
Engineering displays	**190**	Consumer neuroscience	**230**
Human error and prevention	**192**	The power of branding	**232**
		The power of celebrity	**234**
Forensic psychology	**194**		
Psychology and criminal		**The psychology of sports**	**236**
investigations	**196**	Improving skills	**238**
Psychology in the courtroom	**200**	Keeping motivated	**240**
Psychology in prisons	**202**	Getting in the zone	**242**
		Performance anxiety	**244**
Psychology in politics	**204**		
Voting behavior	**206**	**Psychometric tests**	**246**
Obedience and			
decision-making	**208**	**Index**	**248**
Nationalism	**210**		
		Acknowledgments	
Psychology in the		**and picture credits**	**256**
community	**214**		
How community works	**216**		
Empowerment	**218**		
Urban communities	**220**		
Safety in the community	**222**		
Consumer psychology	**224**		
Understanding consumer			
behavior	**226**		

CONTRIBUTORS

Jo Hemmings (consultant editor)
is a behavioral psychologist who
studied at the Universities of
Warwick and London. She has
authored several successful books
on relationships, writes regularly for
national newspapers and magazines,
is a regular on TV and radio, and
runs a counseling practice in
London. She is also the consultant
psychologist on ITV's *Good Morning
Britain* in the UK.

Merrin Lazyan (US consultant)
is a radio producer, writer, editor,
and classical singer who studied
psychology at Harvard University.
She has worked on several fiction
and nonfiction books, spanning a
broad range of topics.

Catherine Collin is a clinical
psychologist and Director of
Outlook SW Ltd (IAPT) and an
Associate Professor (Clinical
Psychology) at Plymouth University.
Catherine's interests lie in primary
care mental health and the cognitive
behavioral therapies.

Joannah Ginsburg Ganz is
a clinical psychotherapist and
journalist who has worked in private
and public settings for the past 25
years. She also regularly contributes
to psychology publications.

Alexandra Black is a freelance
author who writes on a range of
subjects, from history to business.
Her writing career initially took her
to Japan, and she later worked for a
publisher in Australia before moving
to Cambridge, UK.

Foreword

Lying at the intersection of a number of disciplines, including biology, philosophy, sociology, medicine, anthropology, and artificial intelligence, psychology has always fascinated people. How do psychologists interpret human behavior to understand why we do what we do? Why are there so many branches and approaches, and how do they work in a practical sense in our day-to-day lives? Is psychology an art or a science, or a fusion of both?

While theories come and go out of fashion—and new studies, experiments, and research are conducted all the time—the essence of psychology is to explain the behavior of individuals based on the workings of the mind. In these often turbulent and uncertain times, people are increasingly looking to psychology and psychologists to help them make sense of why the powerful and influential behave the way that they do, and the resulting impact that might have on us. But psychology also has huge relevance to those much closer to us than politicians, celebrities, or business magnates—it tells us a great deal about our own families, friends, partners, and work colleagues. It also resonates a great deal in understanding our own minds, leading to a greater self-awareness of our own thoughts and behaviors.

As well as offering us a basic understanding of all the various theories, disorders, and therapies that form part of this ever-changing field of study, psychology plays a huge role in our everyday lives. Whether it is in education, the workplace, sports, or our personal and intimate relationships—and even the way that we spend our money or how we vote—there is a branch of psychology that impacts every single one of us in our daily lives on a constant and continued basis.

How Psychology Works considers all aspects of psychology—from theories to therapies, personal issues to practical applications, all presented in an accessible, stylish, and beautifully simple way. I wish it had been around when I was a psychology student!

Jo Hemmings, consultant editor

WHAT IS PSYCHOLOGY?

There are many different approaches to psychology—
the scientific study of the human mind and how
individuals behave. All seek the key to unlock
people's thoughts, memories, and emotions.

The development of psychology

Most advances in psychology are recent, dating back about 150 years, but its origins lie with the philosophers of ancient Greece and Persia. Many approaches and fields of study have been developed that give psychologists a toolkit to apply to the real world. As society has changed, new applications have also arisen to meet people's needs.

c.1550 BCE The Ebers Papyrus (Egyptian medical papyrus) mentions depression

ANCIENT GREEK PHILOSOPHERS

470–370 BCE Democritus makes a distinction between the intellect and knowledge gained through the senses; Hippocrates introduces the principle of scientific medicine

387 BCE Plato suggests that the brain is the seat of mental processes

350 BCE Aristotle writes on the soul in *De Anima*, and he introduces the tabula rasa (blank slate) concept of the mind

c.300–30 BCE Zeno teaches stoicism, the inspiration for CBT (cognitive behavioral therapy) in the 1960s

705 CE The first hospital for the mentally ill is built in Baghdad (followed by hospitals in Cairo in 800 and Damascus in 1270)

SCHOLARS OF THE EARLY MUSLIM WORLD

c.900 Ahmed ibn Sahl al-Balkhi writes of mental illness, with physical and/or psychological causes; Rhazes practices the first recorded psychotherapy

850 Ali ibn Sahl Rabban al Tabari develops the idea of clinical psychiatry to treat mental patients

1025 Avicenna's *Canon of Medicine* describes many conditions, including hallucinations, mania, insomnia, and dementia

1808 Franz Gall writes about phrenology (the idea that a person's skull shape and placement of bumps on the head can reveal personality traits)

1698 John Locke describes the human mind as a tabula rasa (blank slate) at birth in *An Essay Concerning Human Understanding*

1629–1633 René Descartes outlines his dualistic theory of mind versus matter (pp.24–25) in *Treatise of the World*

1620s Francis Bacon writes on psychological topics, including the nature of knowledge and memory

1590 Rudolph Goclenius first coins the term "psychology"

EUROPEAN PHILOSOPHERS

PSYCHOLOGY AS A FORMAL DISCIPLINE

1879 Wilhelm Wundt founds a laboratory in Leipzig, Germany, dedicated to psychological research, marking the start of formal experimental psychology

mid-1880s Wundt trains Hugo Münsterberg and James McKeen Cattell, who sow the seeds of I/O (industrial/organizational) psychology (pp.176–187)

1890–1920 Methods of teaching in schools are changed with the advent of educational psychology (pp.166–175)

1896 Clinical psychology begins with the first psychological clinic at the University of Pennsylvania

1920s Dr. Carl Diem founds a sports psychology (pp.236–245) laboratory in Berlin

1920s onward The use of psychometric tests to measure intelligence starts individual-differences psychology (pp.146–153)

1920 Jean Piaget publishes *The Child's Conception of the World*, prompting the study of cognition in children

1916 Lewis Terman applies psychology to law enforcement, heralding the beginnings of forensic psychology (pp.194–203)

1913 John B. Watson publishes *Psychology as the Behaviorist Views It*, outlining the principles of behaviorism (pp.16–17)

  BEHAVIORAL

1913 Carl Jung breaks away from his colleague Freud and develops his own theories (p.120) of the unconscious mind

1909 onward Developmental psychology (pp.146–153) emerges prompted by Freud's emphasis on the importance of childhood experiences

1900 Sigmund Freud introduces his theory of psychoanalysis in *The Interpretation of Dreams* (pp.14–15)

  PSYCHOANALYTICAL

1920s Behavioral psychologist John B. Watson begins working in the advertising industry and develops the discipline of consumer psychology (pp.224–235)

Early 1930s Social psychologist Marie Jahoda publishes the first study of community psychology (pp.214–223)

  BIOLOGICAL

1935 Kurt Koffka publishes *Principles of Gestalt Psychology* (p.18 and p.133)

1935 onward Biological psychology (pp.22–23) emerges as a discipline

1938 ECT (electroconvulsive therapy) (pp.142–143) is used for the first time

1939 HFE psychology (pp.188–193) develops in World War II to help operators make and use complex machines and weaponry with accuracy

 **NEUROPSYCHOLOGY**

1950s The first psychoactive drugs are developed; psychopharmacology begins as a treatment for mental illness (pp.142–143)

1950s In his studies of epilepsy, neuroscientist Wilder G. Penfield links chemical activity in the brain with psychological phenomena (pp.22–23)

1952 The first *Diagnostic and Statistical Manual of Mental Disorders* is published

2000 The World Congress of Psychology takes place in Stockholm. Diplomat Jan Eliasson discusses how psychology can help conflict resolution

1990 Jerome Bruner publishes *Acts of Meaning: Four Lectures on Mind and Culture*, drawing on philosophy, linguistics, and anthropology (cultural psychology, pp.214–215)

1976 Richard Dawkins publishes *The Selfish Gene*, popularizing evolutionary psychology (p.22)

2000 Sequencing of the human genome opens up a new area of research into the human mind and body

1980s Health psychology (pp.112–115) becomes a recognized branch of the profession

1965 The Swampscott Conference of Education of Psychologists in Community Mental Health takes place

1960s Interest in community psychology (pp.214–223) surges due to political unrest

1956 George A. Miller applies cognitive psychology (pp.20–21) in *The Magical Number Seven, Plus or Minus Two*

1971 A CT (computed tomography) scan makes the first image of a living brain

Early 1960s Systemic (family) therapy (pp.138–141) emerges as a field of study

1960s Aaron T. Beck pioneers the practice of CBT (p.125)

  COGNITIVE

1954 Abraham Maslow publishes *Motivation and Personality*, hailing humanism (pp.18–19) as a third force in psychology

  HUMANISTIC

1954 Gordon Allport identifies the stages of social prejudice, an aspect of political psychology (pp.204–213)

Psychoanalytical theory

This psychological theory proposes that the unconscious struggles of the mind determine how personality develops and dictates behavior.

What is it?

Founded by Austrian neurologist Sigmund Freud in the early 20th century, psychoanalytical theory proposed that personality and behavior are the outcome of continual conflicts in the mind. The individual is not usually aware of the discord because it takes place at a subconscious level. Freud suggested conflict occurs between three parts of the mind: the id, superego, and ego (below, right).

Freud believed that personality develops from birth in five stages, which he called psychosexual because they involve both sexuality and mental processes. At each stage a person's mind focuses on a different aspect of sexuality, such as oral pleasure when they suck their thumb as a baby. Freud believed that the psychosexual stages trigger a battle between

Topographical model

Freud divided the mind into three levels of consciousness. The conscious mind forms only a small part of the whole. Although it is completely unaware of the thoughts in the unconscious mind, the latter still affect behavior.

Dreams

Dreams are seen as a channel for unconscious thoughts that people cannot usually access because many of them are too disturbing for the conscious mind to cope with.

Conscious mind

This contains the ideas and emotions that people are aware of.

Preconscious mind

This stores information such as childhood memories, which can be accessed through psychoanalysis.

Psychoanalysis

In this therapy (p.119), the client tells the analyst about their childhood memories and dreams in order to unlock the unconscious mind and reveal how it is controlling or triggering undesirable behavior.

Unconscious mind

This hides most of a person's impulses, desires, and thoughts.

biology and social expectations, and the mind must resolve this conflict before a person can move on to healthy mental development.

Evaluation

Although Freud's model has been hugely influential in highlighting the role of the subconscious (psychoanalysis, p.119), it has proved controversial because it focuses on sexuality as the driver of personality. Many critics view his model as too subjective and too simplistic to explain the complex nature of the mind and behavior.

DEFENSE MECHANISM

What is it?	*What happens?*	*How does it work?*
Freud argued that people subconsciously employ defense mechanisms when faced with anxiety or unpleasant emotions. These mechanisms help them to cope with memories or impulses that they find stressful or distasteful by tricking them into thinking that everything is fine.	The ego uses defense mechanisms to help people reach a mental compromise when dealing with things that cause internal conflict. Common mechanisms that distort a sense of reality include denial, displacement, repression, regression, intellectualization, and projection.	Denial is a common defense mechanism used to justify a habit an individual feels bad about, such as smoking. By saying that they are only a "social smoker," they can allow themselves to have a cigarette while not admitting that they are in fact addicted to smoking.

Structural model

The conscious mind is just the tip of the iceberg, a small part of a hidden whole. Psychoanalytical theory is based on the concept that the unconscious mind is structured in three parts—the id, ego, and superego—which "talk" to one another to try to resolve conflicting emotions and impulses.

Conscious

Superego
This wants to do the right thing. It is the moral conscience that takes on the role of a strict parent.

Ego
This is the voice of reason, negotiating with the id and the superego.

Id
This strives for instant gratification, is childlike, impulsive, and hard to reason with.

Unconscious

✓ NEED TO KNOW

> **Inferiority complex** When self-esteem is so low that a person cannot function normally. The idea was developed by neo-Freudian Alfred Adler.

> **Pleasure principle** What drives the id—the desire to obtain pleasure and avoid pain.

> **Neo-Freudians** Theorists who built on Freud's psychoanalytic theories, such as Carl Jung, Erik Erikson, and Alfred Adler.

Behaviorist approach

Behavioral psychology analyzes and treats people on the basis that their behavior is learned by interacting with the world and that the influence of the subconscious is irrelevant.

What is it?

The starting point for behavioral psychology is a focus on only observable human behavior, leaving out thought and emotion. This approach rests on three main assumptions. First, people learn their behavior from the world around them, and not from innate or inherited factors. Second, because psychology is a science, measurable data from controlled experiments and observation should support its theories. Third, all behavior is the result of a stimulus that triggers a particular response. Once the behavioral psychologist has identified a person's stimulus-response association, they can predict it, a method known as classical conditioning (below). In therapy (pp.122–129), the therapist uses this prediction to help the client change their behavior.

Evaluation

The strength of the behaviorist approach—that it can be scientifically proven, unlike Freud's psychoanalytic approach (pp.14–15), for example—has also been seen as its weakness. Many of the behavioral experiments were carried out on rats and dogs, and humanists (pp.18–19) in particular rejected the assumption that people in the world acted in the same way as animals in laboratory conditions.

Behavioral psychology also takes little account of free will or biological factors such as testosterone and other hormones, reducing human experience to a set of conditioned behaviors.

Themes of behaviorism

John Watson developed behavioral psychology in 1913. His theory agreed with the early 20th-century trend toward data-backed science rather than concentrating on the subjective workings of the mind, and the behaviorist approach was influential for decades. Later psychologists interpreted behavioral theory along more flexible lines, but objective evidence remains a cornerstone of research.

CLASSICAL CONDITIONING

Pavlov noted that his dogs salivated at the sight of food and started ringing a bell at the same time as feeding them. Soon, the dogs salivated merely at the sound of the bell, which they now associated with food.

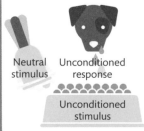

| Neutral stimulus | Unconditioned response | Conditioned stimulus | Conditioned response |

Unconditioned stimulus

METHODOLOGICAL BEHAVIORISM

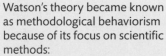

EXTERNAL

Watson's theory became known as methodological behaviorism because of its focus on scientific methods:

❭ He viewed psychology as a science, its goals being the prediction and control of behavior.

❭ It is the most extreme theory of behaviorism because it rules out any influence from a person's DNA or internal mental state.

❭ It assumes that when people are born their minds are a blank slate and they learn all their behavior from the people and things around them (classical conditioning, left). For example, a baby smiles back when their mother smiles, or cries if their mother raises her voice.

OPERANT CONDITIONING

This method for inducing behavior change, in this case training a dog, involves positive or negative actions on the part of the owner to reinforce or punish the dog's behavior.

❯ **Positive reinforcement** Giving a reward encourages good behavior. For example, the dog receives a treat for sitting on command. It quickly learns that repeating that behavior will earn it another treat.

❯ **Positive punishment** The owner does something unpleasant to discourage bad behavior. When the dog pulls ahead on the lead, its collar feels uncomfortably tight around its throat.

❯ **Negative reinforcement** The owner removes something bad to encourage good behavior. The lead goes slack when the dog walks close to its owner. The dog learns to walk to heel without pulling and so avoid the choking sensation.

❯ **Negative punishment** Taking away something that the dog enjoys is used to discourage undesired behaviors. For example, the owner turns their back on the dog to deprive it of attention if it jumps up. The dog learns not to jump up.

RADICAL BEHAVIORISM

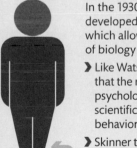

EXTERNAL   **BIOLOGY**

In the 1930s B. F. Skinner developed radical behaviorism, which allowed for the influence of biology on behavior:

❯ Like Watson, Skinner believed that the most valid approach to psychology was one based on scientifically observing human behavior and its triggers.

❯ Skinner took classical conditioning a step forward with the idea of reinforcement— behavior that is reinforced by a reward is more likely to be repeated (operant conditioning, above).

PSYCHOLOGICAL BEHAVIORISM

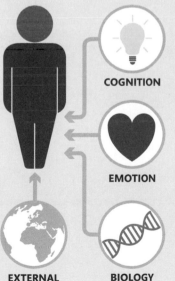

COGNITION

EMOTION

EXTERNAL   **BIOLOGY**

Conceived by Arthur W. Staats, psychological behaviorism gained dominance over four decades. It informs current practice in psychology, especially in education:

❯ A person's personality is shaped by learned behaviors, genetics, their emotional state, how their brain processes information, and the world around them.

❯ Staats researched the importance of parenting in child development.

❯ He showed that early linguistic and cognitive training resulted in advanced language development and higher performance in intelligence tests when children were older.

Humanism

Unlike other psychological approaches, humanism places central importance on the individual's viewpoint, encouraging the question "How do I see myself?" rather than "How do others see me?"

What is it?

Whereas behavioral psychology is concerned with observing external actions and psychoanalysis delves into the subconscious, humanism is holistic, focusing on how a person perceives their own behavior and interprets events. It centers on a person's subjective view of themselves and who they would like to be, rather than the objective view of an observer.

Pioneered by Carl Rogers and Abraham Maslow in the 1950s, humanism offers an alternative way of trying to fathom human nature. It assumes that personal growth and fulfillment are primary goals in life, and that emotional and mental well-being comes from achieving this. The principle of free will, exercised in the choices a person makes, is also key.

"The good life is a process, not a state of being."

Carl Rogers, American humanist psychologist

Evaluation

Rogers and other humanist psychologists suggested a number of new methods of investigation, such as open-ended questionnaires in which there were no "right" answers, casual interviews, and the use of diaries to record feelings and thoughts. They reasoned that the only way to really get to know someone was to talk to them.

Humanism is the theory that underpins person-centered therapy (p.132)—one of the most common therapies for depression. The humanistic approach is also used in education to encourage children to exercise free will and make choices for themselves, and in researching and understanding motivation.

However, humanism ignores other aspects of the individual such as their biology, the subconscious mind, and the powerful influence of hormones. Critics also say that the approach is unscientific, because its goal of self-realization cannot be accurately measured.

GESTALT PSYCHOLOGY

Influenced by humanism, gestalt psychology examines in detail how the mind takes small pieces of information and builds them into a meaningful whole. It emphasizes the importance of perception—the laws that govern how each person perceives the world.

Part of gestalt assessment involves showing clients a series of images to discover how their eye perceives each one. The Rubin Vase illusion is the best known of these, and illustrates the law of "figure" and "ground": a person's mind always works to distinguish a figure (words, for example) from its background (a white page), and in doing so, makes a decision about priority and what to focus on.

THE RUBIN VASE ILLUSION offers the viewer a perceptual choice between seeing two faces in profile and seeing a white vase.

Road to fulfillment

Carl Rogers identified three parts to personality that determine a person's psychological state: self-worth, self-image, and the ideal self. When a person's feelings, behavior, and experience match their self-image and reflect who they would like to be (ideal self), they are content. But if there is a mismatch (incongruence) between these aspects, they are dissatisfied.

INDIVIDUAL OR GROUP?

Humanism is rooted in Western ideas of personal identity and achievement, sometimes called individualism. In contrast, collectivism subordinates the person to the group.

Individualism

❯ Identity defined in terms of personal attributes—such as outgoing, kind, or generous

❯ Own goals take priority over those of the group

Collectivism

❯ Identity defined by which group someone belongs to

❯ Family, then workplace, are most important groups

❯ Goals of group take priority over individual's

SELF-ACTUALIZATION

SELF-ACTUALIZATION

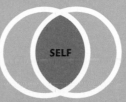

SELF

When a person's perception of who they are aligns with who they want to be, they achieve self-actualization. This satisfies their need to reach and express their full potential.

INCREASINGLY CONGRUENT

SELF-IMAGE | IDEAL SELF

With more common ground between self-image and ideal self, a person has greater self-worth and adopts a more positive frame of mind.

INCONGRUENT

SELF-IMAGE | IDEAL SELF

If there is little overlap between how a person sees themselves (self-image) and what they would like to be (ideal self), they feel unhappy, with low self-worth.

Cognitive psychology

A branch of psychology that considers the mind to be like a complex computer, the cognitive approach analyzes the way people process information and how that dictates their behavior and emotions.

What is it?

When the computer arrived in offices in the late 1950s, it sparked comparisons between artificial information processing and the operation of the human mind. Psychologists reasoned that in the same way that a computer accepts data, codes it for storage, and retrieves it, the human mind takes in information, changes it to make sense of it, stores it, and recalls it when needed. This computer analogy came to be the foundation for cognitive psychology.

The theories behind cognitive psychology can apply to virtually every aspect of daily life. Examples include the brain receiving and processing sensory information to make a judgment (such as recognizing that a carton of milk has soured from its bad smell); reasoning with logic to reach a decision (such as whether to buy an expensive shirt that may last longer than a cheap one); or learning how to play a musical instrument, which requires the brain to make new connections and store new memories.

Evaluation

Although cognitive psychology emphasizes internal processes, it aims to be strictly scientific, relying on laboratory experiments to back up any theory. What happens in controlled experiments, however, can be difficult to apply to real-life scenarios. Similarly, the assumption that the human mind functions like

PROCESSING (mediational mental event)

After receiving information via the senses, the brain must sort through it to analyze it and decide what to do with it. Cognitive psychologists call this process mediational because it happens between ("mediates") the environmental stimulus and the brain's eventual response to that stimulus. In the case of a car breakdown, the brain might analyze the smell of burning rubber, and connect it with an earlier memory of a similar smell.

Information processing

Using evidence from controlled experiments, psychologists have built theoretical models of how the mind deals with information. According to these models, the human brain handles information in the same sequence a computer uses to handle data—from input, through transformation of the data, to retrieval.

INPUT (from environment)

A person's sense organs detect stimuli from the external world and send messages to the brain as electrical impulses containing information. For example, if a person's car breaks down, their brain focuses on warning signs, such as unexpected sounds from the engine, visual cues like smoke, or the smell of burning rubber.

a computer does not take into account realities such as people getting tired and emotional, and critics claim it treats humans as machines, reducing all behavior to a cognitive process such as committing things to memory. Critics have also pointed out that this approach ignores the roles of biology and genetics.

However, cognitive psychology has proved useful for treating memory loss and selective attention disorders. It is also valuable in understanding child development, allowing educators to plan appropriate content for each age group, and to decide the best tools for delivering it. In the legal system, cognitive psychologists are regularly called on to assess eyewitness reports in order to determine whether a witness has accurately recalled a crime.

OUTPUT
(behavior and emotion)
When the brain has retrieved enough information, it can make a decision about what response to make, in the form of either a behavioral or an emotional reaction. In the example of the car, the brain recalls memories of previous breakdowns, together with any relevant mechanical information stored, and then runs through a mental checklist of possible causes and solutions. It remembers that the smell of burning rubber previously indicated a broken fan belt. The person pulls over, turns off the ignition, and opens the hood to check.

"Disconnected facts in the mind are like unlinked pages on the Web: they might as well not exist."
Steven Pinker, Canadian cognitive psychologist

COGNITIVE BIAS

When the mind makes an error in the course of thought processing, it results in a skewed judgment or reaction, known as a cognitive bias. This may be related to memory (poor recall, for example) or lack of attention, usually because the brain is making a mental shortcut under pressure. Biases are not always bad—some are the natural outcome of having to make a quick decision for survival purposes.

Examples of bias

> **Anchoring** Placing too much importance on the first piece of information heard.

> **Base-rate fallacy** Abandoning original assumptions in favor of a new piece of information.

> **Bandwagon effect** Overriding own beliefs in order to go along with what other people are thinking or doing.

> **Gamblers' fallacy** Mistakenly believing that if something is happening more often now, it will happen less often in the future—for example, if the roulette wheel consistently falls on black, thinking it is bound to fall on red before long.

> **Hyperbolic discounting** Choosing a smaller reward now, rather than patiently waiting for a larger reward.

> **Neglect of probability** Disregarding true probability, for example, avoiding air travel for fear of a plane crash, but fearlessly driving a car even though it is statistically far more dangerous.

> **Status quo bias** Making choices to keep a situation the same or alter it as little as possible, rather than risking change.

Biological psychology

Based on the premise that physical factors, such as genes, determine behavior, this approach can explain how twins brought up separately exhibit parallel behavior.

What is it?

Biological psychology assumes that people's thoughts, feelings, and behavior all derive from their biology, which includes genetics as well as the chemical and electrical impulses that wire the brain to the nervous system. This assumption implies that the blueprint laid down in the womb—people's physiological structure and DNA—dictates their personality and behavior as they go through life.

Some of these ideas are based on the results of twin studies, which have shown that twins separated at birth and brought up in different households display remarkably similar behavior in adult life. Biopsychologists argue that this phenomenon can be explained only if the twins' genetics influence them so strongly that not even the role of their parents, friends, life experiences, or environment have much impact.

An example of biological psychology in action is the research into how teenagers behave. Scans of teenage brains using imaging technology have revealed that adolescent brains process information in a different way than adult brains. These differences help to offer a biological explanation for why teenagers can be impulsive, sometimes lack good judgment, and can become overly anxious in social situations.

Evaluation

Many of the ideas in biological psychology emphasize nature over nurture. As a result, critics consider the approach to be oversimplistic, giving undue weight to the influence of biology and built-in physical attributes. Little credit is given to the influence of events or people on an individual as they grow up. On the other hand, few argue with the rigorous scientific backbone of the approach, which places importance on the systematic testing and validation of ideas. And biopsychologists have enabled important medical advances—using research from neurosurgery and brain imaging scans, they have made positive contributions to treatment for patients with both physical and mental problems, including Parkinson's disease, schizophrenia, depression, and drug abuse.

EVOLUTIONARY PSYCHOLOGY

Psychologists in this field explore why people's behavior and personality develop differently. They investigate how individuals adapt their language, memory, consciousness, and other complex biological systems to best cope with the environment they find themselves in. Key ideas include:

> **Natural selection** This has its origins in Charles Darwin's hypothesis that species adapt over time or evolve mechanisms that facilitate survival.

> **Psychological adaptations** This looks at mechanisms people use for language acquisition, for differentiating kin from non-kin, for detecting cheats, and for choosing a mate based on certain sexual or intelligence criteria.

> **Individual differences** This seeks to explain the differences between people—for example, why some people are more materially successful than others.

> **Information processing** This evolutionary view suggests that brain function and behavior have been molded by information taken in from the external environment, and so are the product of repeatedly occurring pressures or situations.

Different approaches

Biopsychologists are interested in how the body and biological processes shape behavior. Some focus on the broad issue of how physiology explains behavior, whereas others concentrate on specific areas such as the medical applications of the theory, or experiments to determine whether an individual's genetics dictate their behavior.

"In the last analysis the entire field of psychology may reduce to biological electrochemistry."

Sigmund Freud, Austrian neurologist

Physiological

This approach is based on the assumption that biology shapes behavior. It seeks to discover where certain types of behavior originate in the brain, how hormones and the nervous system operate, and why changes in these systems can alter behavior.

Medical

This branch explains and treats mental disorders in terms of physical illness. Disorders are considered to have a biological basis, such as a chemical imbalance in the body or damage to the brain, rather than causes linked to environmental factors.

Genetics

This field attempts to explain behavior in terms of patterns that are laid down in each person's DNA. Studies of twins (especially twins separated at birth and raised in different homes) have been used to show that traits such as IQ are inherited.

How the brain works

Studies of the brain have given valuable insight into the vital correlation between brain activity and human behavior, as well as revealing the complex process by which the brain itself is brought to life.

Connecting brain and behavior

Understanding the biology of the brain and how it works became vital with the rise of neuroscience in the 20th century. Studies in this field confirmed that the brain itself is fundamentally intertwined with human behavior, and prompted the emergence of specialist fields, such as neuropsychology. This relatively new branch of science combines cognitive psychology (the study of behavior and mental processes) with brain physiology, and examines how specific psychological processes relate to the brain's physical structure. Investigating the brain in this light raises the age-old question of whether mind and body can be separated.

The relationship between brain and mind has been debated since the time of ancient Greece and Aristotle, when prevailing philosophical thought labeled the two entities as distinct. This theory, which René Descartes reiterated in the 17th century with his concept of dualism (right), permeated studies of the brain until well into the 20th century.

Modern neurological research and advances in technology have enabled scientists to trace certain behaviors to specific areas of the brain, and to study connections between the different regions. This has radically advanced knowledge of the brain and its effect on behavior, mental function, and disease.

Mind controlling brain

Dualism argues that the nonphysical mind and the physical brain exist as separate entities, but are able to interact. It considers that the mind controls the physical brain, but allows that the brain can at times influence the normally rational mind, for example, in a moment of rashness or passion.

SPECIALIZATION OF THE CEREBRAL HEMISPHERES

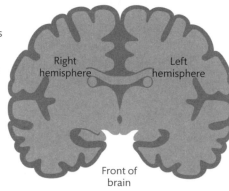

CEREBRAL CORTEX
Nerve fibers cross over at the base of the brain, so each hemisphere controls the opposite side of the body.

Right hemisphere

Left hemisphere

Front of brain

Left hemisphere

❭ This controls and coordinates the right side of the body.

❭ It is the analytical side of the brain.

❭ It is responsible for tasks relating to logic, reasoning, decision-making, and speech and language.

Right hemisphere

❭ This controls muscles on the left side of the body.

❭ It is the creative side of the brain.

❭ It deals with sensory inputs, such as visual and auditory awareness, creative and artistic abilities, and spatial perception.

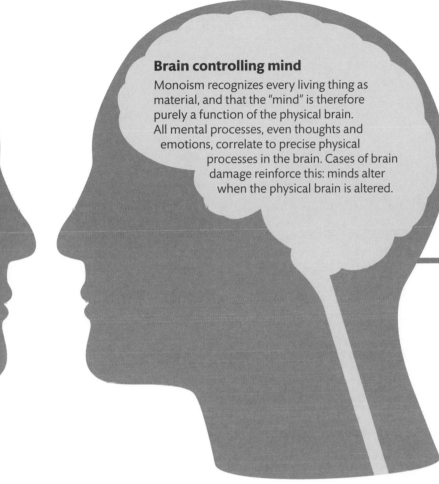

Brain controlling mind

Monoism recognizes every living thing as material, and that the "mind" is therefore purely a function of the physical brain. All mental processes, even thoughts and emotions, correlate to precise physical processes in the brain. Cases of brain damage reinforce this: minds alter when the physical brain is altered.

> "I think, therefore I am."
>
> René Descartes,
> French philosopher

Mind-body dualism

Humans are innately reluctant to reduce consciousness to pure biology. But the scientific evidence shows that the physical firing of neurons generates our thoughts. Two schools of thought, monoism and dualism, dominate the question of whether the mind is part of the body, or the body part of the mind.

Brain studies

Linking a behavior to a specific area of the brain first began with 19th-century studies of people with brain damage, as changes in behavior could be correlated directly to the site of injury. In one case, a worker survived injury to his frontal lobe, and the ensuing changes in his character suggested the formation of personality occurs in that area of the brain. The two linguistic functions of Broca's and Wernicke's areas (p.27) were named after the surgeons who dissected the brains of two patients who had linguistic problems when alive. Each brain showed malformations in a specific area, indicating where spoken language is generated (Broca's area) and understood (Wernicke's area). However, evidence of interconnections between regions suggests certain functions may be linked to more than one area. Roger Sperry's work in the 1960s on the cerebral hemispheres was a landmark in brain research. Studying patients whose hemispheres had been surgically divided, he found each side had specialized cognitive skills (left). He also realized that each hemisphere could be independently conscious.

However, all brain studies have limitations—they show correlations between brain activity and behavior, not absolutes. Surgical procedure on, or damage to, one part of the brain may affect other areas, which could account for observed behavioral changes. Equally, tests on brain-damaged patients offer no experimental control and can only observe behavior occurring after the damage.

Mapping the brain

One of the most complex systems in nature, the human brain controls and regulates all our mental processes and behaviors, both conscious and unconscious. It can be mapped according to its different neurological functions, each of which takes place in a specific area.

The hierarchy of mental processing is loosely reflected in the brain's physical structure: high-level cognitive processes take place in the upper areas, while more basic functions occur lower down. The largest and uppermost region (the cerebral cortex) is responsible for the highest-level cognitive function, including abstract thought and reasoning. It is the capacity of their cerebral cortex that separates humans from other mammals. The central limbic areas (below) control instinctive and emotional behavior, while structures lower in the brain stem maintain vital bodily functions, such as breathing.

Functional divisions

The cerebral cortex (also called the cerebrum) divides into two separate but connected hemispheres, left and right. Each one controls a different aspect of cognition (pp.24–25). Further divisions include four paired lobes (one pair on either hemisphere), each of which is associated with a specific type of brain function.

The frontal lobe is the seat of high-level cognitive processing and motor performance; the temporal lobe is involved in short- and long-term memories; the occipital lobe is associated with visual processes; and the parietal lobe deals with sensory skills.

Brain-imaging techniques, such as fMRI (functional magnetic resonance imaging), measure activity in the different brain areas, yet their value to psychologists can be limited. Those studying fMRI results need to be aware, for example, of the issue of "reverse inference": just because a particular part of the brain is shown to be active during one cognitive process does not mean it is active because of that process. The active area might simply be monitoring a different area, which is in fact in control of the process.

Locating brain function

Psychologists and neurologists can map neurological function when small areas of the brain are stimulated. Using brain-scanning techniques, such as fMRI or CT, they study and record the sensation and movements this stimulation produces.

The limbic system

This complex set of structures is involved in processing emotional responses and the formation of memories.

Hypothalamus

Involved in regulating body temperature and water levels and key behavioral responses.

Olfactory bulb

Relays messages about smell to the central limbic areas for processing.

Amygdala

Processes emotions; affects learning and memory.

Thalamus

Processes and sends data to higher brain areas.

Hippocampus

Converts short-term memories into long-term ones.

FRONTAL LOBE

Broca's area
Area in the left hemisphere; vital to the formation of articulated speech.

PARIETAL LOBE

TEMPORAL LOBE

Wernicke's area
Plays a key role in the comprehension of spoken language

OCCIPITAL LOBE

Cerebellum
Involved in balance and posture; coordinates sensory input with muscle response.

Brain stem
Main control center for key bodily functions, such as swallowing or breathing.

Motor cortex
This is the primary area of the cerebral cortex involved in motor function. It controls voluntary muscle movements, including planning and execution.

Sensory cortex
Information gathered by all five senses is processed and interpreted here. Sensory receptors from around the body send neural signals to this cortex.

Primary visual cortex
Visual stimuli are initially processed in this cortex, enabling recognition of color, movement, and shape. It sends signals on to other visual cortices to be processed further.

Dorsolateral prefrontal cortex
This area is linked to various high-level mental processes, including "executive functions"— the processes involved in self-regulation or mental control.

OFC (orbital frontal cortex)
Part of the prefrontal cortex, the OFC connects with the sensory and limbic areas; it plays a role in the emotional and reward aspect of decision-making.

Supplementary motor cortex
One of the secondary motor cortices, this area is involved in planning and coordinating any complex movements. It sends information to the primary motor cortex.

Tempo-parietal junction
Located between the temporal and parietal lobes, this area processes signals from limbic and sensory areas, and has been linked with the comprehension of "self."

Lighting up the brain

The human brain contains around 86 billion specialized nerve cells (neurons) that "fire" chemical and electrical impulses to allow communication between them and the rest of the body. Neurons are the core building blocks of the brain, and connect to form complex pathways through the brain and central nervous system.

Neurons separate at a narrow junction called a synapse. In order to pass a signal on, the neuron must first release biochemical substances, known as neurotransmitters, which fill the synapse and activate the neighboring cell. The impulse can then flow across the synapse in a process known as synaptic transmission. In this way the brain sends messages to the body to activate the muscles, and the sensory organs are able to send messages to the brain.

Forming pathways

A neuron's unique structure enables it to communicate with up to 10,000 other nerve cells, creating a complex, interconnected neural network that allows information to travel at great speed. Studies of synaptic

transmission indicate that pathways within this vast network link to specific mental functions. Every new thought or action creates a new brain connection, which strengthens if it is used repeatedly, and it is then more likely that the cells will communicate along that pathway in the future. The brain has "learned" the neural connections associated with that particular activity or mental function.

Acetylcholine

The effects of this neurotransmitter are mostly excitatory, and activate the skeletal muscles; it is also linked to memory, learning, and sleep.

86 billion neurons exist in the brain

Neurotransmitters

Many different types of neurotransmitters are released at a synapse, and may have either an "excitatory" or an "inhibitory" effect on a target cell. Each type is linked with a specific brain function, such as regulating mood or appetite. Hormones have a similar effect but are transmitted by blood, whereas neurotransmitters are transmitted across the synaptic cleft.

Glutamate

The most common neurotransmitter, glutamate has an excitatory effect and links to memory and learning.

Adrenaline

Released in stress situations, adrenaline creates an energy surge that increases heart rate, blood pressure, and blood flow to the larger muscles.

Norepinephrine

Similar to adrenaline, this excitatory neurotransmitter is mainly associated with the fight-or-flight mechanism; it is also linked to stress resilience.

GABA

The brain's main inhibitory neurotransmitter, GABA slows the firing of neurons and is calming.

Serotonin

With an inhibitory effect, serotonin is linked to mood enhancement and calmness. It regulates appetite, temperature, and muscle movement.

Dopamine

With either an inhibitory or an excitatory effect, dopamine plays a key role in reward-motivated behavior and links to mood.

Endorphins

Released by the pituitary gland, endorphins have an inhibitory effect on the transmission of pain signals; they are associated with pain relief and feelings of pleasure.

CHEMICAL EFFECTS AND OVERLAPS

These three neurotransmitters have distinct yet interrelated roles.

> All affect mood.

> Norepinephrine and dopamine are both released in stressful situations.

> Serotonin moderates a neuron's response to the excitatory effects of dopamine and norepinephrine.

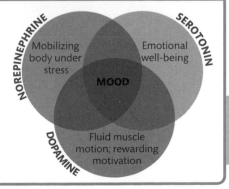

How memory works

Every experience generates a memory—whether it lasts depends on how often it is revisited. Intricate neural connections allow memories to form, and these can strengthen, aiding recall, or fade away.

What is memory?

A memory is formed when a group of neurons fire in a specific pattern in response to a new experience—these neural connections can then refire in order to reconstruct that experience as a memory. Memories are categorized into five types (right). They are briefly stored in the short-term (working) memory but can fade unless the experience is of emotional value or importance, in which case it is encoded (below) in the long-term memory. In recalling a memory, the nerve cells that first encoded it are reactivated. This strengthens their connections and, if done repeatedly, solidifies the memory. A memory's component parts, such as related sounds or smells, reside in different areas of the brain, and in order to retrieve the memory all of these brain parts must be activated. During recall a memory can merge accidentally with new information, which fuses irrevocably with the original (known as confabulation).

Endel Tulving explained memory as two distinct processes: storing information in long-term memory, and retrieving it. The link between the two means that being reminded of the circumstances in which a memory was stored can act as a trigger to recall the memory itself.

How memories form

The process of laying down (encoding) a memory depends on many factors. Even once encoded a memory can take two years to be firmly established.

0.2 SECONDS

1. Attention

Focusing attention on an event helps to solidify the memory: the thalamus activates neurons more intensely, while the frontal lobe inhibits distractions.

0.25 SECONDS

2a. Emotion

High emotion increases attention, making an event more likely to be encoded into a memory. Emotional responses to stimuli are processed in the amygdala.

0.2–0.5 SECONDS

2b. Sensation

Sensory stimuli are part of most experiences, and if of high intensity they increase the chances of recollection. Sensory cortices transfer signals to the hippocampus.

TYPES OF MEMORY

> **Episodic memory** Recalling past events or experiences, usually closely linked with sensory and emotional information.

> **Semantic memory** Retaining factual information, such as the name of a capital city.

> **Working memory** Storing information temporarily; capable of holding between five and seven items at any one time; also known as short-term memory.

> **Procedural (body) memory** Using learned actions that require no conscious recall, such as riding a bicycle.

> **Implicit memory** Bringing back an unconscious memory that influences behavior, such as recoiling from a stranger reminiscent of someone unpleasant.

CASE STUDY: BADDELEY'S DIVERS

Studies by psychologists indicate that in retrieving memories humans are aided by memory cues. British psychologist Alan Baddeley conducted an experiment in which a group of divers were asked to learn a list of words—they learned some words on dry land and some underwater. When they were later asked to recall the words, most divers found recall easier in the physical environment in which they had first memorized them, so it was easier to remember the words learned underwater when they went underwater. Baddeley's experiment suggested that context itself could provide a memory cue. Similarly, when a person goes to collect an object from another room but on arriving cannot recall what they were looking for, often returning to the original room triggers that memory cue.

"Memory is the treasury and guardian of all things."

Cicero, Roman politician

3. Working memory

Short-term memory stores information until needed—it is kept active by two neural circuits that incorporate the sensory cortices and the frontal lobes.

4. Hippocampal processing

Important information transfers to the hippocampus, where it is encoded. It can then loop back to the brain area that first registered it, to be recalled as a memory.

5. Consolidation

The neural firing patterns that encode an experience carry on looping from the hippocampus to the cortex—this firmly fixes (consolidates) it as a memory.

How emotions work

The emotions an individual feels on a daily basis dictate the type of person they feel they are. And yet it is a series of biological processes in the brain that generate every feeling a person has.

What is emotion?

Emotions impact hugely on people's lives—they govern their behavior, give meaning to their existence, and are at the core of what it is to be considered human. Yet in reality emotions result from physiological responses in the brain triggered by different stimuli—the psychological significance read into emotions is an entirely human construct. Emotions evolved to promote human success and survival by initiating certain behaviors: for example, feelings of affection prompt the desire to find a mate, reproduce, and live in a group; fear generates a physiological response to avoid danger (fight-or-flight); reading emotions in others makes social bonding possible.

Processing emotion

The limbic system (p.26), located just under the cortex, generates all emotions. They are processed via two routes, conscious and unconscious (below). The primary receptor that "screens" the emotional content of all incoming stimuli is the amygdala, which signals to other areas of the brain to produce an

Conscious and unconscious emotive routes

Humans experience their emotional responses through an unconscious route, which is designed to prepare the body for rapid action (fight-or-flight), or via a conscious route, which enables a more considered response to a situation. The amygdala responds to threat and can detect stimuli before the person is even aware of it, provoking an automatic, unconscious reaction. A simultaneous, but slower, transmission of sensory information to the cortex creates a conscious secondary route for the same stimulus, and can modify this initial reaction.

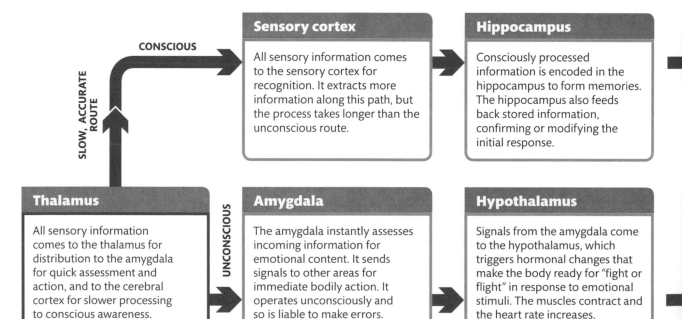

CONSCIOUS

SLOW, ACCURATE ROUTE

UNCONSCIOUS

Sensory cortex

All sensory information comes to the sensory cortex for recognition. It extracts more information along this path, but the process takes longer than the unconscious route.

Hippocampus

Consciously processed information is encoded in the hippocampus to form memories. The hippocampus also feeds back stored information, confirming or modifying the initial response.

Thalamus

All sensory information comes to the thalamus for distribution to the amygdala for quick assessment and action, and to the cerebral cortex for slower processing to conscious awareness.

Amygdala

The amygdala instantly assesses incoming information for emotional content. It sends signals to other areas for immediate bodily action. It operates unconsciously and so is liable to make errors.

Hypothalamus

Signals from the amygdala come to the hypothalamus, which triggers hormonal changes that make the body ready for "fight or flight" in response to emotional stimuli. The muscles contract and the heart rate increases.

appropriate emotional response. Connections between the limbic system and the cortex, in particular the frontal lobes, enable emotions to be processed consciously and experienced as valuable "feelings."

Each emotion is activated by a specific pattern of brain activity—hatred, for example, stimulates the amygdala (which is linked to all negative emotion) and areas of the brain associated with disgust, rejection, action, and calculation. Positive emotion works by reducing activity in the amygdala and those cortical regions linked to anxiety.

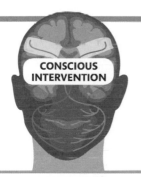

CONSCIOUS INTERVENTION

CONSCIOUS FACIAL EXPRESSIONS
The motor cortex allows a person to control facial expression and so hide or express genuine emotion.

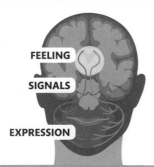

FEELING

SIGNALS

EXPRESSION

REFLEX FACIAL EXPRESSIONS
The emotional reaction caused by the amygdala sparks spontaneous, uncontrolled facial expressions.

EMOTIVE BEHAVIORS AND RESPONSES

Typical behavioral patterns in response to emotion have evolved in order to neutralize any perceived threat, through either fight or appeasement. In contrast, moods last longer, are less intense, and involve conscious behaviors.

	POSSIBLE STIMULUS	BEHAVIOR
ANGER	Challenging behavior from another person	Provokes unconscious response and rapid emotion; "fight" reaction prompts dominant and threatening stance or action
FEAR	Threat from stronger or more dominant person	Provokes unconscious response and rapid emotion; "flight" response avoids threat, or a show of appeasement indicates lack of challenge to dominant person
SADNESS	Loss of loved one	Conscious response dominates; longer-term mood; backward-looking state of mind and passivity avoid additional challenge
DISGUST	Unwholesome object such as rotting food	Provokes unconscious rapid response; aversion prompts swift removal of self from unhealthy environment
SURPRISE	Novel or unexpected event	Provokes unconscious rapid response; attention focuses on object of surprise to glean maximum information that guides further conscious actions

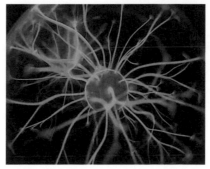

EVERY EMOTION sparks a slightly different pattern of activity in the brain.

"Human behavior flows from ... desire, emotion, knowledge."

Plato, ancient Greek philosopher

PSYCHOLOGICAL DISORDERS

The distressing symptoms of a psychological disorder often go hand in hand with circular thoughts, feelings, and actions. When the symptoms form a recognizable pattern, a doctor can diagnose and treat a person.

Diagnosing disorders

The medical diagnosis of a mental health condition is a complex process of matching an individual's pattern of physical and psychological symptoms to behaviors associated with a disorder, or disorders. Some conditions, such as a learning disability or neuropsychological problems, are easily identified. Functional disorders that affect personality and conduct are more difficult, however, as they involve numerous biological, psychological, and social factors.

What are mental health disorders?

Mental health disorders are characterized by the presence of unusual or abnormal mood, thinking, and behaviors that cause an individual significant distress or impairment, and disrupt their ability to function. Impairment occurring as the result of common stressors such as bereavement would not be considered a disorder. Diverse social and cultural factors impacting behaviors might also rule out the presence of mental health problems.

CATEGORIES OF DISORDERS

> Mood disorders (pp.38–45)
> Anxiety disorders (pp.46–55)
> Obsessive compulsive and related disorders (pp.56–61)
> Trauma- and stress-related disorders (pp.62–65)
> Neurodevelopmental disorders (pp.66–69)
> Psychotic disorders (pp.70–75)
> Neurocognitive disorders (pp.76–79)

> Addictive and impulse-control disorders (pp.80–85)
> Dissociative disorders (pp.86–89)
> Eating disorders (pp.90–95)
> Communication disorders (pp.96–97)
> Sleep disorders (pp.98–99)
> Motor disorders (pp.100–101)
> Personality disorders (pp.102–107)
> Others (pp.108–109)

Disorders can be classified into diagnostic groups (above); the two main works used to identify, categorize, and organize them are the World Health Organization's *International Classification of Disease (ICD-10)* and the American Psychiatric Association's *Diagnostic and Statistical Manual of Mental Disorders (DSM-5)*.

1in4 people will be affected by mental or neurological disorders in their lifetime

Assessment of a mental health condition

Clinical diagnosis is made only after a careful assessment process that includes observation and interpretation of a person's behaviors and discussion with them and, if relevant, their family, caregivers, and specialist professionals. Putting a name to a person's distress can help them—and their support systems—gain a deeper understanding of their difficulties and how to manage them better, but it can also negatively shape a person's outlook and contribute to self-fulfilling prophecies.

Physical examination
A GP will first eliminate physical illness that could be causing symptoms. Medical examination can also reveal intellectual disabilities or speech disorders due to physical abnormalities. Imaging techniques may be used to test for brain injury or dementia, and blood tests can reveal a genetic predisposition to certain disorders.

Clinical interview
If no physical illness is identified, an individual may be referred to a mental health specialist. They will ask the client about their life experiences, their family history, and recent experiences that relate to their problem. The conversation will also aim to uncover any predisposing factors, strengths, and vulnerabilities.

Psychological tests
Particular aspects of a person's knowledge, skill, or personality will be evaluated through a series of tests and/or tasks, usually in the form of checklists or questionnaires standardized for use on very specific groups. For example, such tests may measure adaptive behaviors, beliefs about the self, or traits of personality disorders.

Behavioral assessment
A person's behavior will also be observed and measured, normally in the situation where their difficulties occur, to gain an understanding of the factors that precipitate and/or maintain their symptoms. The person might also be asked to make their own observations by recording a mood diary or using a frequency counter.

Depression

This is a common condition that may be diagnosed when a person has been feeling down and worried—and has lost pleasure in daily activities—for more than two weeks.

What is it?

The symptoms of depression can include continuous low mood or sadness, having low self-esteem, feeling hopeless and helpless, being tearful, feeling guilt-ridden, and being irritable and intolerant of others.

A person with depression is unmotivated and uninterested, finds it difficult to make decisions, and takes no enjoyment from life. As a result, the individual may avoid the social events that they usually enjoy, thus missing out on social interaction, which can cause a vicious circle which sees them spiraling further downward.

Depression can make it difficult for a person to concentrate and remember things. In extreme cases the sense of hopelessness may lead to thoughts of self-harm or even suicide.

Internal and external causes

A wide range of biological, social, and environmental factors can cause depression. External causes predominantly encompass life events that can have a negative impact on a person, and often act in combination with internal causes—those within an individual—to trigger depression.

EXTERNAL CAUSES

Money, or the lack of it, and the stress caused by financial concerns and worries about debt.

Stress when a person cannot cope with the demands placed on them.

Relationship problems leading to depression in the longer term.

Job/unemployment impacting status and self-esteem, perception of a positive future, and ability to engage socially.

INTERNAL CAUSES
Personality traits, such as neuroticism and pessimism.
Childhood experiences, especially if the person felt out of control and helpless at the time.
Family history, if a parent or sibling has had depression.
Long-term health problems, such as heart, lung, or kidney disease; diabetes; and asthma.

Pregnancy and birth and the overwhelming prospect of parenthood for new mothers.

Bereavement following the death of a family member, friend, or pet.

Loneliness as a result of health or disability, especially in the elderly.

Bullying among children and adults, whether physical or verbal, face to face or online.

Alcohol and drugs due to the physiological, social, and economic consequences of addiction.

> "... depression is so insidious ... it's impossible to ever see the end."
>
> Elizabeth Wurtzel, American author

Many internal and external factors (left), such as childhood experiences and life events, physical illness, or injury, can cause depression. It can be mild, moderate, or severe and is extremely common—according to the World Health Organization, more than 350 million people suffer from it globally.

How is it diagnosed?

A doctor can diagnose by asking the person questions about their particular symptoms. One objective is to find out how long the symptoms have been going on. The doctor may also suggest blood tests to rule out any other illness that may cause the symptoms of depression.

Subsequent treatment depends on the severity of the depression, but the main option is to undergo psychotherapy. Antidepressants may be offered to help the person cope with everyday life. For mild to moderate depression, exercise can be helpful. In severe cases, hospital admission or medication for psychotic symptoms (pp.70–75) may be needed.

⊕ TREATMENT

> **Cognitive and behavioral therapies** such as behavioral activation, cognitive behavioral therapy (p.125), compassion focused, acceptance and commitment (p.126), and cognitive (p.124) therapies.

> **Psychodynamic psychotherapy** (pp.118–121) and counseling.

> **Antidepressants** (pp.142–143) on their own or alongside therapy.

FEELINGS OF LONELINESS result from depression and cause a person to feel completely alone, helpless, and isolated.

Bipolar disorder

This condition is characterized by extreme swings—highs (mania) and lows (depression)—in a person's energy and activity levels, which is why it was originally called manic depression.

What is it?

There are four types of bipolar disorder: bipolar 1 is severe mania lasting for more than a week (the person may need hospitalization); bipolar 2 causes swings between a less severe mania and low mood; cyclothymia features longer-term hypomanic and depressive episodes lasting for up to two years; and unspecified bipolar disorder is a mixture of the three types. During a mood swing an individual can undergo extreme personality changes, which puts social and personal relationships under severe strain.

The main cause of bipolar is commonly believed to be an imbalance of the chemicals involved in brain function. Known as neurotransmitters, these chemicals include norepinephrine, serotonin, and dopamine, and relay signals between nerve cells (pp.28–29). Genetics also play a role: bipolar disorder runs in families, and it can develop at any age. It is thought that 2 in every 100

Patterns of depression and mania

There are distinct phases to the mood swings of bipolar disorder. The extent and timescale of fluctuations and the way moods manifest themselves and affect personality can vary widely.

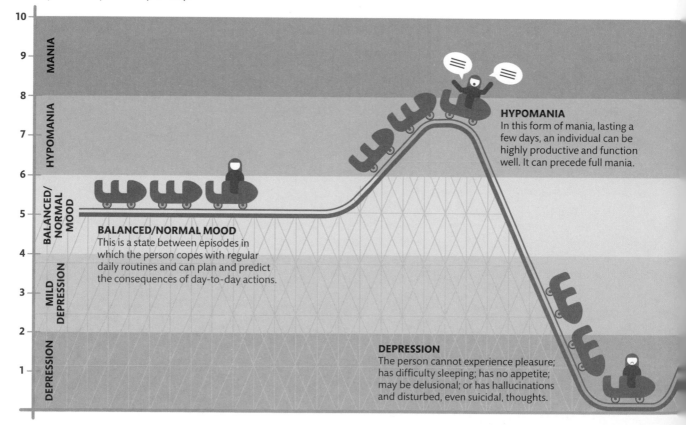

MANIA

HYPOMANIA

BALANCED/NORMAL MOOD

MILD DEPRESSION

DEPRESSION

BALANCED/NORMAL MOOD
This is a state between episodes in which the person copes with regular daily routines and can plan and predict the consequences of day-to-day actions.

HYPOMANIA
In this form of mania, lasting a few days, an individual can be highly productive and function well. It can precede full mania.

DEPRESSION
The person cannot experience pleasure; has difficulty sleeping; has no appetite; may be delusional; or has hallucinations and disturbed, even suicidal, thoughts.

people have an episode at some stage; some have only a couple in their lifetime, whereas others have many. Episodes may be triggered by stress; illness; or hardships in everyday life, such as relationship difficulties or problems with money or work.

How is it diagnosed?

The affected person is assessed by a psychiatrist or clinical psychologist, who asks about the symptoms and when they first occurred. Signals leading up to an episode are explored, too. The doctor also looks to eliminate other conditions that can cause mood swings. The individual is usually treated with medication and lifestyle management techniques.

⊕ TREATMENT

❯ **Cognitive behavioral therapy** (p.125).

❯ **Lifestyle management** including regular exercise; better diet; sleep routines, which may improve mood regulation; and use of diaries and daily awareness methods, which may help the individual to recognize signs of mood changes.

❯ **Mood stabilizers** (pp.142–143) taken long term to minimize likelihood of mood swings; dosage often adjusted during episodes of hypomania, mania, or depression.

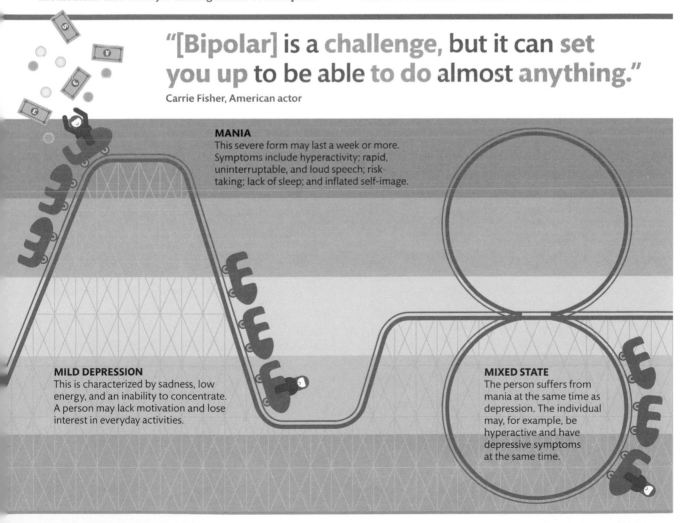

"[Bipolar] is a **challenge,** but it can **set you up** to be able **to do** almost **anything.**"

Carrie Fisher, American actor

MANIA
This severe form may last a week or more. Symptoms include hyperactivity; rapid, uninterruptable, and loud speech; risk-taking; lack of sleep; and inflated self-image.

MILD DEPRESSION
This is characterized by sadness, low energy, and an inability to concentrate. A person may lack motivation and lose interest in everyday activities.

MIXED STATE
The person suffers from mania at the same time as depression. The individual may, for example, be hyperactive and have depressive symptoms at the same time.

Perinatal mental illness

Occurring at any time during pregnancy and up to a year after giving birth, perinatal mental illnesses include PPD (postpartum depression), sometimes called postnatal depression, and postpartum psychosis.

What is it?

Feeling tearful or irritable just after giving birth is so common it is dubbed the "baby blues," but these feelings last for only a couple of weeks. What sets PPD apart from baby blues is the length of time it lasts. It is a longer-term moderate to severe depression that can develop in new mothers (and occasionally fathers) at any time in the year after birth. Symptoms include constant low mood or mood swings, low energy levels, difficulty bonding with the baby, and frightening thoughts. The individual may cry easily and profusely and feel acutely fatigued yet have sleep problems. Feelings of shame and inadequacy, worthlessness, and fear of failure as a parent are common. In severe cases, panic attacks, self-harm, and thoughts of suicide occur. However, most individuals make a full recovery. Untreated, PPD may last for many months or longer.

PPD can develop suddenly or slowly, and is usually caused by hormone and lifestyle changes and fatigue. It is not clear why some people develop PPD, but risk factors appear to include difficult childhood experiences, low self-esteem, a lack of support, and stressful living conditions.

How is it diagnosed?

To determine whether an individual has PPD, a doctor, midwife, or health professional assesses symptoms using an efficient and reliable screening questionnaire such as the Edinburgh Postnatal

85%
of new mothers experience the "baby blues"

Depression Scale, which rates mood and activity levels over the previous seven days. Other assessment scales are used to assess mental well-being and functioning.

Good clinical judgment is needed when interpreting the results of these questionnaires as new parents are likely to be less active simply as a result of their new responsibilities.

POSTPARTUM PSYCHOSIS

An extremely serious condition, postpartum psychosis (also known as puerperal psychosis) affects 1–2 women per 1,000 births. It usually occurs in the first few weeks after delivery, but may begin up to six months after birth. Symptoms often develop rapidly and include confusion, high mood, racing thoughts, disorientation, paranoia, hallucinations, delusions, and sleep disturbance. The individual may also have obsessive thoughts about the baby, and attempt to self-harm or harm the baby. Immediate treatment is needed because of the potentially life-threatening thoughts and behaviors associated with the disorder. Treatment comprises hospitalization (usually in a highly monitored mother-and-baby treatment unit), medication (antidepressants and antipsychotics), and psychotherapy.

 ## TREATMENT

> **Cognitive and behavioral therapies** (pp.122–129) in a group, one-on-one, or as guided self-help; one-on-one counseling.

> **Lifestyle management,** such as talking to partner, friends, and family; resting; regular exercise; and eating healthily and regularly.

> **Antidepressants** (pp.142–143) alone or with psychotherapy.

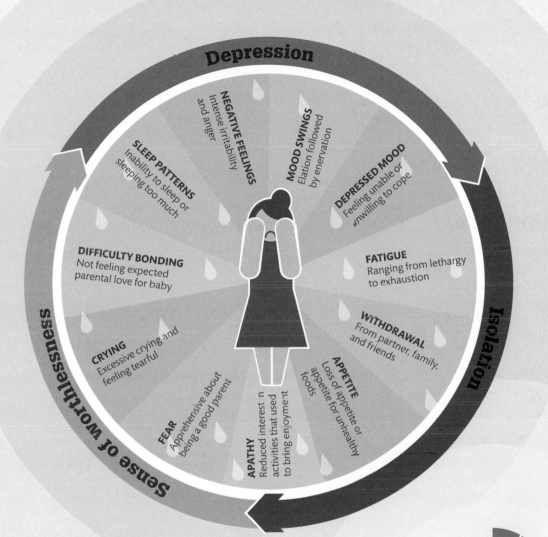

Depression

Isolation

Sense of worthlessness

NEGATIVE FEELINGS
Intense irritability
and anger

MOOD SWINGS
Elation followed
by enervation

DEPRESSED MOOD
Feeling unable or
unwilling to cope

SLEEP PATTERNS
Inability to sleep or
sleeping too much

FATIGUE
Ranging from lethargy
to exhaustion

DIFFICULTY BONDING
Not feeling expected
parental love for baby

WITHDRAWAL
From partner, family,
and friends

CRYING
Excessive crying and
feeling tearful

APPETITE
Loss of appetite or
appetite for unhealthy
foods

FEAR
Apprehensive about
being a good parent

APATHY
Reduced interest in
activities that used
to bring enjoyment

Range of symptoms

The symptoms of postpartum depression
are similar to those of anxiety and general
depression. Symptoms can make it difficult
to complete day-to-day activities and
routines, and can affect an individual's
relationship with their baby, partner,
family, and friends.

DMDD (disruptive mood dysregulation disorder)

DMDD is a childhood disorder characterized by almost constant anger and irritability combined with regular and severe temper tantrums.

What is it?

DMDD is a recently identified disorder that children with a history of chronic irritability and serious temper outbursts are now recognized as having. The child is sad, bad-tempered, and/or angry almost every day. The outbursts are grossly out of proportion with the situation at hand, occur several times every week, and happen in more than one place (at home, at school, and/or with peers). Strained interactions that occur only between a child and their parents, or a child and their teacher, do not indicate DMDD.

How is it diagnosed?

For a diagnosis of DMDD, the symptoms must be evident consistently for more than a year, and interfere with a child's ability to function at home and at school. One cause can be that the child misinterprets other people's expressions, in which case training in facial-expression-recognition can be offered. Diagnosed children are generally under the age of 10, but not younger than 6 or older than 18. One to 3 percent of children under the age of 10 have symptoms.

Disruptive behavior

Children with DMDD regularly have severe temper tantrums, inconsistent with their developmental stage, three or more times a week in at least two different settings.

DESTROYS things and/or throws them around room

SHOUTS ABUSE at teachers, peers, or parents

ANGRY AND IRRITABLE almost all of the time

Children with DMDD were once identified as having pediatric bipolar disorder, but they do not present with the episodic mania or hypomania of that disorder. They are unlikely to develop bipolar, but are at a higher risk of depression and anxiety as adults.

✚ TREATMENT

❯ **Psychotherapy** (pp.118–141) for both child and family to explore emotions and develop mood management techniques.

❯ **Lifestyle management** including positive behavior support to establish better communication and minimize outburst triggers.

❯ **Antidepressants** or antipsychotics (pp.142–143) to support psychotherapy.

2013 the year DMDD was recognized

SAD (seasonal affective disorder)

SAD is a form of seasonal depression linked to changing levels of light that typically starts in fall as the days shorten. It is also known as "winter depression" or "hibernation state."

What is it?

The nature and severity of SAD vary from person to person, and for some it can have a significant impact on their day-to-day life. Typically the symptoms come and go with the seasons, and always begin at the same time of year, often in the fall. Symptoms include low mood, a loss of interest in everyday activities, irritability, despair, guilt, and feelings of worthlessness. People with SAD lack energy, feel sleepy during the day, sleep for longer than normal at night, and find it hard to get up in the morning. As many as one in three people are affected.

SAD's seasonal nature can make diagnosis difficult. Psychological assessment looks at a person's mood, lifestyle, diet, seasonal behavior, thought changes, and family history.

⊕ TREATMENT

> **Psychotherapies,** such as cognitive behavioral therapy (p.125) and counseling.
> **Lifestyle management** by improving access to light—sitting near windows when inside, using a sunlight-simulating light bulb, and daily outdoor activity.

Seasonal cause and effect

Sunlight level affects a part of the brain called the hypothalamus by altering the production of two chemicals: melatonin (which controls sleep) and serotonin (which changes mood).

Winter pattern

> **Melatonin increases** so person is tired and wants to sleep.
> **Serotonin production drops,** causing person to feel low.
> **Desire to stay in bed** and sleep can lead to reduced social contact.
> **Craving carbohydrates** can cause overeating and weight gain.
> **Constant daytime fatigue** affects work and family life.

Secretion of melatonin by the pineal gland is triggered by darkness/inhibited by light and controlled by the hypothalamus.

Summer pattern

> **Melatonin drops** so person has more energy.
> **Serotonin production** increases, improving mood and outlook.
> **Sleep is good,** but not excessive, so person has more energy.
> **Diet improves** as cravings subside.
> **Improved energy** results in increased activity and more social contact.

Spring · Summer · Fall · Winter

Panic disorder

Panic attacks are an exaggerated reaction to the body's normal response to fear or excitement. With panic disorder, a person regularly experiences such attacks for no obvious reason.

What is it?

The normal reaction to fear or excitement causes the body to produce the hormone adrenaline to prepare for "fight or flight" from the source of fear. If a person has a panic attack, apparently normal thoughts or images trigger the brain's fight-or-flight center, resulting in adrenaline racing around the body causing symptoms such as sweating, increased heart rate, and hyperventilation. Attacks last about 20 minutes and can be very uncomfortable.

The individual may misinterpret these symptoms, saying they feel as if they are having a heart attack or even dying. The fear can further activate the brain's threat center so more adrenaline is produced, worsening symptoms.

Individuals who have recurring panic attacks can fear the next one so much that they live in a constant state of "fear of fear." Attacks may, for example, be set off by fear of being in a crowd or a small space, but often they are triggered by internal sensations that have nothing to do with the outside world. As a result, everyday tasks can become difficult and social situations daunting. Those with panic disorder may avoid certain places or activities, so the problem persists because the person can never "disconfirm" their fear.

What are the causes?

One in 10 people suffer from occasional panic attacks; panic disorder is less common. Traumatic life experiences, such as a bereavement, can trigger the disorder. Having a close family member with panic disorder is thought to increase the risk of developing it. Environmental conditions such as high carbon dioxide levels may also cause attacks. Some illnesses, for example an overactive thyroid, can produce symptoms similar to panic disorder, and a doctor will rule out such illnesses before making a diagnosis.

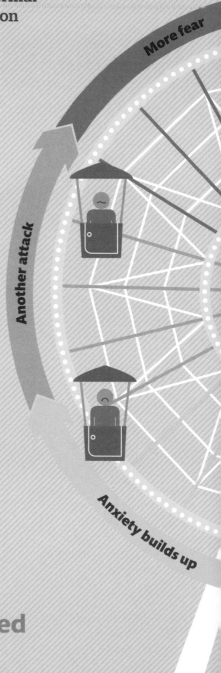

More fear

Another attack

Anxiety builds up

 **TREATMENT**

> **Cognitive behavioral therapy** (p.125) to identify triggers, prevent avoidance behavior, and learn to disprove feared outcomes.

> **Support groups** to meet others with the disorder and get advice.

> **Selective serotonin reuptake inhibitors** (SSRIs) (pp.142–143).

2%
of people are affected by panic disorder

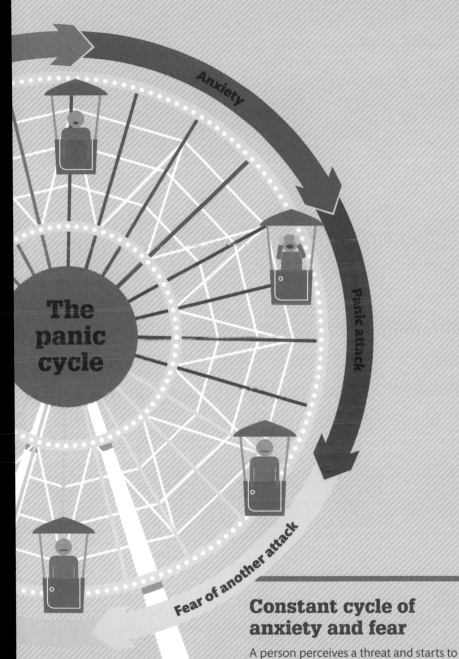

The panic cycle

Anxiety

Panic attack

Fear of another attack

Constant cycle of anxiety and fear

A person perceives a threat and starts to panic. The physical symptoms develop, worsening the anxiety and therefore the symptoms, which in turn increase the likelihood of a repeat attack.

SYMPTOMS OF A PANIC ATTACK

The symptoms result from the action of the autonomic nervous system—the part not under conscious control (pp.32–33).

Increased heart rate

Adrenaline causes the heart to pump faster to move blood containing oxygen to where it is needed. This can result in chest pains.

Feeling faint

Breathing is faster and shallower to increase oxygen, causing hyperventilation and lightheadedness.

Sweating and pallor

Sweating increases to cool the body. The person may also become pale as blood is diverted to where it is needed most.

Choking sensation

Faster breathing feels like choking—oxygen level rises but not enough carbon dioxide is exhaled.

Dilated pupils

The pupil (black part of the eye) becomes dilated to let in more light, making it easier to see to escape.

Slowed digestion

As digestion is not crucial for "flight," it slows. The sphincters (valves) relax, which makes the sufferer feel nauseous.

Dry mouth

The mouth can feel very dry as body fluids are concentrated in the parts of the body where they are most needed.

Specific phobias

A phobia is a type of anxiety disorder. Specific phobias manifest themselves when a person anticipates contact with, or is exposed to, the object, situation, or event they fear.

What are they?

Specific, simple phobias (as opposed to the complex ones, agoraphobia and claustrophobia, pp.50–51) are the most common psychological disorders in children and adults. A phobia is much more than fear and arises when a person develops an exaggerated or unrealistic sense of danger about a situation or an object. The fear may not make any sense, but the individual feels powerless to stop it. Anticipated or actual exposure (even to an image) can cause extreme anxiety or a panic attack. Symptoms include rapid heart rate, breathing difficulties, and a feeling of being out of control.

A combination of genetics; brain chemistry; and other biological, psychological, and environmental factors can give rise to a phobia. It can often be traced back to a frightening event or stressful situation a person either witnessed or was involved in during early childhood. A child can also "learn" a phobia through seeing other family members demonstrate phobic behavior.

Specific phobias often develop during childhood or adolescence and may become less severe with age. They can also be associated with other psychological conditions such as depression (pp.38–39), obsessive compulsive disorder (pp.56–57), and post-traumatic stress disorder (p.62).

How are they diagnosed?

Many affected individuals are fully aware of their phobia, so a formal diagnosis is not necessary and they do not need treatment—avoiding the object of their fear is enough to control the problem. However, in some people habitual avoidance of a feared object can also maintain or worsen the phobia, and seriously impact aspects of their lives. A GP can refer them to a specialist with expertise in behavioral therapy.

SPECIFIC PHOBIAS are very treatable with gradual, guided exposure to the feared object or situation.

8.7%
of adult Americans are affected by a specific phobia

TREATMENT

› **Cognitive behavioral therapy** (p.125) to overcome a phobia using a system of graded steps to work toward the goal of confronting the feared object or situation without fear; anxiety management techniques to master each step.

› **Mindfulness** to raise tolerance of anxiety and of thoughts or images associated with the distress.

› **Anti-anxiety medication** or antidepressants (pp.142–143) alongside therapy if the phobia is impairing day-to-day living.

Types of specific phobia

There is a wide variety of objects or situations that can trigger a phobia. Specific, so-called "simple," phobias fall into five groups: blood-injection-injury, natural environment, situational, animal, and "other" types. With the exception of the first type, specific phobias are two to three times more common in females than males.

BLOOD-INJECTION-INJURY

A unique group of phobias in which the sight of blood or needles causes a vasovagal reaction—a reflex action that slows down the heart rate, reducing blood flow to the brain—that can result in fainting. Unlike all other phobias, this is as common in males as it is in females.

NEEDLES

BLOOD

NATURAL ENVIRONMENT

A person with a phobia from this group has an irrational fear of a natural event, which they often associate with imagery of potentially catastrophic outcomes. Examples of this type of phobia include storms; deep water; germs; and fear of heights, such as being near a cliff edge.

WATER

HEIGHTS

LIGHTNING

SITUATIONAL

These are a group of phobias of being in a specific situation, which can range from visiting the dentist's office to stepping into an old elevator, flying, driving over a bridge or through a tunnel, or getting into a car.

FLYING

BRIDGES

ANIMAL

This group of phobias includes insects, snakes, mice, cats, dogs, and birds, among other animals. It could be rooted in a genetic predisposition for survival from animals that were a threat to human ancestors.

SNAKES

SPIDERS

RATS

OTHER PHOBIAS

Thousands of people are tormented by an array of phobias, including fear of vomiting; a specific color, for example, anything that is yellow or red (including foodstuffs); the number 13; the sight of a belly button or toes; sudden loud noises; costumed characters, such as clowns; trees; or contact with cut flowers.

TREES

CLOWNS

Agoraphobia

This is an anxiety disorder characterized by a fear of being trapped in any situation in which escape is difficult or rescue is unavailable if things go wrong.

What is it?

Agoraphobia is a complex phobia that is not, as many think, simply a fear of open spaces. The individual dreads being trapped, and avoids whatever triggers the terror of being unable to escape. The result can be a fear of traveling on public transport, being in an enclosed space or a crowd, going shopping or to health appointments, or leaving the house. The associated panic attack brought on by such an experience is accompanied by negative thoughts—for example, the person may think that as well as being trapped they are going to look ridiculous, because they are out of control in public. The symptoms, or fear of them, are disruptive and result in avoidance behaviors that make leading a normal life hard.

Agoraphobia can develop if an individual has a panic attack, then worries excessively about a repeat experience. In the UK, one-third of those who have panic attacks go on to develop agoraphobia. Biological and psychological factors are the probable cause. Experiencing or witnessing a traumatic event, mental illness, or an unhappy relationship may play a part.

Treatment can help—about one-third are cured and 50 percent find that symptoms improve. A GP first excludes other conditions that may be causing the symptoms.

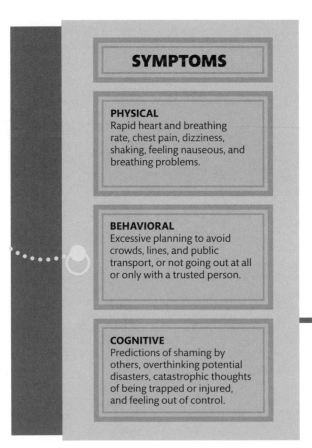

SYMPTOMS

PHYSICAL
Rapid heart and breathing rate, chest pain, dizziness, shaking, feeling nauseous, and breathing problems.

BEHAVIORAL
Excessive planning to avoid crowds, lines, and public transport, or not going out at all or only with a trusted person.

COGNITIVE
Predictions of shaming by others, overthinking potential disasters, catastrophic thoughts of being trapped or injured, and feeling out of control.

"Nothing diminishes anxiety faster than action."

Walter Inglis Anderson, American painter, writer, and naturalist

⊕ TREATMENT

> **Intensive psychotherapy** such as cognitive behavioral therapy (p.125) to explore the thoughts that maintain the phobia; behavioral experiments to gather evidence that defuses strongly held beliefs.

> **Self-help groups** using safe visual material to work on exposure to the feared situation; teaching how to manage a panic attack by breathing slowly and deeply.

> **Lifestyle management** such as exercise and a healthy diet.

Types of symptoms

The symptoms of agoraphobia are classified into three types: the physical symptoms that a person experiences in the feared situation; behavioral patterns associated with the fear; and cognitive symptoms—the thoughts and feelings a person has when anticipating or living with the fear. The combination can make it difficult for a person to function day to day.

Claustrophobia

An irrational fear of becoming trapped in a confined space or even the anticipation of such a situation, claustrophobia is a complex phobia that can cause extreme anxiety and panic attacks.

What is it?

For a person with claustrophobia, being confined induces physical symptoms similar to those of agoraphobia (opposite). The fear also increases negative thoughts of running out of oxygen or suffering a heart attack with no chance of escape. Many individuals also experience feelings of dread and fear of fainting or losing control.

Claustrophobia may be caused by conditioning (pp.16–17) following a stressful situation that occurred in a small space. This might be traced back to childhood, when, for example, an individual was confined in a tiny room or was bullied or abused. The condition can also be triggered by unpleasant experiences at any stage of life, such as turbulence on a flight or being trapped in an elevator. The individual fears a repeat of being confined and overimagines what could happen in a small space. As a result they plan their daily activities carefully to minimize the likelihood of "becoming trapped."

Sometimes claustrophobia is observed in other family members, which suggests a genetic vulnerability to the disorder and/or a learned associated response.

⊕ TREATMENT

> **Cognitive behavioral therapy** (p.125) to reevaluate negative thoughts through exposure to the feared situation in small steps so the individual realizes that the worst fear does not occur.

> **Anxiety management** to cope with anxiety and panic by using breathing techniques, muscle relaxation, and visualization of positive outcomes.

> **Anti-anxiety medication** or antidepressants (pp.142–143) prescribed in extreme cases.

FEAR OF CONFINED SPACES is normal if the threat is genuine, but a person with claustrophobia has an irrational fear regardless of actual danger.

GAD (generalized anxiety disorder)

People with this disorder experience continual unrestrained and uncontrollable worry (even when no danger is present), to the extent that day-to-day activity and functioning can become impaired.

What is it?

An individual with GAD worries excessively about a wide range of issues and situations. Symptoms include "threat" reactions such as heart palpitations, trembling, sweating, irritability, restlessness, and headaches. GAD can also cause insomnia and difficulty in concentrating, making decisions, or dealing with uncertainty.

The person may become obsessed with perfectionism, or with planning and controlling events. The physical and psychological symptoms can have a debilitating effect on social interactions, work, and everyday activities, leading to lowered confidence and isolation. Worries may revolve around family or social matters, work, health, school, or specific events. A person with GAD experiences feelings of anxiety most days, and as soon as they resolve one worry another appears. They overestimate the likelihood of bad or dangerous things happening and predict the worst possible outcome. The individual may even report positive beliefs about the helpfulness of worry, such as "Worrying makes it less likely that bad things will happen." Long-term or habitual avoidance of fearful situations or places compounds the disorder, because the individual never gathers evidence that their fears are unfounded, thus maintaining the worry.

Social fears

Health or money worries

Anticipation of dangers and disasters

Perfectionism

Women are 60% more likely to develop GAD than men

Balancing worries

Anxiety becomes a problem when a person is weighed down with worries for the majority of days in a six-month period or longer.

⊕ TREATMENT

> **Cognitive behavioral therapy** (p.125) to identify triggers, negative thoughts, habitual avoidance, and safety behaviors.

> **Behavioral therapy** (p.124) to identify new behavioral goals, with achievable steps.

> **Group therapy** with assertiveness training and building self-esteem to help counteract unhelpful beliefs and unfounded fears.

Social anxiety disorder

Individuals with this condition experience an overwhelming fear of being judged or of doing something embarrassing in social situations. The disorder can cause disabling self-consciousness.

What is it?

An individual with social anxiety disorder (also called social phobia) experiences excessive nerves or dread of social situations. They may be anxious only in specific circumstances, such as speaking or performing in public, or experience distress in all social situations.

The person tends to be extremely self-conscious and worries about others evaluating them negatively. They dwell on past social incidents, obsessing about how they might

have come across. Social anxiety causes the person to overplan and rehearse for anticipated situations, which may lead to odd or awkward behavior. Individuals may then gather evidence to support their fears, because difficult situations often arise as a result of the person's anxiety or over-rehearsal.

This disorder leads to isolation and depression and can seriously affect social relationships. It can also have a negative impact on performance at work or school.

TREATMENT

> **Cognitive behavioral therapy** (p.125) to recognize and change negative thought patterns and behaviors.
> **Group therapy** for the opportunity to share problems and practice social behavior.
> **Self-help** including affirmations, rehearsing before social events, and using video feedback to disprove negative assumptions.

SYMPTOMS BEFORE SOCIAL INTERACTION
The individual may prepare and rehearse excessively in advance, planning topics of conversation or how to present themselves in a specific way.

DURING INTERACTION
Physical symptoms such as trembling, rapid breathing, racing heart, sweating, or blushing occur as the body's "fight or flight" system is activated. In extreme cases, the person may experience a panic attack.

AFTER INTERACTION
The person conducts a detailed, negative, and self-critical appraisal of the social situation, dissecting conversations and body language and giving them a negative slant.

Separation anxiety disorder

This anxiety disorder can develop in children whose natural concern about being separated from their parent, primary caregiver, or home persists beyond the age of two years.

What is it?

Separation anxiety is a normal adaptive reaction that helps to keep babies and toddlers safe while they attain competence to cope with their environment. However, it can be a problem if it persists for more than four weeks and interferes with age-appropriate behavior.

The child becomes distressed when they need to leave a primary caregiver and fears that harm will come to that person. Situations such as school and social occasions can also be a trigger. Affected children may experience panic attacks, disturbed sleep, clinginess, and inconsolable crying. They may complain of physical problems such as stomachache, headache, or just feeling unwell for no apparent reason. Older children may anticipate feelings of panic and struggle to travel independently.

Separation is the most common anxiety disorder in children under 12 years old. It can also affect older children, and it may be diagnosed in adulthood. The disorder can develop after a major stressor such as the loss of a loved one or pet, moving, changing schools, or parents' divorce. Overprotective or intrusive parenting can contribute.

Separation anxiety is very treatable with behavioral therapies that include building planned separations into times of the day when the person is feeling least vulnerable.

Being alone

Worries about losing their primary caregiver are common, and the child may relive their daytime fears in nightmares. They may refuse to sleep alone or suffer from insomnia.

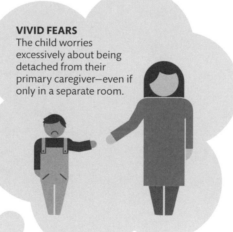

VIVID FEARS
The child worries excessively about being detached from their primary caregiver—even if only in a separate room.

UNWANTED BURDEN
Anxious feelings may manifest themselves as physical pains as the child struggles to fix their panic of separation onto something tangible.

 TREATMENT

> **Cognitive behavioral therapy** (p.125) for anxiety management; assertiveness training for older children and adults.

> **Parent training and support** to promote and reinforce short periods of separation that are then extended gradually.

> **Anti-anxiety medication** and antidepressants (pp.142–143) for older individuals, in combination with environmental and psychological interventions.

Selective mutism

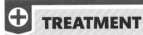

This is an anxiety disorder in which people are unable to talk in certain social situations, but are able to speak at other times. It is usually first recognized between the ages of three and eight years.

What is it?

Selective mutism is associated with anxiety, and children who are affected by it struggle with excessive fears and worries. They are generally able to speak freely where they feel comfortable but are unable to talk in specific situations, when they do not engage, go still, or have a frozen facial expression when expected to talk. This inability to speak is not the result of a conscious decision or a refusal.

The mutism can be triggered by a stressful experience, or it can stem from a speech or language disorder, or hearing problem, that makes social situations involving communication particularly stressful. Whatever the cause, everyday activities are difficult, as are relationships within the family or school. Treating the condition can prevent it from persisting into adulthood—the younger the child is when diagnosed, the easier it is to treat.

If symptoms persist for more than a month, the child should be seen by a GP, who can refer them for speech and language therapy. A specialist asks whether there is a history of anxiety disorders, a likely stressor, or a hearing problem. Treatment depends on how long the child has had the condition, the presence of learning difficulties or anxieties, and the support that is available.

⊕ TREATMENT

> **Cognitive behavioral therapy** (p.125) using positive and negative reinforcements to build speech and language skills; graded exposure to specific situations to reduce anxiety, removing pressure on the child to speak.

> **Psychoeducation** (p.113) can provide information and support for parents and caregivers, relieve general anxiety, and reduce chances of the disorder persisting.

"It is a child suffering in silence."

Dr. Elisa Shipon-Blum, American president of Selective Mutism Anxiety Research and Treatment Center

State of fear

Children with selective mutism literally "freeze" when they are expected to talk, and make little or no eye contact. The condition is more common in children who are learning a second language.

OCD (obsessive compulsive disorder)

This is a debilitating anxiety-related condition characterized by intrusive and unwelcome obsessive thoughts that are often followed by repetitive compulsions, impulses, or urges.

What is it?

OCD is often marked by thoughts that reflect an excessive sense of responsibility for keeping others safe and an overestimation of the perceived threat an intrusive thought signifies. OCD is cyclical (below) and often starts with an obsessive thought, which the person focuses on, in turn raising anxiety levels. Checking everything is in order and following rituals can provide relief, but the distressing thought returns.

The obsessive thoughts and compulsions are time-consuming, and individuals may struggle to function day to day or have a disrupted social or family life. The disorder may be triggered by an event in the

OBSESSIONS (THOUGHTS)

Fear of causing harm

Excessive attention paid to thoughts about actions that could cause harm.

Intrusive thoughts

Obsessive, repetitive, and even disturbing thoughts about causing harm.

Fear of contamination

Thinking that something is dirty or germ-ridden and will cause illness or death to the person or someone else.

Fear related to order or symmetry

Concern that harm could result unless tasks are done in a specific order.

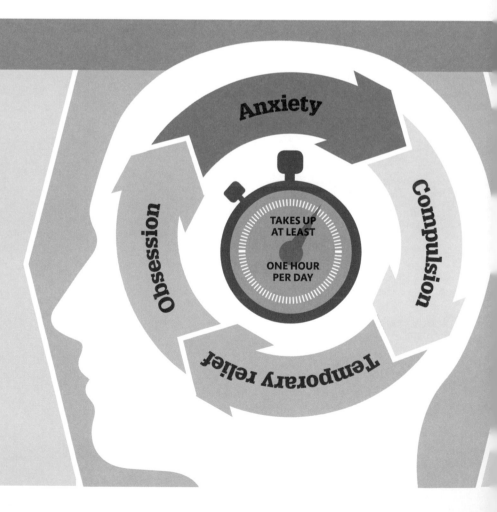

Anxiety

Obsession

Compulsion

Temporary relief

TAKES UP AT LEAST ONE HOUR PER DAY

person's history that they felt highly responsible for. Family history, differences in the brain, and personality traits also play a part. An examination of thoughts, feelings, and behavior patterns determines OCD, but its similarity to other anxiety disorders can make diagnosis difficult.

With pure OCD, a person has intrusive and disturbing thoughts about harming people, but rather than performing observable compulsions, their compulsions take place in the mind.

> "An **average person** can have **four thousand thoughts** a day, and **not all** of them are **useful** or **rational**."
>
> David Adam, British author

⊕ TREATMENT

> ❯ **Cognitive behavioral therapy** (p.125) involving exposure to triggers and learning how to control responses.

> ❯ **Anti-anxiety medication** and/or antidepressants (pp.142–143) to help relieve symptoms of depression and anxiety.

> ❯ **Specialist residential treatment** in addition to therapy and medication for extremely severe cases of OCD.

COMPULSIONS (BEHAVIORS)

Rituals

Following rituals such as counting or tapping to prevent harm and provide relief from the cycle of fear.

Constant checking

Examining household appliances, lights, taps, locks, windows (to counter fear of causing harm by fire), driving routes (fear of having run a person over), or people (fear of upsetting someone).

Correcting thoughts

Trying to neutralize thoughts to prevent disasters.

Reassurance

Repeatedly asking others to confirm everything is OK.

FOLLOWING RITUALS and constant checking that everything is in order and safe are the main features of OCD.

Hoarding disorder

Also known as compulsive hoarding, this disorder is characterized by the excessive acquisition of, and/or the inability or unwillingness to dispose of, large quantities of objects.

What is it?

Hoarding disorder may begin as a way of coping with a stressful life event. The individual with does not discard worn-out possessions, for fear either of needing them again or of something bad happening to other people if they get rid of anything. They store sentimental items because they believe that discarding them will keep emotional needs from being met. The individual continues to accumulate items even when space is running out. Hoarding can be hard to treat because the person does not see it as a problem and experiences such overwhelming discomfort at reducing the clutter that they avoid any attempt to do so. Alternatively, the person may be aware of the problem but too ashamed to seek help or advice.

Hoarding may be part of other disorders such as OCD (pp.56–57), severe depression (pp.38–39), or psychotic disorders (pp.70–75). In assessment, the doctor questions the person about their feelings on acquiring objects and their overestimation of responsibility for causing harm by discarding items.

 ### TREATMENT

> **Cognitive behavioral therapy** (p.125) to examine and weaken the thoughts that maintain the hoarding behavior and allow adaptive or flexible alternatives to emerge.
> **Lifestyle management** at home to motivate reducing clutter for health and safety reasons.
> **Antidepressants** (pp.142–143) to decrease the associated anxiety and depression.

Living with hoarding

A person with hoarding disorder may let junk mail, bills, receipts, and heaps of paper pile up. The resulting clutter can pose a health and safety risk and makes it hard to move from room to room, which is distressing for the individual and affects their, and their family's, quality of life. This may lead to isolation and impaired or difficult relationships with other people.

BDD (body dysmorphic disorder)

In this condition a person has a distorted perception of how they look. The individual typically spends an excessive amount of time worrying about their appearance and how others view them.

What is it?

BDD is an anxiety disorder that can have a huge impact on daily life. An individual with BDD worries obsessively about how they look. They often focus on a specific aspect of their body, for example, viewing a barely visible scar as a major flaw or seeing their nose as abnormal, and are convinced that others view the "flaw" in the same way. The person may spend a great deal of time concealing an aspect of their appearance, seeking medical treatment for the part of the body believed to be defective, and/or diet or exercise excessively.

BDD affects about 1 in every 50 people in the US, can occur in all age groups, and is seen in males and females in equal numbers. It is more common in people with a history of depression (pp.38–39) or social anxiety disorder (p.53), and it often occurs alongside OCD (pp.56–57) or generalized anxiety disorder (GAD, p.52). BDD may be due to brain chemistry or genetics, and past experiences may play a role in triggering its development. In assessment, the doctor asks the person about their symptoms and how they affect them and may refer them to a mental health specialist for further treatment.

TREATMENT

> **Cognitive behavioral therapy** (p.125) to identify self-appraisal related to the problem body part and weaken the beliefs that maintain it.

> **Antidepressants** and anti-anxiety medication (pp.142-143) alongside therapy.

Breaking the cycle

Treatment for BDD can be highly successful and focuses on breaking the cycle of thoughts, feelings, and behaviors that maintain it. The length of time treatment takes depends on the severity of the condition.

TRIGGER
Seeing their reflection, misinterpreting body language, or someone's passing comment can start the cycle.

EFFORTS TO CHANGE APPEARANCE
Safety behaviors or social avoidance prevail. The person may apply excessive makeup or use clothing to conceal the perceived defective attribute; seek cosmetic surgery; use extreme diet and exercise to change body shape; and avoid social situations, thus increasing feelings of isolation.

AUTOMATIC THOUGHTS
Negative thoughts dominate, for example, "I am defective and defective people are worthless, so I am worthless."

Negative self-image

LOW MOOD
The perceived constant social threat leads to chronic anxiety and depression.

Skin-picking and hair-pulling disorders

Also known as excoriation and trichotillomania respectively, these are impulse-control disorders in which a person has recurrent, irresistible urges to pick at their skin or pull out their body hair.

What are they?

The expressed aim of skin pickers or hair pullers is to achieve perfect hair or skin, but the reverse is the result. Both behaviors can cause physical damage.

A person with trichotillomania may pull hair from their scalp and/or other parts of their body such as eyebrows, eyelashes, and legs (and sometimes also from pets), which can result in noticeable hair loss. They may also swallow the hair, which can cause vomiting, stomach pain, and bleeding that can lead to anemia. Skin picking can result in scabs, abrasions, and lesions that may become infected. Both of these

conditions can also be associated with OCD (pp.56–57).

Skin picking and hair pulling often begin as a reaction to an immediate stress or may be a response to a traumatic experience or abuse. The behavior can be learned from other members of the family with similar habits or develop by chance and become associated with stress relief, which is a powerful behavioral reinforcement. Females are more likely to be affected, and symptoms often start in girls aged 11–13 years.

Hair pulling or skin picking can cause significant impairment or disruption in daily life for affected

individuals. They may avoid routine activities or work, have difficulty concentrating, become socially isolated, and suffer financial strain.

TREATMENT

> **Behavioral therapies** to promote healthy stress management. Habit reversal training, combining awareness with alternative behavior, and stimulus control using a different activity while an urge dissipates.

> **Antidepressants** (pp.142–143) prescribed along with therapy.

Repetitive behavior

Habits associated with these disorders often begin as a response to stress or anxiety but become addictive—the more that a person pulls or picks, the greater their urge to do it, in spite of the various negative consequences.

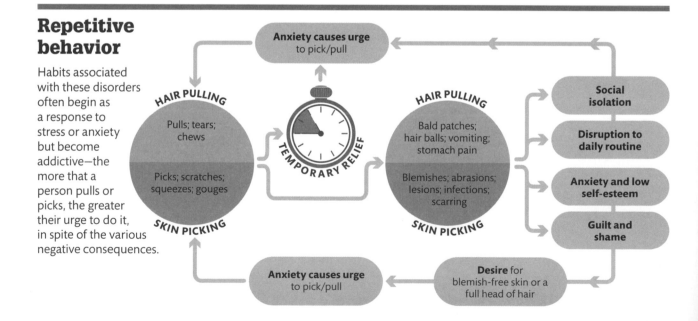

Illness anxiety disorder

Previously known as hypochondria, this condition involves a person worrying excessively about becoming seriously ill, even if thorough medical examinations reveal nothing.

What is it?

Hypochondria is considered to be two separate conditions: illness anxiety disorder if there are no symptoms or they are mild, or somatic symptom disorder (pp.108–109) if there are major physical symptoms causing emotional stress. People with illness anxiety disorder become excessively preoccupied with their health. Some have exaggerated feelings about an existing condition (about 20 percent do have heart, respiratory, gastrointestinal, or neurological problems). Others experience unexplained symptoms. They convince themselves that these symptoms indicate a serious illness that has been missed by medical teams.

Illness anxiety is a long-term condition that fluctuates in severity and may worsen with age or stress. It can be triggered by a major life event.

Someone who is anxious or depressed is more prone to the disorder. Assessment and treatment focus on stopping avoidance and reassurance behaviors (below), reevaluating health beliefs, and increasing the person's tolerance of uncertainties.

Endless checks

Disbelief in medical opinion reaffirms the person's anxiety and results in extra focus on the body part or illness, which causes panic and physical symptoms. Safety behaviors, such as avoiding situations for fear of exposure to disease, and reassurance from others provide brief respite.

⊕ TREATMENT

> **Behavioral therapies** such as attention training to keep from overattending to body sensations and help reevaluate beliefs.

> **Antidepressants** (pp.142–143) prescribed along with therapy.

VICIOUS CYCLE OF ILLNESS ANXIETY

PAIN/SENSATION TRIGGER

MISINTERPRET SIGNS

Stomach cancer!

RESEARCH ILLNESS

CHECK BODY FREQUENTLY

POSSIBLE AVOIDANCE

...FROM DOCTOR

CONSTANTLY SEEK REASSURANCE ...

... FROM FAMILY

TEMPORARY RELIEF

PTSD (post-traumatic stress disorder)

This is a severe anxiety disorder that may develop anytime after a person experiences or witnesses a terrifying or life-threatening event, or series of events, over which they have little or no control.

What is it?

PTSD is seen in people who have been in military combat or a serious incident, or suffered prolonged abuse or the unexpected injury or death of a family member. The event itself activates the fight-or-flight reflex in the brain and body, putting the person on hyperalert to deal with the consequences of the trauma and protect them from a repeat of the episode. An individual with PTSD feels that the threat remains, so their heightened response is maintained, causing an array of unpleasant symptoms including panic attacks, involuntary flashbacks, nightmares, avoidance and emotional numbing, anger, jumpiness, insomnia, and difficulty concentrating. These symptoms usually develop within a month of the event (but may not appear for months or years) and last for more than three months. PTSD can lead to other mental health problems, and excessive alcohol and drug use is common.

Watchful waiting is advisable at first to see if the symptoms subside within three months as treatment too early can exacerbate PTSD.

⊕ TREATMENT

❯ **Trauma-focused therapy** such as cognitive behavioral therapy (p.125) or eye movement desensitization and reprocessing (p.136) to help reduce the sense of current threat by working on memory of the event.

❯ **Compassion-focused therapy** to self-soothe from shame-based thoughts and images. Group therapy for vulnerable groups such as war veterans.

Brain changes

PTSD is a survival reaction. The symptoms result from an aim to help survive further traumatic experiences, and include raised levels of stress hormones and other changes in the brain.

PREFRONTAL CORTEX
Trauma affects the function of the prefrontal cortex, changing behaviors, personality, and complex cognitive functions such as planning and decision-making.

HYPOTHALAMUS
In PTSD, the hypothalamus sends signals to the adrenal glands (on the kidneys) to release the hormone adrenaline into the bloodstream and increase the chances of survival.

HIPPOCAMPUS
PTSD increases stress hormones, which reduce activity in the hippocampus and make it less effective in memory consolidation. Both the body and mind remain hyperalert because the decision-making ability is reduced.

AMYGDALA
PTSD increases the function of the amygdala, activating the fight-or-flight response and increasing sensory awareness.

ASR (acute stress reaction)

Also called acute stress disorder, ASR can appear quickly after an exceptional physical or mental stressor such as a bereavement, a road traffic incident, or an assault, but does not usually last long.

What is it?

Symptoms of ASR are anxiety and dissociative behavior following exposure to a traumatic and unexpected life event. The person may feel disconnected from themselves, have difficulty handling emotions, suffer mood swings, become depressed and anxious, and have panic attacks. They often experience difficulty sleeping, poor concentration, and recurrent dreams and flashbacks, and may avoid situations that trigger memories of the event. Some individuals have physiological symptoms such as raised heart rate, breathlessness, excessive sweating, headaches, chest pain, and nausea.

ASR is described as acute because the symptoms come on fast, but do not usually last.

Symptoms of ASR can begin within hours of the stress and are resolved within a month; if they last longer they may turn into PTSD (opposite).

ASR may resolve without therapy. Talking things over with friends or relatives can help those with the disorder understand the event and put it into context. Individuals may benefit from psychotherapies, too.

80%
of people with ASR develop PTSD 6 months later

⊕ TREATMENT

⟩ **Psychotherapies** such as cognitive behavioral therapy (p.125) to identify and reevaluate thoughts and behaviors that maintain anxiety and low mood.

⟩ **Lifestyle management** including supportive listening and stress-relieving practices such as yoga or meditation.

⟩ **Beta-blockers** and antidepressants (pp.142–143) to ease physical symptoms in combination with psychotherapy.

REGULAR MEDITATION can benefit the relationship that those with ASR have with uncomfortable mental experiences and calm the fight-or-flight response.

HOW DOES ASR DIFFER FROM PTSD?

ASR and PTSD are similar, but the time frames are different. The symptoms of ASR occur within a month of an event and they usually resolve within the same month. The symptoms of PTSD may or may not develop within a month of the event or events. PTSD is not diagnosed unless the symptoms have been evident for more than three months. There is an overlap between what the symptoms are. However, in ASR symptoms involving feelings, such as dissociation, depression, and anxiety, predominate. With PTSD the symptoms relate to a prolonged or persistent response to the fight-or-flight mechanism (pp.32–33). There is a higher risk of ASR developing in a person who has had PTSD or mental health issues in the past, and ASR can lead to PTSD.

Adjustment disorder

This is a short-term, stress-related psychological disorder that can follow a significant life event. Typically, a person's reaction is stronger, or more prolonged, than expected for the type of event.

What is it?

Any stressful event can trigger anxiety, difficulty sleeping, sadness, tension, and inability to focus. However, if an individual finds an event especially hard, their reaction can be stronger and persist for months. In a child, the disorder can follow family conflicts, problems at school, and hospitalization. The child may become withdrawn and/or disruptive, and complain of unexplained pain or illness. Adjustment disorder is not the same as PTSD or ASR (pp.62–63)

because the stress trigger is not as severe. It normally resolves within months as a person learns how to adapt to a situation and/or the stressor is removed. There is no way to predict whether one person is more likely to develop adjustment disorder than another. It comes down to how they respond to an event and their personal history.

A GP initially assesses whether an individual's symptoms may be due to another condition, such as ASR, before referring them for a psychological assessment.

⊕ TREATMENT

> **Psychotherapies** such as cognitive behavioral therapy (p.125) and/or family or group therapies (pp.138–141) to help identify and respond to stressors.

> **Antidepressants** (pp.142–143) to lessen symptoms of depression, anxiety, and insomnia, along with a psychotherapy.

Causes and outcome

Some life events are known to lead to adjustment difficulties of varying severity. Examples are the death of a friend or family member, divorce or relationship breakdown, moving, illness or injury, financial worries, or job stress.

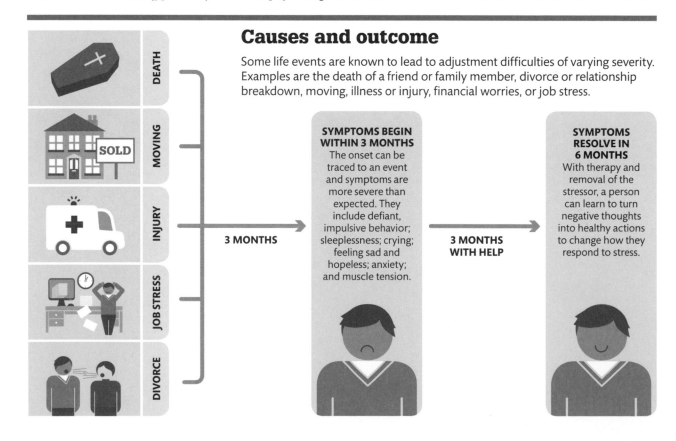

DEATH

MOVING — SOLD

INJURY

JOB STRESS

DIVORCE

3 MONTHS

SYMPTOMS BEGIN WITHIN 3 MONTHS
The onset can be traced to an event and symptoms are more severe than expected. They include defiant, impulsive behavior; sleeplessness; crying; feeling sad and hopeless; anxiety; and muscle tension.

3 MONTHS WITH HELP

SYMPTOMS RESOLVE IN 6 MONTHS
With therapy and removal of the stressor, a person can learn to turn negative thoughts into healthy actions to change how they respond to stress.

Reactive attachment disorder

This disorder can result in children who do not bond with a caregiver in infancy. Unidentified reactive attachment disorder can be a precursor to lifelong impaired personal development.

What is it?

Attachment theory (pp.154–157) states that developing a strong emotional and physical bond with a primary caregiver is key to a child's healthy personal development. Without such a bond a child can become increasingly detached, withdrawn, and distressed, and the physical symptoms relating to stress become obvious.

Persistent disregard of a child's basic physical needs, frequent changes of primary caregivers, and childhood abuse can disrupt a child's ability to form social and emotional bonds. The child can develop markedly disturbed ways of relating socially, and may be unable to initiate or respond to social interactions.

Disinhibited responses, such as a disregard for convention and impulsive behavior, used to be included in the assessment of this disorder, but these are now considered as a separate diagnosis of disinhibited social engagement disorder.

Long-term impact

Early neutral, negative, or even hostile environments are likely to have a long-term negative impact and affect a person right through to adulthood. An individual's ability to make and maintain healthy relationships in later life is seriously compromised. Reactive attachment disorder can develop in early infancy, and the vulnerability it creates is associated with a wide range of disorders that affect both children and adults (below).

TREATMENT

> **Cognitive and behavioral therapies** including cognitive behavioral therapy (p.125) to examine habitual appraisals, dialectical behavior therapy (p.126) to help severely affected adults, family therapy (pp.138–141) to promote good communication, anxiety management, and positive behavior support.

Associated disorders

Undiagnosed reactive attachment disorder is an underlying factor in a number of psychological problems that emerge in childhood or adulthood under clinical assessment.

DEPRESSION
This can develop because a person with reactive attachment disorder sees a constant disparity between expectation and reality.

LEARNING DIFFICULTIES
Social isolation creates a hostile environment that can make an individual more likely to have developmental disorders.

LOW SELF-ESTEEM
Without any positive reciprocal interactions in infancy, neutral or negative ones can predominate later, which can affect self-esteem.

RELATIONSHIP ISSUES
Not developing healthy attachments in childhood makes it difficult to form meaningful relationships in adulthood.

SOCIAL DIFFICULTIES
If a person feels different from their peers, they can be disruptive and are more susceptible to isolation or bullying.

SUBSTANCE ABUSE
Individuals who have suffered a disrupted infancy or childhood commonly seek support through drugs.

ADULT

CHILD

ADHD (attention deficit hyperactivity disorder)

This neurodevelopmental disorder is diagnosed in children with behavioral symptoms (inattentiveness, hyperactivity, and impulsivity) that are inconsistent with their age.

What is it?

This is a condition that makes it difficult for a child to sit still and concentrate, and it is usually noticeable before the age of six. The effects of ADHD can persist into adolescence and adulthood. Adults may also be diagnosed with the preexisting condition, when persistent problems in higher education, employment, and relationships reveal it. However, the symptoms may not be as clear as they are in children (right). The level of hyperactivity decreases in adults with ADHD, but they struggle more with paying attention, impulsive behavior, and restlessness.

The evidence for what causes ADHD is inconclusive, but it is thought to include a combination of factors. Genetics may play a part, which explains why it runs in families. Observations of brain scans also indicate differences in brain structure, and have identified unusual levels of the neurotransmitters dopamine and norepinephrine (pp.28–29). Other possible risk factors include premature birth, low birthweight, and exposure to environmental hazards. The condition is more common in people with learning difficulties. Children with ADHD may also display signs of other conditions such as ASD (pp.68–69), tic disorders or Tourette's (pp.100–101), depression (pp.38–39), and sleep disorders (pp.98–99). Surveys have shown that worldwide this condition affects more than twice as many boys as girls.

Identifying ADHD

A GP cannot officially diagnose ADHD, but if they suspect a child has the disorder they refer them for specialist assessment. The child's patterns of hyperactivity, inattention, and impulsive behavior are observed over a six-month period before a treatment plan is prepared.

HYPERACTIVITY

> **Difficulties sitting still** The child cannot stay seated (or quiet) in situations where it is expected, such as the classroom.

> **Constant fidgeting** The child may twitch limbs, torso, and/or head, whether sitting or standing.

> **Lack of volume control** The child shouts and makes loud noises during normal everyday activities.

> **Little or no sense of danger** This may result in the child running and climbing in environments where these behaviors are neither safe nor appropriate.

> ## "... an ADHD brain [is] like a browser with way too many open tabs."
> Pat Noue, ADHD Collective

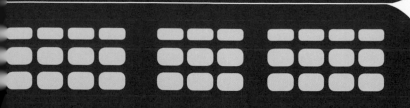

INATTENTIVENESS

> **Concentration difficulties** This causes the child to make errors of judgment and mistakes. Along with constant movement, this can cause injury.
> **Clumsiness** The child is prone to dropping and breaking things.
> **Easily distracted** The child appears not to be listening and is unable to complete tasks.
> **Poor organizational skills** The child's inability to concentrate has an impact on organizational abilities.
> **Forgetfulness** This results in the child losing things.

IMPULSIVITY

> **Interrupting** The child disrupts conversations regardless of the speaker or situation.

> **Inability to take turns** The child is unable to wait their turn in conversations and games.

> **Excessive talking** The child may change a topic often or focus obsessively on one.

> **Acting without thinking** The child is unable to wait in line or keep up with group pace.

⊕ TREATMENT

> **Behavioral therapies** (pp.122–129) to help the child and their family manage day to day; psychoeducation (p.113) for families and caregivers.
> **Lifestyle management** such as improving physical health and reducing stress to calm the child.
> **Medication** can calm (not cure) the person so that they are less impulsive and hyperactive. Stimulants (pp.142–143) increase dopamine levels and trigger the area of the brain involved in concentration.

MANAGING ADHD

There are a number of ways that parents can help their child to handle the condition.

> **Create predictable routines** to calm an ADHD sufferer. Schedule daily activities and keep them consistent. Make sure school timetables are clearly set, too.
> **Set clear boundaries** and make sure the child knows what is expected of them; praise positive behavior right away.
> **Give clear instructions,** either visual or verbal, whichever the child finds easier to follow.
> **Use an incentive scheme,** for example, have a star/points chart whereby a child can earn privileges for good behavior.

ASD (autism spectrum disorder)

ASD describes a spectrum (range) of lifelong disorders that affect a person's ability to relate to other people—and their emotions and feelings—making social interaction difficult.

What is it?

ASD is generally diagnosed in childhood and can present in a variety of ways. A parent or caregiver may notice that a baby does not use vocal sounds or an older child has problems with social interaction and nonverbal communication. Symptoms such as repetitive behaviors, problems talking, poor eye contact, tidying or ordering rituals, bizarre motor responses, repetition of words or sentences, a restricted repertoire of interests, and sleep problems are common. Some children with ASD may also have depression (pp.38–39) or ADHD (pp.66–67).

Genetic predisposition, premature birth, fetal alcohol syndrome, and conditions such as muscular dystrophy, Down syndrome, and cerebral palsy are known to be associated with ASD. A GP first examines the child to rule out physical causes for the symptoms, then refers them for specialist diagnosis. Information is gathered about all aspects of the child's behavior and development, at home and school. There is no cure, but specialized therapies such as speech therapy and physical therapy can help. One in every 68 people in the US has ASD and it is identified in more girls than boys.

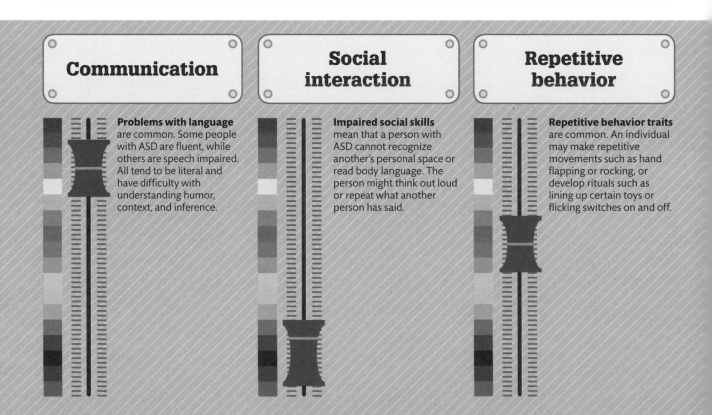

Communication

Problems with language are common. Some people with ASD are fluent, while others are speech impaired. All tend to be literal and have difficulty with understanding humor, context, and inference.

Social interaction

Impaired social skills mean that a person with ASD cannot recognize another's personal space or read body language. The person might think out loud or repeat what another person has said.

Repetitive behavior

Repetitive behavior traits are common. An individual may make repetitive movements such as hand flapping or rocking, or develop rituals such as lining up certain toys or flicking switches on and off.

HIGH-FUNCTIONING AUTISM AND ASPERGER'S

High-functioning autism (HFA) and Asperger's syndrome (AS) are both terms that are applied to people with characteristics of ASD, but who are of above average intelligence with an IQ of more than 70. However, they exist as two separate diagnoses, as those with HFA have delayed language development, which is not present in AS. Diagnosis of HFA or AS may be missed in children as they are socially awkward with a manner that is not easily understood. The ASD traits they share of perfectionism and obsessive interest in a specific subject can mean that they become experts in their area of interest. Like ASD, those with HFA or AS also require strict routines and have sensitivities to certain stimuli, awkwardness, and difficulty behaving appropriately and communicating in social situations; the severity of these symptoms will differ in each individual. Long-term difficulties arise with social and intimate relationships, both at school and into adulthood.

⊕ TREATMENT

> **Specialist interventions and therapies** can assist with self-harming, hyperactivity, and sleep difficulties.

> **Educational and behavioral programs** can support the learning of social skills.

> **Medication** (pp.142–143) can help with associated symptoms—melatonin for sleep problems, SSRIs for depression, and methylphenidate for ADHD.

Degrees of ASD

ASD manifests itself in different ways and to different degrees in each person. Autistic author and academic Stephen M. Shore said, "If you've met one individual with autism, you've met one individual with autism."

> ## "... in science or art, a dash of autism is essential."

Hans Asperger, Austrian pediatrician and researcher of autism

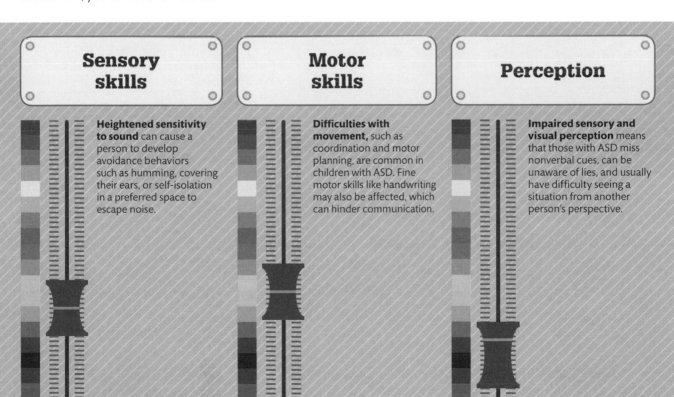

Sensory skills

Heightened sensitivity to sound can cause a person to develop avoidance behaviors such as humming, covering their ears, or self-isolation in a preferred space to escape noise.

Motor skills

Difficulties with movement, such as coordination and motor planning, are common in children with ASD. Fine motor skills like handwriting may also be affected, which can hinder communication.

Perception

Impaired sensory and visual perception means that those with ASD miss nonverbal cues, can be unaware of lies, and usually have difficulty seeing a situation from another person's perspective.

Schizophrenia

This is a long-term condition that affects the way a person thinks. It is characterized by feelings of paranoia, hallucinations, and delusions, and significantly impacts a person's ability to function.

What is it?

The word schizophrenia comes from the Greek, and literally means "split mind," which has led to the myth that people with the condition have split personalities, but they do not. Instead they suffer from delusions and hallucinations that they believe are real. There are different types of schizophrenia. The main ones are paranoid (hallucinations and delusions); catatonic (unusual movements, switching between being very active and being very still); and disorganized, which has aspects of both. Despite popular belief, individuals with schizophrenia are not always violent. They are, however, more likely to abuse alcohol and drugs, and it is these habits, combined with their condition, that can cause them to become aggressive.

Schizophrenia appears to result from a combination of physical, genetic, psychological, and environmental factors. MRI scans have identified abnormal levels of neurotransmitters dopamine and serotonin (pp.28–29) and unusual brain structure, and there might be a correlation between the condition and pregnancy or birth complications. It is also thought that excessive cannabis use in young adulthood can be a trigger.

Popular theories regarding the causes of schizophrenia in the second half of the 20th century included family dysfunction theories, such as the "double bind" (when people are faced with contradictory, irreconcilable demands for courses of action), high levels of parent/caregiver "expressed emotion" (not tolerating those with the disorder), and learning the schizophrenic role through labeling. Since then, mental health specialists have observed that hearing voices or feeling paranoid are common reactions to trauma, abuse, or deprivation. Stress can trigger acute schizophrenic episodes, and learning to recognize their onset can help with management of the condition.

⊕ TREATMENT

> **Community mental health teams** such as social workers, occupational therapists, pharmacists, psychologists, and psychiatrists work together to develop ways to help a person stay stable and progress.

> **Medication** in the form of antipsychotics (pp.142–143) is prescribed to reduce mostly positive symptoms, but it does not cure the condition.

> **Cognitive behavioral therapy** (p.125) and the technique of reality testing can help with management of symptoms such as delusions. New developments use imagery to defuse stress that negative symptoms cause.

> **Family therapy** (pp.138–141) can improve relationships and coping skills within the family and educate anyone involved in a person's care.

Positive symptoms (psychotic)

These symptoms are classed as positive because they are additions to a person's mental state and represent new ways of thinking and behaving that only develop with the condition.

 > **Hearing voices** is common, and can occur occasionally or all the time. The voices may be noisy or quiet, disturbing or negative, known or unknown, and male or female.

 > **Hallucinations** involve seeing things that are not there but seem very real to the person, and are often violent and very disturbing.

 > **Feeling sensations** can cause a person to be convinced that they have unpleasant creatures such as ants crawling on or under their skin.

 > **Smelling and tasting things** that cannot be identified can arise, and there may be difficulty discriminating between smells and tastes.

 > **Delusions**—fixed beliefs—are held despite evidence to the contrary. The person may think they are famous and/or being chased or plotted against.

 > **Feelings of being controlled** by, for example, a religious or dictatorial delusionist, can overwhelm a person. The beliefs can make them act differently.

How is it diagnosed?

Schizophrenia is diagnosed through clinical interviews and specialist checklists during which the symptoms (below) are assessed. The earlier the condition is diagnosed and treatment begun, the better, so that there is less time for its extreme impact on personal, social, and work life to build up. While schizophrenia is not curable, people can overcome it enough to function day to day. A personalized treatment plan that caters to the specific needs of the individual with schizophrenia is required for people with such a complex mental health issue.

Around **1.1%** of the global adult population has schizophrenia

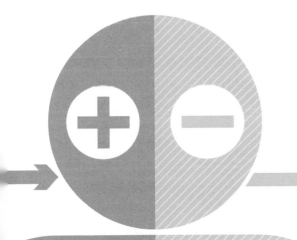

Negative symptoms (withdrawal)

These symptoms are called negative because they represent a loss of certain functions, thoughts, or behaviors that a healthy person exhibits, but that are absent in those with schizophrenia.

 ❯ **Difficulty communicating** with others can result in changed body language, a lack of eye contact, and incoherence.

 ❯ **"Flattened" emotions** result in a significantly reduced range of response. The person will take no pleasure in activities.

 ❯ **Tiredness** may result in lethargy, change in sleep patterns, staying in bed, or sitting in the same place for long periods.

 ❯ **Absence of willpower or motivation** makes it difficult or even impossible for a person to engage in normal day-to-day activity.

 ❯ **Poor memory and concentration** means that the individual is unable to plan or set goals and has difficulty keeping track of thoughts and conversations.

 ❯ **Inability to cope** with everyday tasks results in disorganization. The individual stops looking after themselves, domestically or personally.

 ❯ **Becoming withdrawn** from social and community activities can disrupt the individual's social life.

Symptoms of schizophrenia

These are classified as positive or negative. Positive symptoms are psychotic additions to an individual, whereas negative symptoms can look like the withdrawal or flat emotions seen with depression. Schizophrenia is likely if a person has experienced one or more symptoms from both domains for most of the time for a month.

Schizoaffective disorder

This is a long-term mental health condition in which a person suffers both the psychotic symptoms of schizophrenia and the deregulated emotions that characterize bipolar disorder at the same time.

What is it?

While symptoms may vary from person to person, one episode will feature both psychotic and mood symptoms (manic, depressive, or both) for part of the time and a period with only psychotic or mood symptoms for most of the time over a period of at least two weeks.

Schizoaffective disorder can be triggered by traumatic events that took place when a person was too young to know how to cope or was not being cared for in a way that made it possible to develop coping skills. Genetics may play a part, too. It is more common in women and usually begins in early adulthood.

A mental health professional will assess the symptoms and will want to know how long they have been present, and what triggers them. This chronic condition impacts every aspect of a person's life, but symptoms can be managed. Family interventions to raise awareness of the disorder can improve communication and support.

⊕ TREATMENT

❯ **Medication** is needed long-term; usually combinations of mood stabilizers plus antidepressants for depressive types or antipsychotics for manic types (pp.142–143).

❯ **Cognitive behavioral therapy** (p.125) can help a person make links between thoughts, feelings, and actions; learn the cues preceding behavior change; sand develop coping strategies.

The different forms

People with this disorder experience periods of psychotic symptoms—such as hallucinations or delusions—with mood disorder symptoms of either a manic type or a depressive type, but sometimes both. The condition features cycles of severe symptoms followed by periods of improvement.

1% of the population is likely to develop schizoaffective disorder

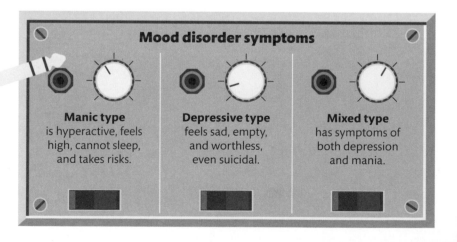

Mood disorder symptoms

Manic type is hyperactive, feels high, cannot sleep, and takes risks.

Depressive type feels sad, empty, and worthless, even suicidal.

Mixed type has symptoms of both depression and mania.

Psychotic symptoms

❯ **Hallucinations** Hearing voices and seeing things that are not there.

❯ **Delusions** False, fixed beliefs in things that are not true.

Catatonia

An episodic condition that affects both behavior and motor skills, catatonia is characterized by abnormal psychomotor functioning and extreme unresponsiveness when awake.

What is it?

Catatonia is a state of immobility that can persist for days or weeks. Those with the condition may have an extremely negative outlook and may not respond to external events, become agitated, have difficulty speaking due to extreme anxiety, and refuse to eat or drink. Symptoms also include feelings of sadness, irritability, and worthlessness, which can occur nearly every day. An individual may lose interest in activities, lose or gain weight suddenly, have trouble getting to sleep or out of bed, and feel restless. Decision making is impaired and suicidal thoughts are common.

This condition can have a psychological or neurological cause, and may be associated with depression (pp.38–39) or psychotic disorders. It is estimated that 10–15 percent of people with catatonia also have symptoms of schizophrenia (pp.70–71), while about 20–30 percent of individuals with bipolar disorder (pp.40–41) may experience catatonia during their illness—mostly during their manic phase.

Diagnosing catatonia

A mental health professional observes an individual and looks for a number of symptoms. At least 3 out of the 12 symptoms described (right) must be present to confirm a diagnosis of catatonia.

⊕ TREATMENT

❯ **Medication** prescribed depends on the symptoms, but includes antidepressants, muscle relaxers, antipsychotics, and/or tranquilizers such as benzodiazepines, but these carry a risk of dependency (pp.142–143). Outside help is needed to ensure compliance with medication and to teach living skills.

❯ **Electroconvulsive therapy** may be used when medication is ineffective. This involves transmitting an electric current through the person's brain (pp.142–143).

Mutism
Silent and apparently unwilling or unable to speak.

Echolalia
Constantly repeats what other people have said.

Grimacing
Makes distorted facial expressions that show disgust, dislike, and even pain.

Stupor
Immobile, lacks expression, and does not respond to stimuli.

Catalepsy May be rigid, have a seizure, or be completely unresponsive in this trancelike state.

Waxy flexibility Limbs can be moved by someone else and will remain in the new position.

Agitation
Movement may be purposeless and risky.

Mannerism
Strikes poses or makes idiosyncratic movements.

Posturing
Moves from one unusual position to another.

Stereotypy
Frequent persistent, repetitive movements.

Negativism
Resistant to any outlook other than a negative one.

Echopraxia
Constantly mimics other people's movements.

Delusional disorder

This is a very rare form of psychosis that causes a person to experience complex and often disturbed thoughts and delusions that are not true or based on reality.

What is it?

Previously known as paranoid disorder, delusional disorder is marked by an individual's inability to distinguish what is real from what is imagined. The delusions may be misinterpretations of experienced events, and are either not true or highly exaggerated. They may be nonbizarre and relate to situations that could occur, such as being followed, poisoned, deceived, or loved from a distance, or may be bizarre delusions that are impossible, for example, a belief in an imminent alien invasion.

Delusional disorder can make it hard for a person to concentrate, socialize, and live a normal life, because it can cause dramatic changes in a person's behavior that result in conflict with those around them. Individuals may become so preoccupied with their delusions that their lives are disrupted. However, others continue to function normally and, apart from the subject of their delusion, do not behave in an obviously odd manner. Some people experience hallucinations—seeing, hearing, tasting, smelling, or feeling things that are not really there.

Thematic delusions

Delusions are fixed beliefs that do not change, even when a person is presented with conflicting evidence, and characteristically follow particular themes (right). Individuals are likely to display the delusion for a month or longer, and most do not admit they are problematic. The person may appear completely normal as long as an outsider does not touch on the belief.

Erotomanic
A delusion in which a person believes that another individual, often someone famous, is in love with them; may lead to stalking behavior.

Somatic
A person with these delusions has physical or bodily sensations—for example, as a result of believing insects are crawling under their skin.

Grandiose
An individual with grandiose delusions believes they have a great unrecognized talent or knowledge, for example, they may be a special messenger, guru, or God.

Psychological disorders known to trigger delusional episodes include schizophrenia (pp.70–71), bipolar disorder (pp.40–41), severe depression (pp.38–39) or stress, and lack of sleep. General medical conditions that can cause them are HIV, malaria, syphilis, lupus, Parkinson's, multiple sclerosis, and brain tumors. Misuse of substances such as alcohol or drugs can also trigger delusional episodes in some people.

How is it diagnosed?

A doctor will first take a complete medical history of the individual. They will ask about symptoms and will want to know how a delusion affects a person's day-to-day functioning, any family history of mental health conditions, and details of medications and/or illegal substances a person has been taking.

⊕ TREATMENT

> **Medication** (pp.142–143) prescribed may include antipsychotic drugs to reduce the delusional symptoms and antidepressants such as selective serotonin reuptake inhibitors (SSRIs) to help with the depression that can be associated with the disorder.

> **Psychotherapies** such as cognitive behavioral therapy (p.125) to help examine the strongly held beliefs and support changes needed.

> **Self-help groups and social support** to reduce the stress that results from living with this disorder and to help those around them, and family, social, and/or school intervention to help develop social skills to reduce the impact of the disorder on quality of life.

Only **0.2%** of people will ever **experience delusions**

Persecutory
A person with these delusions feels that they are being persecuted or mistreated—for example, stalked, drugged, spied on, or the victim of slander.

Jealous
People with this delusion have a morbid but unfounded belief that their partner has been unfaithful or is deceiving them.

Mixed or unspecified
Themes are said to be mixed if several types of delusions are present but no particular one predominates. In some cases the delusion does not fall into any of the main categories and is unspecified.

Dementia

This is an (as yet) incurable, degenerative disorder, also known as mild or major neurocognitive impairment. It is characterized by memory disorders, personality changes, and impaired reasoning.

What is it?

The term dementia describes a set of symptoms that affect the brain and gradually become more severe. Symptoms include difficulties with concentration, problem solving, carrying out a sequence of tasks, planning, or organizing, as well as general confusion.

A person with dementia may lose track of days or dates, and find it hard to follow a conversation or recall the right word for something. They may also be unable to judge distances or see objects in three dimensions. Dementia may cause people to feel insecure and lose their self-confidence and can result in depression.

Many different conditions, such as Alzheimer's, cardiovascular disease, Lewy bodies, and disorders of the front and side lobes of the brain, cause the symptoms.

Dementia is mainly seen in older adults, but can occur in people in their 50s (known as early onset), and sometimes even younger.

There is no single assessment for dementia. The GP uses memory and thinking tests and may order a scan to confirm which areas of the brain are damaged. Treatment aims to alleviate symptoms and slow their progression.

More than 30% of people over 65 develop dementia

Motor skills
If the areas of the brain responsible for movement are damaged, muscle control lessens.

Emotions
Inability to control or express feelings can cause low self-esteem and depression.

CAUSES

> **Alzheimer's disease** causes abnormal proteins to build up around brain cells and damage their structure. This disrupts the chemical messages that pass between the cells so the cells gradually die. Symptoms progress as more parts of the brain are affected.

> **Vascular dementia** can result from cardiovascular disease. It occurs when blood flow to the brain is impaired (for example, by a stroke), causing problems with reasoning, planning, judgment, and memory.

> **Mixed dementia** results when Alzheimer's and vascular dementia occur at the same time.

> **Dementia with Lewy bodies** has similar symptoms to Alzheimer's and Parkinson's disease. Also known as Pick's disease, it occurs when protein bodies form in nerve cells and often causes hallucinations and delusions.

> **Frontotemporal dementia** is a rarer form that affects the temporal (side) and frontal lobes of the brain. It alters personality and behavior, and makes use of language difficult.

Social skills
The inability to concentrate and follow conversation can make it difficult to relate to people.

Memory
Short-term memory is affected first, but long-term memory also fails as the disease progresses.

Speech
Speaking and control of language become hard, which can be disconcerting for others.

Decision making
Memory loss, poor concentration, and confusion can make decision making hard or impossible.

Judgment
No longer feeling in control or able to plan anything leads to loss of faith in own judgment.

Concentration
Lack of focus can make daily routines and independent living very difficult.

Empathy
Struggling to make sense of what is happening leaves little room for thinking of others.

⊕ **TREATMENT**

❯ **Cognitive stimulation and reality orientation therapy** for short-term memory.

❯ **Behavioral therapy** (p.124) to help carry out daily routines.

❯ **Validation therapy**—the main caregiver reading out loud, respectful statements.

❯ **Cholinesterase inhibitors** (pp.142–143) to boost memory and judgment.

How it affects a person

Because every person is different, their experience of dementia is, too. The diagnosis is based on a person's history and how the symptoms affect their ability to cope day to day.

PEOPLE WITH DEMENTIA feel insecure, lose confidence in themselves, and need help preparing for the road ahead.

CTE (chronic traumatic encephalopathy)

Also known as post-concussion syndrome, this is a degenerative condition of the brain characterized by physiological and psychological disturbances following closed head injuries.

What is it?

CTE is most often seen in service personnel or people who take part in high-impact contact sports, such as football, rugby, or boxing, and there is no cure. Physical symptoms include headache, dizziness, and pain. Psychological symptoms are memory loss, confusion, impaired judgment, impulse-control problems, and even hallucinations. An individual may become aggressive and have difficulty maintaining relationships. Signs of Parkinson's and dementia (pp.76–77) can emerge later. The disturbances may develop early, or emerge years after the head trauma. A preventive approach is advisable, with the use of protective headgear and the introduction of rules that disallow contact above chest or shoulder height in sport.

At the moment it is possible to diagnose CTE only after death. Tests, brain scans, and biomarkers are being developed to help identify the condition earlier.

TREATMENT

> **Psychotherapies** such as cognitive behavioral therapy (p.125) and mindfulness-based stress reduction (p.129).

> **Lifestyle management** including rest and recuperation after initial head injury, followed by a gradual return to activities, stopped if symptoms return.

> **Antidepressants** (p.142–143) if psychological symptoms warrant them.

CTE was identified in 99% of former US National Football League players

Cumulative effect of head injury

Multiple blows to the unprotected skull can lead to irreversible injury. In a study of 100 people with mild head injury, 20–50 showed symptoms of CTE three months after the initial injury, and about 1 in 10 still had problems a year later.

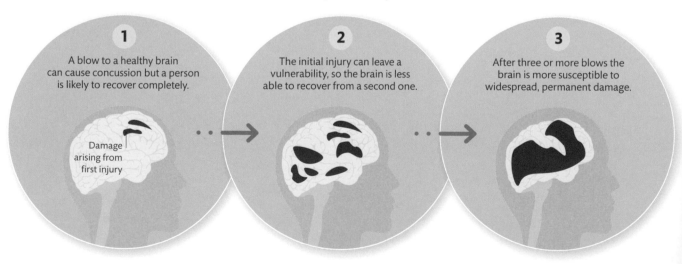

1 A blow to a healthy brain can cause concussion but a person is likely to recover completely.

Damage arising from first injury

2 The initial injury can leave a vulnerability, so the brain is less able to recover from a second one.

3 After three or more blows the brain is more susceptible to widespread, permanent damage.

Delirium (acute confusional state)

This is an acutely disturbed state of mind characterized by lethargy, restlessness, delusions, and incoherence, which can result from a variety of causes including illness, poor diet, or intoxication.

What is it?

Delirium can have a serious impact on day-to-day life but is usually short-term. An individual has difficulty concentrating and may be confused as to where they are. They may move more slowly or quickly than usual and experience mood swings. Other symptoms include not thinking or speaking clearly, difficulty sleeping or feeling drowsy, reduced short-term memory, and loss of muscle control.

Delirium may occur at any age, but it is more common in the elderly and can be confused with dementia (pp.76–77). It is generally a short-term physical or emotional problem, but it can be irreversible. It is also possible to have dementia and delirium at the same time.

Causes vary, but likely reasons are a medical condition, such as a chest or urinary tract infection, or a metabolic imbalance, such as low sodium. Delirium can also follow severe illness, surgery, pain, dehydration, constipation, poor nutrition, or a change in medication.

How is it diagnosed?

A doctor checks the symptoms and assesses movement, cognitive processes, and speech. Some practitioners use observational methods to diagnose or rule out delirium, by watching the person's behavior over an entire day. Physical tests may be carried out to check for underlying illness.

(pp.76–77)

⊕ TREATMENT

- ⟩ **Reality orientation therapy,** involving the use of repeated visual and verbal orientation cues delivered in a respectful manner, to help the person understand their surroundings and situation.

- ⟩ **Lifestyle management** including routine and scheduled activity with exercise to minimize confusion and help the individual regain some day-to-day control.

- ⟩ **Antibiotics** prescribed if illness is identified as the cause, together with rehydration if necessary.

Up to 50% of elderly patients in the hospital suffer from delirium

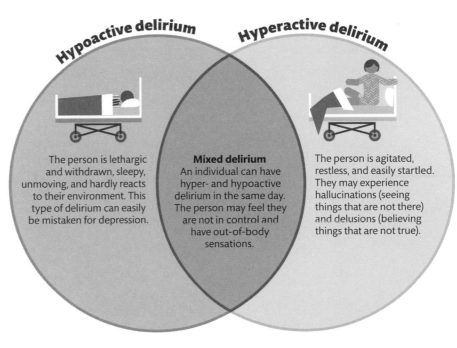

Hypoactive delirium

The person is lethargic and withdrawn, sleepy, unmoving, and hardly reacts to their environment. This type of delirium can easily be mistaken for depression.

Mixed delirium
An individual can have hyper- and hypoactive delirium in the same day. The person may feel they are not in control and have out-of-body sensations.

Hyperactive delirium

The person is agitated, restless, and easily startled. They may experience hallucinations (seeing things that are not there) and delusions (believing things that are not true).

Substance use disorder

This is a serious condition in which the use of alcohol or drugs, or both, leads to physical and psychological problems that affect the individual's working or home life for the worse.

What is it?

Also known as drug use disorder or substance abuse, this condition can cause wide-ranging impairments and psychological distress. Symptoms and signs of substance abuse (whether alcohol or drugs) include taking drugs regularly, maybe daily, to function; taking drugs even when alone; continuing to use drugs even when the person knows it is harming their own health, family, or work; making excuses to use drugs and reacting with aggression to inquiries about their substance use; being secretive about using drugs; losing interest in other activities; impaired ability to work; neglecting to eat or attend to physical appearance; confusion; lethargy; depression; financial problems; and criminal activity such as stealing money.

In the longer term, overconsumption of alcohol can cause weight gain and high blood pressure and increase the risk of depression (pp.38–39), liver damage, problems with the immune system, and some cancers. Drugs can be associated with mental health issues such as depression, schizophrenia (pp.70–71), and personality disorders (pp.102–107).

Alcohol or drug abuse usually begins as a voluntary behavior, encouraged or tolerated within the person's social and cultural climate. Peer pressure, stress, and family dysfunction can escalate the problem. A child with a family member who has chemical-dependency issues may be at a higher risk of the disorder for either environmental or genetic reasons or both.

How is it diagnosed?

Diagnosis begins with the person recognizing that they have a problem; denial is a common symptom of addiction. Empathy and respect are more likely to induce a person to accept that they have substance use disorder than orders and confrontation. The GP or specialist grades the person's behavior (below) while the individual is using the substance.

TREATMENT

❯ **Psychotherapies,** such as cognitive behavioral therapy (p.125) or acceptance and commitment therapy (p.126), to look at the thinking and behaviors that maintain the addiction and change a person's relationship with their thoughts.

❯ **Psychosocial support** through attending meetings with peer groups, such as Alcoholics Anonymous, to motivate and encourage a person to stop substance abuse and improve their quality of life.

❯ **Residential inpatient units** in severe cases to limit a person's activities during detoxification and provide medication necessary to help manage any extreme withdrawal symptoms.

Behavior patterns

The diagnosis of this disorder, whatever the substance, is based on a set of 11 behaviors related to its use. The severity of the disorder is based on how many of these behaviors are present: 0–1 = no diagnosis; 2–3 = mild substance use disorder; 4–5 = moderate substance use disorder; 6+ = severe substance use disorder.

Alcohol use

Use of other substances

Impaired control

> **1.** Uses substance for longer and/or in larger amounts than originally intended.

> **2.** Wants to cut down, but cannot do so.

> **3.** Spends longer and longer getting, using, and recovering from using the substance.

> **4.** Has intense cravings for the substance, which makes it difficult for the person to think about anything else.

Social impairment

> **5.** Continues to use despite knowing the problems it causes with life at home or work.

> **6.** Continues to use despite arguments with family or the loss of friendships it causes.

> **7.** Gives up social and recreational activities as a result, so spends less time with friends and family, and becomes increasingly isolated.

Risky use

> **8.** While under the influence, engages in risky sexual behavior or puts themselves or others in danger, for example, by driving, operating machinery, or swimming.

> **9.** Continues to use while aware that the substance is making psychological or physical problems worse (for example, drinking even when liver damage has been diagnosed).

Pharmacological criteria

> **10.** Becomes tolerant to the substance, so needs increasing amounts to achieve the same effects. Different drugs vary in terms of how quickly tolerance develops.

> **11.** Suffers withdrawal such as nausea, sweating, and shaking if the intake is stopped.

29.5million

people in the **world** have drug use disorder

United Nations Office on Drugs and Crime, World Drug Report 2017

Impulse-control and addiction

Impulse-control disorders are diagnosed in people who cannot withstand the urge to perform problematic behaviors. In addiction, a pleasurable activity becomes compulsive and interferes with daily life.

What are they?

The basic concepts underlying impulsive and addictive behaviors overlap. Some psychologists think that impulse-control disorders should be classed as addictions.

In impulse-control disorders, a person perpetuates their behavior regardless of the consequences, and they become less and less able to control their inner urges. Usually, a person feels an increasing tension or arousal before the action, pleasure or relief while doing it, and regret or guilt in the aftermath. Environmental and neurological factors both play a part in the development of the disorders and they may be triggered by stress.

The recognized impulse-control disorders are compulsive gambling (opposite), kleptomania (p.84), pyromania (p.85), hair pulling (p.60), and intermittent explosive disorder (below). Sex, exercise, shopping, and Internet addictions (below) share similar traits.

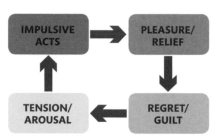

Impulse-control disorders and addictions

DISORDER	WHAT IS IT?	TREATMENT
INTERMITTENT EXPLOSIVE DISORDER	Tendency to short but violent outbursts even though there is no real trigger for the behavior.	Impulse-control training to identify cues and change responses; adapt environment.
SEX ADDICTION	Intense focus on sex and how to obtain it, regardless of the negative impact on everyday life.	Psychotherapies can support the development of alternative emotional coping strategies.
EXERCISE ADDICTION	Uncontrollable compulsion to exercise beyond health needs that can result in injury or illness.	Behavioral therapy to manage stress with more adaptive activities and planned exercise.
SHOPPING ADDICTION	Stress-triggered, irresistible urge to shop, followed by euphoria that provides only temporary relief.	Behavioral therapy to support changes in thinking and responses to break the cycle.
COMPUTER/ INTERNET ADDICTION	Preoccupation that leads to more time spent online, and mood problems if that time is restricted.	Behavioral therapy to become aware of problem and develop ways to cope with real world.

Gambling disorder

Also known as compulsive gambling, this is an impulse-control disorder that exists when a person repeatedly gambles despite the significant problems or distress it causes themselves and others.

What is it?

The thrill of winning releases dopamine (p.29) from the reward center in the brain. For some people the act of gambling becomes addictive and they need ever bigger wins to achieve the same thrill.

Once a gambling disorder takes hold, the cycle is difficult to break. The disorder may start from desperation for money, the need to experience the highs, the status associated with success, and the atmosphere of a gambling environment. The person can become irritable if they attempt to cut down, and then may gamble because of the distress. Severe disorders can take hold through a financial desperation to recoup lost money. Even when the person finally wins again, it is rarely enough to cover losses. Aside from significant financial loss, excessive gambling can impact badly on relationships. It can also cause anxiety, depression, and suicidal thoughts. Physical signs can include sleep deprivation, weight gain or loss, skin problems, ulcers, bowel problems, headaches, and muscle pains. Because most people do not admit they have a problem, a major component of treatment is helping them to acknowledge it. The true prevalence of the disorder is not known because so many hide their habit.

1% of the American population are pathological gamblers

Thrill of winning

| DESIRE FOR EASY MONEY | SOCIAL STATUS OF SUCCESS | DOPAMINE RELEASED BY WINNING | PLAYS AGAIN FOR MORE REWARDS | INCREASES SIZE OF STAKES |

AFFECTS RELATIONSHIPS	PHYSICAL SYMPTOMS	DEPRESSION/ ANXIETY
INABILITY TO SLEEP	SUICIDAL THOUGHTS	SUFFERS WITHDRAWAL SYMPTOMS
STRUGGLES WITH WORK	LIES TO COVER EXTENT OF PROBLEM	RETURNS TO TRY TO RECOUP LOSSES

DEBT INCREASES

⊕ TREATMENT

> **Cognitive behavioral therapy** (p.125) to help people learn to resist the beliefs and behaviors that maintain the disorder.

> **Psychodynamic therapy** (p.119) to help grasp the meaning and consequences of the behavior.

> **Self-help groups** and counseling to help understand how the behavior affects others.

Kleptomania

An individual with kleptomania has an irresistible and repeated compulsion to steal items. These episodes of stealing occur unexpectedly, without planning.

What is it?

A person with kleptomania steals on impulse and often throws the stolen goods away, because they are mostly interested in the act of stealing. Kleptomania is distinguished from shoplifting in that most shoplifters plan the theft, usually because they want an item but do not have enough money to buy it.

Many people with kleptomania live secret lives of shame because they are afraid to seek help; up to 24 percent of those arrested for shoplifting are thought to suffer from it. Kleptomania is associated with other psychiatric problems such as depression, bipolar disorder, generalized anxiety disorder, eating and personality disorders, substance abuse, and other impulse-control disorders. There is evidence to link kleptomania with the neurotransmitter pathways associated with behavioral addictions and mood-enhancing neurochemicals like serotonin.

There is no specific cure for kleptomania, but psychotherapy and/or medication may help break the cycle of compulsive stealing.

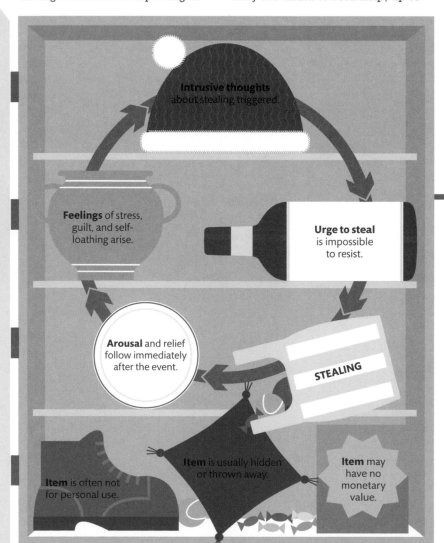

Intrusive thoughts about stealing triggered.

Feelings of stress, guilt, and self-loathing arise.

Urge to steal is impossible to resist.

Arousal and relief follow immediately after the event.

STEALING

Item is often not for personal use.

Item is usually hidden or thrown away.

Item may have no monetary value.

Perpetual pattern

A person with kleptomania may report feeling tense before they steal, then pleased and gratified as they do it. The subsequent guilt can increase the tension again.

⊕ TREATMENT

> **Psychotherapies** such as behavior modification, family (pp.138–141), cognitive behavioral (pp.122–129), and psychodynamic therapies (pp.118–121) to explore the underlying causes and put in place more appropriate ways of dealing with distress.

> **Selective serotonin reuptake inhibitors** (SSRIs) (pp.142–143) along with therapy.

Pyromania

A person with pyromania sets fires purposely. This very rare impulse-control disorder is triggered by stress, and the action provides relief from tension or distress.

What is it?

Also known as firesetting, pyromania is an obsessive desire to light fires. It can be a chronic (long-term) problem, or restricted to several occurrences during a period of unusual stress. A person with pyromania is excessively fascinated with making fires and situations involving fire, as well as witnessing or assisting in the fire's aftermath.

Individual factors that contribute to pyromania may include antisocial behaviors and attitudes, sensation and/or attention seeking, lack of social skills, and inability to cope with stress. Parental neglect or emotional detachment, parental psychological disorders, peer pressure, and stressful life events can all be triggers in both children and adults. Interviews with affected children and teens often identify a chaotic household, in which case a whole-family approach to treatment is required.

Destructive cycle

The cycle of obsession and gratification is difficult to break.

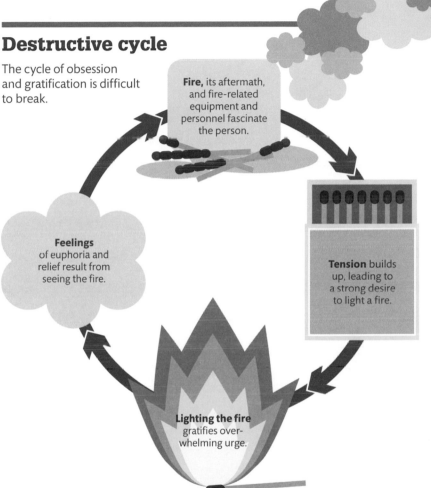

Fire, its aftermath, and fire-related equipment and personnel fascinate the person.

Tension builds up, leading to a strong desire to light a fire.

Lighting the fire gratifies overwhelming urge.

Feelings of euphoria and relief result from seeing the fire.

⊕ TREATMENT

❯ **Cognitive and behavioral therapies** (pp.122–129) tailored to children to include problem-solving and communication skills, anger management, aggression replacement training, and cognitive restructuring; long-term, insight-oriented psychotherapy for adults.

PYROMANIA IN CHILDREN, TEENS, AND ADULTS

❯ **In children and teens** firesetting may be a cry for help, or part of a larger pattern of aggression. Teens may be influenced by antisocial adults in their community. Some are diagnosed with psychotic or paranoid disorders (pp.70–75), and others may be cognitively impaired.

❯ **In adults** pyromania has been linked to symptoms that include depressed mood, thoughts of suicide, and poor interpersonal relationships. It is often associated with psychological problems such as OCD (pp.56–57).

DID (dissociative identity disorder)

In this rare and severe condition, a person's identity is fragmented into two or more distinct personality states. The parts do not join up into a whole.

What is it?

A person with DID has a splintered identity, rather than a growth of separate personalities, which is why the name of the condition was changed from its previous term of multiple personality disorder.

The individual feels as though they have different people within (called alters). Each alter has its own persona, with its own pattern of thinking and communicating, even down to different handwriting and physical requirements, such as wearing glasses. Someone with DID finds it hard to define what they are like, and may refer to themselves as "we." They have no control over when and which alter takes over, and for how long.

Dissociative experiences

An individual with DID uses dissociation—disconnection from the world around them—as a defense mechanism. They may feel as if they are floating away, watching themselves from outside. As if in a movie, the person observes rather than feels their emotions and parts of their body. The world around a person affected by DID may seem unreal and hazy, with objects changing appearance.

The individual has significant and frequent gaps in memory, unable to recall personal information in a way that is more extreme than forgetfulness. They may not remember people, places, and events in their lives from the distant and recent past, yet vividly relive other things that have happened. The person has moments of absence while carrying out day-to-day activities and may travel somewhere but be unable to remember how they got there.

The person regularly experiences symptoms of personality change and dissociation. These symptoms are thought to be a way of coping that often goes back to severe and prolonged trauma experienced in childhood, but the dissociation disrupts everyday life long after the trauma has ceased. Affected individuals continue to use the dissociation as a way of coping in all stressful situations in later life.

How is it diagnosed?

If a specialist suspects DID, they will complete mental health questionnaires that capture and rate the person's symptoms.

The aberrant and inexplicable behavior that characterizes DID is distressing and confusing for the individual and impacts negatively on work, social life, and intimate relationships. DID often exists alongside anxiety and depression (pp.38–39), panic attacks, OCD (pp.56–57), hearing voices, and suicidal feelings.

Identity alteration

Each alter, as the identity fragments of someone with DID are called, has distinct patterns of perception and personality that recur and take control of the individual's behavior. Typically the personalities know each other and communicate, sometimes criticizing one another. The transition from one to another is sudden and the person has no control over which one is in charge, but certain stressors can make a particular alter emerge.

 TREATMENT

> **Psychotherapies,** such as cognitive behavioral therapy (p.125), to reappraise the trauma and develop psychological flexibility to help deconstruct the personalities and reunite them into one. Treatment is long-term.

> **Dialectical behavior therapy** (p.126) to treat any self-harming and suicidal behaviors.

> **Anti-anxiety medication** and antidepressants (pp.142–143) often prescribed to help the person cope with associated conditions.

8–13 the typical number of identities in people with dissociative identity disorder

A younger self
may talk in a childlike way or even be unable to talk.

Opposing attitude
from the host's identity provides a different perspective on life events.

Different name
can denote a switch to the thinking patterns of another alter.

LIZ

SWITCHING BETWEEN ALTERS

Another gender or age
changes memories or perceptions of events.

Different appearance,
for example, hair color or clothing style, can change the host's persona.

The host identity
is the one main alter that a person may feel is most like them. This host identity may not remember facts about their personal history when a different alter is in control.

Change of role
can enable a view of life events from another standpoint.

Depersonalization and derealization

These are two related dissociative disorders. Depersonalization makes a person feel disconnected from their thoughts, feelings, and body, whereas derealization makes them feel disconnected from their environment.

What are they?

The feelings that result from these two conditions can be very disturbing and seriously interfere with a person's ability to function. Some people fear they are going mad, or become depressed, anxious, or panicky. People with depersonalization describe feeling like a robot and not in control of their speech or movement, as if they are an outside observer of their own thoughts or memories. They may also feel that their body is distorted. With derealization a person can feel alienated and disconnected from their surroundings. In some, the symptoms for these disorders are mild and short-lived, whereas in others they may persist for months or even years.

Little is known about what causes these disorders, but biological and environmental factors may play a role. Some people appear to be more prone to them, because they are neurologically less reactive to emotions or they may have a personality disorder (pp.102–107). The disorders can be triggered by intense stress, trauma, or violence.

If symptoms are present, a clinical assessment will include a full medical history and physical examination to rule out illness or side effects of medication, and questionnaires will be completed to identify associated symptoms and possible triggers. An individual is diagnosed with depersonalization and/or derealization disorder only when they persistently or repeatedly suffer from distorted perceptions of detachment from themselves or their environment. Many people experience a temporary feeling of dissociation from their thoughts or surroundings at some point in their lifetime, but fewer than 2 percent of people will be identified as having one, or both, of these disorders.

THE "REAL" PERSON

THE "OBSERVER"

⊕ TREATMENT

> **Psychotherapies,** particularly cognitive behavioral therapy (p.125), psychodynamic therapy (pp.118–121), or mindfulness meditation (p.129) can help a person understand why the feelings occur, learn coping strategies to manage the situations that trigger them, and gain control over symptoms.

> **Medication,** such as antidepressants (pp.142–143), can be prescribed to treat any associated disorders, including anxiety and depression.

Out-of-body experience

A person can be so dissociated from reality that they feel as if they are observing themselves in a movie and cannot relate to the individual in the real world.

Dissociative amnesia

This is an often short-term, dissociative disorder in which a person becomes separated from their personal memories following stress, trauma, or illness.

What is it?

Dissociative amnesia is often linked to overwhelming stress, such as witnessing or suffering from abuse, an accident, or a disaster. The resulting severe memory loss often affects specific recollections, such as a certain period during childhood, or something associated with a friend, relative, or peer. Alternatively, the amnesia may focus on a traumatic event, for example, a crime victim may have no memory of being robbed at gunpoint, but can recall details from the rest of that day. A person may develop generalized memory loss and may not remember their name, job, home, family, and friends. They may disappear and be reported missing. They might even create a totally new identity, fail to recognize people or places from their past life, and be unable to explain themselves—this is known as a dissociative fugue.

Clinical diagnosis will involve completing assessment questionnaires that help identify a trigger and enable the individual to capture and rate their symptoms. Physical checks and psychological examinations are also carried out to exclude other medical causes of memory loss.

TREATMENT

> **Psychotherapies,** such as cognitive behavioral therapy, dialectical behavior therapy, eye movement desensitization and reprocessing, family therapy, and art therapies such as hypnosis or mindfulness meditation can help the person understand and deal with the stress that triggered the disorder, and learn coping strategies (pp.118–141).

> **Medication,** such as antidepressants, may be prescribed for the depression or psychosis that can be associated with the amnesia (pp.142–143).

2–7%
of people have dissociative amnesia

Memory recovery

Most cases of dissociative amnesia are short-term, and while memories may temporarily fall away, they often return suddenly and completely. The recovery may happen on its own, after being triggered by something in the person's surroundings, or in a therapy session.

Anorexia nervosa

With this serious emotional disorder, a person wants to weigh as little as possible. They develop an aversion to food and their appetite reduces as they eat less and less.

What is it?

A person with anorexia becomes so afraid of gaining weight that they cannot eat normally. They may take appetite suppressants, laxatives, or diuretics (to remove body fluid), or make themselves vomit after meals (bulimia nervosa, pp.92–93), but they may also binge (binge-eating disorder, p.94).

Many factors can trigger anorexia. Pressures at school, such as exams or bullying (particularly if the focus is on body weight or shape), can contribute, as can occupations such as dancing or athletics where being thin is considered "the ideal." The disorder can also be a response to stress in childhood or lack of control over life events, such as losing a job, relationship breakdown, or bereavement, which makes the person exert excessive control over internal processes that are within their power.

Anorexia affects more females than males. Many of those who develop it share personality and behavioral traits. They are often emotionally controlled, have a tendency toward depression and anxiety, find it difficult to handle stress, and worry excessively. Many individuals set themselves strict, demanding goals. They may have feelings of obsession and compulsion, but not necessarily OCD (pp.56–57). Living with anorexia can make it hard to maintain relationships. It can also have an irreversible impact on the body and cause infertility or serious pregnancy complications.

How is it diagnosed?

The GP, clinical psychologist, or specialist health professional asks the individual questions about their personal and family history, weight, and eating habits. The person needs treatment as early as possible to reduce the risk of complications. In most cases, the treatment plan involves psychotherapy and individually tailored advice on eating and nutrition. Recovery can take years.

TREATMENTS

> **Multidisciplinary care team,** including a GP, psychiatrists, specialist nurses, and dietitians to ensure that a person gains weight safely and to support family and close friends.

> **Cognitive behavioral therapy** (p.125) to help the person understand and explain their problem and see it as a cycle of triggers, thoughts, feelings, and behaviors. Therapist and patient collaborate on interventions that break the chain of thoughts maintaining anorexia.

> **Cognitive analytic therapy** to examine the way the person thinks, feels, and acts, as well as the events and relationships that underlie their past experiences—often in childhood.

> **Interpersonal therapy** to resolve problems with attachment and relating to other people.

> **Focal psychodynamic therapy** to explore how early-childhood experiences may have affected the person.

> **In-patient treatment** for severe cases; supervised weight gain through strict daily routines and eating plans, often including group therapy for peer support.

Symptoms of anorexia

All symptoms relate to self-esteem, body image, and feelings, and divide into three main categories: cognitive (feelings and thoughts), behavioral, and physical.

46%
of people with anorexia **recover fully**

Perceived body weight
is too high and the person
feels compelled to lose
weight.

Actual body weight
and BMI are much
lower than is healthy
for their age and
height.

> Expresses a fear of gaining weight and becomes obsessed with body shape.

> Believes that being thin is good and is convinced that they are overweight.

> Measures self-worth in terms of body weight and shape.

> Obsesses about food and the perceived negative consequences of eating.

> Becomes irritable, moody, and unable to concentrate (partly due to hunger), which impacts school or work.

> Behaves obsessively around food and diets, and counts calories excessively. Avoids "fatty" foods and/or eats only low-calorie foods. May skip meals.

> Avoids eating in front of others, and/or purges after eating.

> Lies about how much they eat.

> Repeatedly weighs themselves or checks their body shape in the mirror.

> Exercises obsessively.

> Becomes socially withdrawn.

> Obvious weight loss.

> Irregular or absent periods in females.

> Poor dental health and smelly breath due to persistent vomiting.

> Soft, fine, "downy" hair growing on the body, while head hair falls out.

> Has difficulty sleeping but is very tired.

> Is weak, light-headed, and dizzy.

> Has stomach pains, and is constipated and bloated.

> Has swollen hands and feet.

Bulimia nervosa

A serious eating disorder, bulimia is characterized by a person controlling their weight through severely restricting intake, then binge eating and purging the body of the food.

What is it?

People with bulimia have an abnormal fear of putting on weight and so become obsessed with food and dieting. Unlike those with anorexia (pp.90–91), they are usually at or near a normal weight for their height and build. However, like a person with anorexia, they have a distorted self-image and believe they are too fat.

A person with bulimia may often appear tense or anxious and behave furtively, rapidly consuming large amounts of food in secret before disappearing to the bathroom to make themselves vomit. This behavior is a mechanism for coping with life events—although in fact it makes daily living a struggle—and is linked to depression, anxiety, and social isolation. Pressure to conform to body shapes promoted by the fashion and beauty industries and a family history of bulimia increase the risk. Bulimia is more common in females, but incidence in males is rising. Puberty and self-consciousness are often triggers, and boys and girls in their teens are especially vulnerable to bulimia if teased as an overweight child.

Bulimia can cause irreversible damage to the heart, bowels, teeth, and fertility. Treatment depends on the severity of the condition, and recovery can be a long process.

DIAGNOSING BULIMIA

Doctors all over the world use the so-called SCOFF questionnaire (developed in the UK) to diagnose anorexia (pp.90–91) or bulimia. Two or more "yeses" indicate a likely case.

> Does the person make themselves **Sick** (vomit) after eating?

> Has the person lost **Control** over how much they eat?

> Have they lost more than **One** stone (13lb) within three months?

> Does the person believe they are **Fat** even though others have told them they are too thin?

> Does **Food** dominate their life?

Binge–purge cycle

The person has a low self-opinion and sees losing weight as a way of gaining self-worth. They may also exercise fanatically to burn off the additional calories and avoid social occasions that involve food.

Causes

> The individual may have a caregiver who thinks looks are important and criticizes their weight or appearance.

> The person may want to take control of an aspect of their lives, particularly if recovering from a traumatic event.

> Images of celebrities with flawless, thin bodies trigger the start of a strict diet.

> Despair sets in when the person cannot keep to the diet.

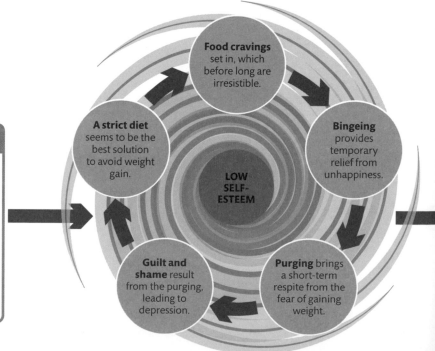

Food cravings set in, which before long are irresistible.

A strict diet seems to be the best solution to avoid weight gain.

Bingeing provides temporary relief from unhappiness.

LOW SELF-ESTEEM

Purging brings a short-term respite from the fear of gaining weight.

Guilt and shame result from the purging, leading to depression.

⊕ TREATMENT

> **Psychotherapies** such as group therapy, self-help, or one-on-one cognitive behavioral therapy (p.125) or interpersonal therapy.
> **Antidepressants** (pp.142–143) prescribed along with therapy.
> **In-patient treatment** needed in extreme cases.

1.5%
of American women have or have had bulimia in their lifetime

Physical effects

> Frequent weight gain and loss.
> Bad breath, stomach pain, sore throat, and damaged tooth enamel from acid levels in vomit.
> Dry skin and hair, hair loss, brittle nails, lethargy, and other signs of poor nutrition.
> Heart strain, hemorrhoids, and weak muscles from misuse and overuse of laxatives and diuretics.
> Irregular/absent periods in females.
> Feeling bloated and/or constipated.
> Bloodshot eyes.
> Calluses on the back of hands from induced vomiting.

PEOPLE WITH BULIMIA feel as if they have no control over eating habits, which increases their fear of weight gain.

Binge-eating disorder

With this condition, a person regularly overeats to cope with low self-esteem and misery, although in fact the persistent, uncontrolled binge eating makes depression and anxiety worse.

What is it?

A person with binge-eating disorder regularly eats large amounts quickly when not hungry, alone or secretly, and feels shame and self-disgust after a binge. They feel they have no control over how much and how often they eat.

Low self-esteem, depression, anxiety, stress, anger, boredom, loneliness, dissatisfaction with the body, pressure to be thin, traumatic events, and a family history of eating disorders are all factors that increase the risk of developing it. The disorder can also develop after the person follows such a strict diet that they are left very hungry and have food cravings. It is the most common eating disorder in the US.

A GP may diagnose the disorder from the person's weight gain—the most common physical effect.

⊕ TREATMENT

❯ **Psychotherapy** (pp.118–141) in groups or one-on-one.

❯ **Self-help programs** through books, in online courses, as part of a support group, or supervised by a health professional.

❯ **Antidepressants** (pp.142–143) prescribed along with therapy.

Bingeing cycle

People with a binge-eating disorder are using food as an instant, albeit negative, way to relieve emotional pain instead of finding positive methods of tackling the underlying cause. The result is a perpetual cycle of eating, relief, depression, and yet more eating.

Relief from increasingly distressing feelings comes only with thoughts of food.

Anxiety rises and depression sets in as eating provides only short-lived "pain" relief.

The need to eat to relieve depression grows in urgency; the person plans a binge, often buying special foods for that purpose.

Low mood returns with self-disgust because of the guilt and shame associated with binge eating.

The person eats large amounts of food rapidly (regardless of degree of hunger), often in secret, may be in a dazed state while eating, and may feel uncomfortably full afterward.

Anxiety drops as eating temporarily numbs the feelings of stress, sadness, or anger.

 # Pica

An individual with this eating disorder persistently eats substances that are not food, such as dirt or paint. It can lead to serious complications if the substance is dangerous when ingested.

What is it?

Children and adults with pica may eat, for example, animal feces, clay, dirt, hairballs, ice, paint, sand, or metal objects such as paper clips. It is more common in children than adults—between 10 and 32 percent of children age 1–6 years are affected by pica. The odd eating behavior can create complications such as lead poisoning or intestinal damage from sharp objects.

For a doctor to diagnose pica, the pattern of behavior must last for at least one month. After a medical examination to rule out causes such as nutrient deficiency or anemia as the root of the unusual cravings, a specialist health professional evaluates the presence of other disorders such as developmental disabilities or OCD (pp.56–57).

⊕ TREATMENT

❭ **Behavioral therapies** (pp.122–129) to associate healthy eating with positive reinforcement or reward. Positive behavior support to address aspects of family and home environment and minimize recurrence.

❭ **Medication** to enhance dopamine levels; supplements to remedy any nutrient deficiencies.

28% of pregnant women are affected by pica

RARER EATING DISORDERS

Irregular eating habits, eating unusual items, distress or avoidance around eating or mealtimes, or concerns about body weight or shape characterize eating disorders.

NAME	WHAT IS IT?	CAUSES	SYMPTOMS	IMPACT	TREATMENT
PURGING DISORDER	Deliberate vomiting that occurs often enough after eating to affect physical health	Childhood abuse or neglect, social media stresses, or family history	Vomiting after meals, laxative use, obsession with weight/appearance, tooth decay, bloodshot eyes	Anxiety, depression, and suicidal thoughts that affect relationships, work, and self-esteem	Management of medical problems, healthy eating plan, nutrition education, psychotherapy
NIGHT-EATING DISORDER	Urge to eat most of the daily food requirement during the late evening or at night	Depression, low self-esteem, or response to stress or dieting	Insomnia, grazing in the evening, waking in the night to eat	Problems with work, social, or intimate relationships; weight gain or substance abuse	Psychoeducation about the disorder and nutritional and behavioral therapy
RUMINATION DISORDER	Tendency in young children who have intellectual disability to rechew partly digested food	Neglect or abnormal relationship with parent or caregiver; may be attention seeking	Regurgitation and rechewing food, weight loss, poor teeth, stomach pains, raw lips	Usually outgrown in early years; if it persists, impacts daily life	Family therapy and positive behavior support

Communication disorders

This range of conditions affects a person's ability to receive, send, process, and/or understand verbal, nonverbal, and visual concepts and may be apparent in hearing, language, and/or speech.

What are they?

The four main conditions are language, childhood fluency, speech-sound, and SCD (social communication disorders). They are often complex. Some are apparent in babies and toddlers, whereas others may not become obvious until a child is at school.

The causes are wide-ranging. Communication disorders may develop of their own accord or stem from a neurological illness. They can be genetic—20–40 percent of children with a family history of speech and/or language impairment have communication disorders. Prenatal nutrition may be involved. Psychiatric disorders, ASD (pp.68–69), Down syndrome, cerebral palsy, and physical problems including cleft lip or palate and deafness may limit a person's ability to communicate.

How are they diagnosed?

To maximize a child's development potential, early intervention is important; some conditions require lifelong management. A speech and language specialist takes a case history, including information about family background, medical conditions, and information from teachers and caregivers, to prepare a treatment plan.

CAUSES OF COMMUNICATION DISORDERS
More than one causal factor may be involved and the effects can range from mild to profound.

DISORDER	TRIGGER	FAMILY HISTORY OF LANGUAGE IMPAIRMENTS	CHILDHOOD DEVELOPMENT DISORDER	GENETIC SYNDROME	IMPAIRED OR NO HEARING	EMOTIONAL OR PSYCHIATRIC DISORDER	PREMATURE BIRTH	NEUROLOGICAL ILLNESS OR DAMAGE	POOR DIET
LANGUAGE DISORDER		✓	✓	✓	✓	✓	✓	✓	✓
SPEECH-SOUND DISORDER			✓	✓	✓			✓	
CHILDHOOD FLUENCY DISORDER		✓	✓			✓		✓	
SOCIAL COMMUNICATION DISORDER		✓	✓	✓		✓	✓	✓	✓

LANGUAGE DISORDER

The child does not understand others (receptive disorder) or cannot communicate thoughts (expressive disorder) or both (receptive-expressive disorder).

> **Baby does not smile** or babble in response to parents, and only has a few words by 18 months.

> **Child does not play** with others and prefers to be alone. May become shy and distant.

> **Child has difficulty swallowing,** affecting ability to speak.

SPEECH-SOUND DISORDER

The child has difficulty articulating sound patterns and mispronounces words beyond expected age range.

> **Unclear speech,** common in young children, continues beyond the age of eight.

> **Child unable to produce** correct sound patterns even though they can understand speech, so cannot make themselves understood by others.

> **Limited understanding** of rules of speech sounds is apparent.

IMPACT ON THE CHILD

Errors of thinking and communication affect daily interactions. Children become anxious, with low self-confidence.

> **Developmental milestones** are delayed as children learn through communication.

> **Social isolation** occurs because child does not initiate interaction and cannot make friends. May become target of bullies.

> **Behavioral issues** arise as child adopts avoidance techniques and may become aggressive if they cannot resolve speech difficulties.

CHILDHOOD FLUENCY

The child stammers or stutters, repeating words or parts of words, and prolonging speech sounds.

> **Speech** can become blocked as if child is out of breath.

> **Child uses distracting sounds** such as throat clearing or head and body movements to disguise their problem.

> **Anxiety** is increasingly evident as child tries to hide disorder.

> **Child avoids public speaking** as anxiety worsens the stutter.

SCD

The child cannot process verbal and visual information simultaneously.

> **Child cannot adapt language** to suit situation, so can be dogmatic, dominating, and inappropriate when talking to adults or peers.

> **Child lacks nonverbal** communication skills such as taking turns in conversation or other group activities.

> **Child cannot greet people** as they have little or no interest in social interaction.

SOCIAL COMMUNICATION DISORDER OR AUTISM SPECTRUM DISORDER?

SCD (social communication disorder) has many symptoms in common with ASD (autism spectrum disorder). Assessment must rule out ASD before doctors diagnose the child with SCD and establish a treatment plan.

Social communication disorder

Children with SCD find it difficult to learn the basic rules of conversation: how to start one, listen, phrase questions, stay on topic, and know when it is over. SCD can occur alongside other developmental issues such as language impairment, learning disabilities, speech-sound disorder, and ADHD (pp.66–67).

Autism spectrum disorder

Children with ASD find it hard to relate to people, emotions, and feelings. As with SCD, this can result in communication difficulties, impaired social skills, and altered sensory and visual perception. But ASD has an additional defining characteristic of restricted or repetitive behaviors.

Sleep disorders

This is a group of conditions that affects a person's ability to sleep well. Their cause may be psychological or physiological, but they can all result in disturbed thoughts, emotions, and behaviors.

What are they?

Most people experience sleep problems from time to time. The problem becomes a disorder if it occurs regularly and interferes with daily life and mental health. Lack of refreshing sleep can have a negative impact on energy, mood, concentration, and overall health—disorientation, confusion, memory problems, and speech disturbances can result, which may in turn worsen the disorder.

Sleep involves transitions between three different states: wakefulness; REM (rapid eye movement) sleep, which is associated with dreaming; and N-REM (non-rapid eye movement) sleep. Disorders include abnormal occurrences not only during sleep but also just before sleep and immediately on waking. For example, a person may have difficulty falling and/or staying asleep (insomnia) and then feel extremely tired throughout the day. A person's sleep may be disturbed by abnormal behavior or events (parasomnias), such as sleepwalking, nightmares, sleep terrors, restless leg syndrome, sleep paralysis, and sleep aggression. Confusional arousal makes a person behave in a strange and confused way when they wake up. REM sleep behavior disorder is a severe parasomnia that causes sleep-related groaning and often causes a person to physically enact their dreams.

What are the causes?

Sleep disruption can be associated with medications, underlying medical conditions (for example, narcolepsy), and sleep-related breathing conditions. The latter includes a range of anomalies from snoring to obstructive sleep apnea (a condition in which the walls of the throat relax and narrow during sleep, interrupting normal breathing), which causes the person to wake up in distress.

INSOMNIA

PARASOMNIA

NARCOLEPSY

HYPERSOMNOLENCE

WHAT IS IT?

Insomnia is difficulty in getting to sleep and/or staying asleep long enough to feel refreshed the next day. Episodes can be short-lived or continue for months or years. It is more common in older adults.

Parasomnias are a group of unwanted events, experiences, or behaviors that occur while a person is falling asleep, sleeping, or waking. The person remains asleep throughout and has no memory of them.

Narcolepsy is a long-term disorder that can develop if the brain is unable to regulate sleeping and waking. It is characterized by irregular sleep patterns and suddenly falling asleep at inappropriate times.

Hypersomnolence is excessive sleepiness that intrudes on daily functions. It can be mild and transient, or persistent and severe, and it often accompanies depression. It mostly affects teens and young adults.

50–70 million American adults have a sleep disorder

CAUSES	SYMPTOMS	IMPACT	TREATMENT
Triggers include worry and stress, for example, problems at work or home or financial difficulties; a significant event, such as a bereavement; underlying health conditions; and alcohol or drug use.	The person may have trouble falling asleep, wake often during the night, wake early and not go back to sleep, and be unable to nap. Tiredness causes irritability, anxiety, and poor concentration.	The person cannot relax, and excessive fatigue limits daytime activities. Work performance is impaired and relationships suffer. Bedtime can be anxiously anticipated, the stress worsening the insomnia.	Stimulus-control or sleep-restriction therapies and paradoxical intention are behavioral therapies (pp.122–129)—the person tries to stay awake for as long as possible to reduce anxiety around sleep.
Parasomnia often runs in families, so it may be genetic; it is associated with medication or physical conditions such as sleep apnea. REM sleep behavior disorder can follow a brain disease.	Common symptoms are sleepwalking, sleep talking, night terrors, confusional arousal, rhythmic movement, and leg cramps. More severe are night-eating disorder and REM sleep behavior disorder.	The lack of refreshing sleep can result in mental impairment, disorientation, confusion, and memory problems. Those with REM sleep behavior disorder can become violent.	Mild or harmless parasomnias need only practical safeguards such as removing possible sources of injury to sleepwalkers. Medication may be needed for REM sleep behavior disorder.
Narcolepsy may be genetic or caused by a lack of melatonin (the brain chemical that regulates sleep), hormonal changes in puberty or menopause, or stress. It can follow infection or inoculation.	Symptoms include daytime sleepiness, sleep attacks, temporary loss of muscle control in response to emotions such as laughing (cataplexy), sleep paralysis, and hallucinations on falling asleep or before waking.	Narcolepsy disrupts daily life and can be difficult to cope with emotionally. An underactive thyroid gland, and other physical symptoms such as sleep apnea or restless legs, can exacerbate problems.	Adopting a healthy diet and lifestyle, regular bedtime routines, and evenly spaced naps to manage excessive daytime drowsiness can all help.
Hypersomnolence may be genetic or due to drug or alcohol abuse or other sleep disorders such as narcolepsy or sleep apnea. It can follow a tumor, head trauma, or injury in the central nervous system.	The person may be very sleepy during the day despite nighttime sleep of at least seven hours, have recurrent daytime naps or sleep lapses, struggle to wake up after long sleep, or feel unrefreshed after sleeping for 14–18 hours.	The person struggles to function in daily life. They may be anxious, irritable, and restless, and have little appetite and no energy. Thinking and speech are slow, and memory problems can develop.	Physical causes are treated first. If hypersomnolence persists, daytime activity is observed. Tailored behavioral therapies include introducing presleep routines and ordered sleep times, which are then altered gradually.

# Tic disorders

Tics are sudden, painless, nonrhythmic behaviors that are either motor (related to movement) or vocal. A disorder may be diagnosed when tics occur repeatedly and are apparently unconnected to the environment or situation.

What are they?

Tics—small, uncontrollable movements or sounds—are not usually serious and normally improve over time. However, if they persist they can be frustrating and interfere with everyday activities—especially if the person has more than one tic.

Changes in the parts of the brain that control movement are thought to cause tics. There is probably a genetic predisposition, too. Taking drugs such as amphetamines or cocaine can trigger tics, as can medical conditions, including cerebral palsy and Huntington's disease, or psychological disorders such as ADHD (pp.66–67) and OCD (pp.56–57).

Tics are more common in children, but they can begin in adulthood. Statistics vary regarding the prevalence, with 0.3–3.8 percent of children described as having severe tics. Treatment may not be needed if a tic is mild; lifestyle management, such as avoiding stress or tiredness, is often all that is required.

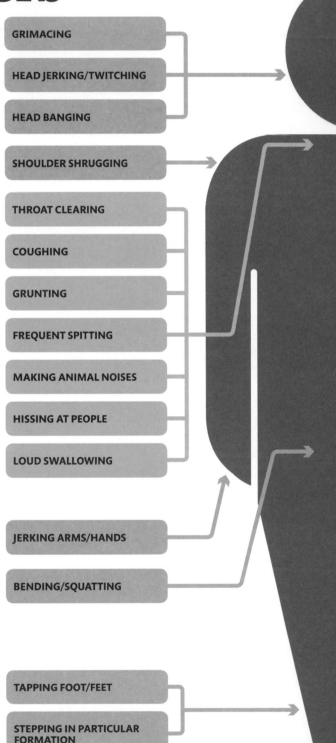

GRIMACING

HEAD JERKING/TWITCHING

HEAD BANGING

SHOULDER SHRUGGING

THROAT CLEARING

COUGHING

GRUNTING

FREQUENT SPITTING

MAKING ANIMAL NOISES

HISSING AT PEOPLE

LOUD SWALLOWING

JERKING ARMS/HANDS

BENDING/SQUATTING

TAPPING FOOT/FEET

STEPPING IN PARTICULAR FORMATION

ADVANCE WARNINGS

Most people have an unusual or uncomfortable feeling before the tic occurs. Individuals often describe this as a rising tension that only the tic itself can release. Some people can suppress their tics for a short period, until the urge to do it becomes too strong, which may result in a more severe tic.

WARNING URGE
> Burning sensation behind eyes
> Tension in a particular muscle
> Dry throat
> Itching

NEED TO RELEASE TENSION

TIC
> Blinking
> Twitching individual muscle
> Grunting
> Twitching body

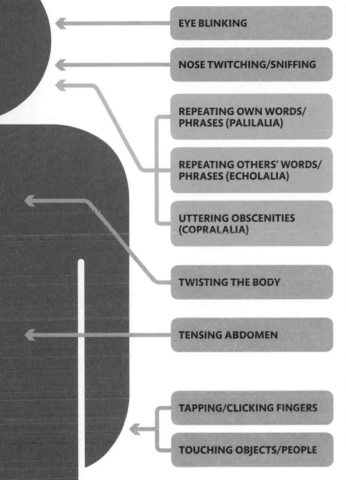

EYE BLINKING

NOSE TWITCHING/SNIFFING

REPEATING OWN WORDS/
PHRASES (PALILALIA)

REPEATING OTHERS' WORDS/
PHRASES (ECHOLALIA)

UTTERING OBSCENITIES
(COPRALALIA)

TWISTING THE BODY

TENSING ABDOMEN

TAPPING/CLICKING FINGERS

TOUCHING OBJECTS/PEOPLE

TOURETTE'S SYNDROME

This is a condition characterized by multiple tics, named after George de la Tourette, who first described it in 1884. For a condition to be classified as Tourette's syndrome, the tics must last for at least a year and at least one must be vocal. Most individuals have a combination of motor and vocal tics, which can be both simple and complex. The syndrome often runs in families.

Tourette's syndrome is thought to be linked to problems with a part of the brain called the basal ganglia, or possibly to a childhood throat infection caused by a streptococcal bacteria. The first stage of diagnosis is to check other possible causes of the symptoms such as allergies or poor eyesight. A neurologist or psychiatrist then rules out conditions such as ASD (pp.68–69) before referring the person for psychotherapy. In a third of cases, the tics reduce, become less troublesome, or disappear over a 10-year period.

"The rhythm of music is very, very important for ... patients with Tourette's."

Oliver Sacks, British neurologist

Simple and complex tics

Tics take many forms. Some affect body movement and others are verbal. They may be simple or complex. A simple tic affects a small number of muscle groups, for example, blinking or clearing the throat. A complex tic involves coordinated patterns of several muscle groups, such as blinking in combination with a shoulder shrug, facial grimace, and spontaneous shouting.

Key
- Motor tics
- Vocal tics

⊕ TREATMENT

- **Behavioral therapies** (pp.122–129) widely used for Tourette's to expose the unpleasant feelings that precede the tic and encourage a response that stops it.
- **Habit reversal training** to teach use of incompatible behaviors in place of the tic, so planned intentional movements compete with the tic and prevent it.
- **Lifestyle management** such as relaxation techniques and listening to music to reduce frequency of tics.
- **Antidepressants** or anti-anxiety medication (pp.142–143) to support behavioral interventions if needed.

PD (personality disorders)

These are disorders in which individuals display persistent and consistent unhealthy patterns of thinking, behavior, and social functioning.

What are they?

Individuals with PD have difficulty not only understanding themselves, but also relating to other people. PD is different from other mental illnesses due to its enduring nature and the fact that it cannot be compared to a physical illness. The individual's behavior varies noticeably from the norm in society, but they may manage their own life without medical help in a way that someone with an extreme condition such as schizophrenia (pp.70–71) cannot. PD often goes hand in hand with substance abuse (pp.80–81), depression (pp.38–39), and anxiety.

The precise causes of personality disorders are not known, but risk factors appear to include a family history of a personality or other mental disorder; an abusive, unstable, or chaotic early life; or a diagnosis of severe aggression and disobedience in childhood. Variations in brain chemistry and structure may also play a role.

There are 10 defined PDs and they are considered to fit into three clusters based on broad similarities within each group.

A doctor does not usually attempt a diagnosis of PD until early adulthood. For a diagnosis to be made, the symptoms (right and pp.104–107) must cause day-to-day problems with functioning and subjective distress, and the person must display some symptoms of at least one of the types.

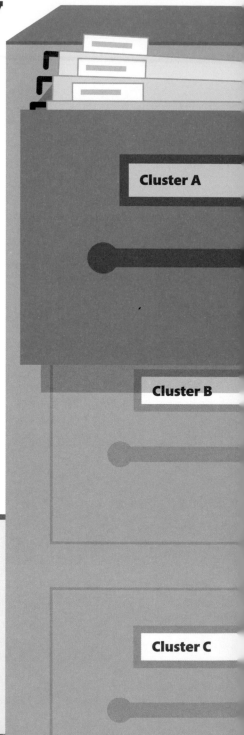

Cluster A

Cluster B

Cluster C

Cluster A: odd/eccentric

A person with a Cluster A personality disorder shows patterns of behavior that most onlookers would regard as odd and eccentric, has difficulty relating to other people, and fears social situations. The individual may not believe that they have a problem. This group includes three personality disorders: paranoid, schizoid, and schizotypal.

Paranoid PD

- ❯ The person is extremely distrustful and suspicious.
- ❯ They think other people are lying to them, trying to manipulate them, or passing on shared confidences.
- ❯ They find hidden meanings in innocent remarks.
- ❯ They have problems maintaining close relationships, often believing that a spouse or partner is unfaithful despite a lack of evidence, for instance.
- ❯ Their suspiciousness and hostility may be expressed in overt argumentativeness; recurrent complaining; or quiet, hostile aloofness.
- ❯ The person's hypervigilance for potential threats makes them appear guarded, secretive, devious, and lacking in tender feelings.

Schizoid PD

- ❯ The person appears cold, detached, and indifferent to other people.
- ❯ They prefer to take part in activities alone.
- ❯ They have little desire to form close relationships of any kind, including sexual ones.
- ❯ They have a limited range of social expression.
- ❯ They cannot pick up social cues or respond to criticism or praise.
- ❯ They have limited ability to experience pleasure or joy.
- ❯ They are more likely to be male than female.
- ❯ They may have a relative with schizophrenia (pp.70–71), but schizoid PD is not as severe a condition.

Schizotypal PD

- ❯ The person becomes very anxious and introverted in social situations, even familiar ones.
- ❯ They make inappropriate responses to social cues.
- ❯ They have delusional thoughts, attaching undue and misguided significance to everyday events. For example, they may be convinced that a newspaper headline contains secret messages for them.
- ❯ They may believe in special powers such as telepathy or their own magical ability to influence another person's emotions and actions.
- ❯ They may have unusual ways of speaking, such as making long, rambling, vague statements or changing the subject partway through.

⊕ TREATMENT

- ❯ **Paranoid PD** Schema-focused cognitive therapy (p.124) to enable links between problems, for example, emotions from childhood memories and current life patterns; also uses cognitive techniques to develop new appraisals. However, high drop-out rates from treatment occur, even if sought, due to difficulty in building rapport and trust between therapist and patient.
- ❯ **Schizoid PD** Cognitive behavioral therapy (p.125) or lifestyle support to reduce anxiety, depression, angry outbursts, and substance abuse; social skills training; medication (pp.142–143) prescribed for low mood or psychotic episodes. However, treatment is rarely sought.
- ❯ **Schizotypal PD** Long-term psychotherapy to build a trusting relationship and cognitive behavioral therapy to help with identification and reevaluation of irrational thoughts; medication prescribed for low mood or psychotic episodes.

PEOPLE WITH PD often do not see themselves as having a problem so seeking treatment is rare.

Cluster B: dramatic/emotional/erratic

A person suffering from a Cluster B personality disorder struggles to regulate their feelings. They are usually overly emotional and unpredictable and display behavior patterns that others see as dramatic, erratic, threatening, and even disturbing. This creates a vicious cycle, as people are uncomfortable near them, so social and personal relationships are difficult to achieve and maintain, which in turn intensifies the initial symptoms.

PSYCHOPATHY

Sometimes considered a subset of antisocial personality disorder (below), psychopathy is one of the hardest disorders to diagnose and is largely resistant to treatment. Psychopathy presents as a specific set of personality traits and behaviors. Mental health professionals can use Robert Hare's Psychopathy Checklist-Revised (PCL-R) to diagnose the disorder by scoring an individual on 20 listed traits with a value of 0, 1, or 2. A score of 30 and above in the US, or 25 and above in the UK, results in a diagnosis of psychopathy. Interpersonal traits include grandiosity, deceit, and arrogance; emotion-based traits, lack of guilt and empathy; and impulsive traits, sexual promiscuity as well as criminal behaviors such as stealing. Individuals lack inhibition and do not learn from experience. They can seem charming at first, but their inability to feel guilt, empathy, or love, along with the presence of casual, reckless attachments and behavior, quickly becomes evident. Many traits—especially the ability to make clear, emotion-free decisions—can be found in successful individuals, particularly in business and sports. Most psychopaths are men, and the disorder is unrelated to the society or culture they come from.

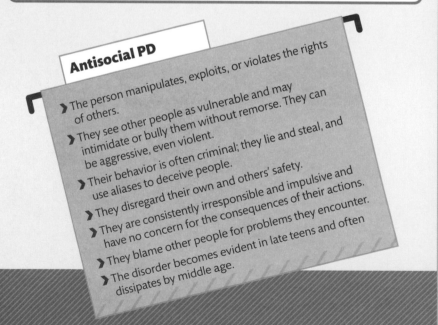

Antisocial PD

> The person manipulates, exploits, or violates the rights of others.
> They see other people as vulnerable and may intimidate or bully them without remorse. They can be aggressive, even violent.
> Their behavior is often criminal; they lie and steal, and use aliases to deceive people.
> They disregard their own and others' safety.
> They are consistently irresponsible and impulsive and have no concern for the consequences of their actions.
> They blame other people for problems they encounter.
> The disorder becomes evident in late teens and often dissipates by middle age.

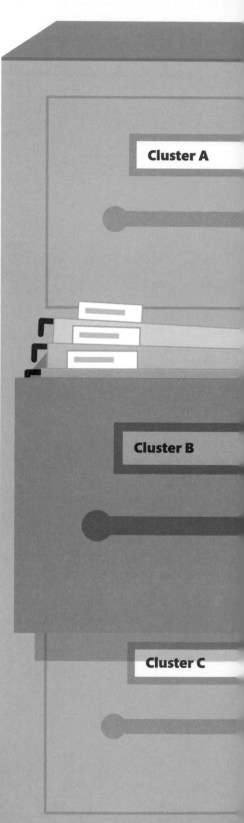

Cluster A

Cluster B

Cluster C

Borderline PD

❯ The person has a fragile self-image.
❯ They are emotionally unstable (also called affect dysregulation), with severe mood swings and frequent, intense displays of anger.
❯ They have intense but unstable relationships with other people.
❯ They fear being alone or abandoned and have long-term feelings of emptiness and loneliness, leading to irritability, anxiety, and depression.
❯ They have disturbed patterns of thinking or perception (called cognitive or perceptual distortions).
❯ They act impulsively, with a tendency to self-harm and suicidal thoughts or attempts.

Histrionic PD

❯ The person is self-centered and regularly seeks attention.
❯ They dress or behave inappropriately, and draw attention to themselves through physical appearance.
❯ Their emotional states rapidly shift, which makes them appear shallow.
❯ They are excessively dramatic, with exaggerated displays of emotion.
❯ They constantly seek reassurance or approval.
❯ They are suggestible (easily influenced).
❯ They believe that their relationships are more intimate than they are.
❯ They may function at a high level in social and work environments.

Narcissistic PD

❯ The person has an exaggerated sense of self-importance, expects to be recognized as superior, and exaggerates their talents.
❯ They are preoccupied with fantasies about success, power, brilliance, beauty, or the perfect partner.
❯ They believe they can associate only with people of equal importance.
❯ They expect special favors and unquestioning compliance from others and take advantage of them to get what they want.
❯ They are unwilling and unable to recognize anyone else's needs and feelings.
❯ They believe they are envied.

⊕ TREATMENT

❯ **Antisocial PD** Cognitive behavioral therapy (p.125); however, person may seek help only when ordered to do so by court because of their criminal behavior.
❯ **Borderline PD** Dialectical behavior and mentalization-based therapies combining psychodynamic (pp.118–121), cognitive behavioral (pp.122–129), systemic (pp.138–141), and ecological approaches, and art therapy (p.137). Group psychotherapy if symptoms are mild; coordinated care program for moderate-to-severe symptoms.
❯ **Histrionic PD** Supportive and solution-focused psychotherapy (pp.118–141) to enable emotion regulation; however, treatment is difficult as individual often exaggerates ability to function.
❯ **Narcissistic PD** Psychotherapy to help the person understand the cause of their emotions and regulate them.

Cluster C: anxious/fearful

This group of personality disorders is characterized by worried, fearful thinking or behavior. A person with one of these disorders struggles with persistent and overwhelming feelings of fear and anxiety and may show patterns of behavior that most people would regard as antisocial and withdrawn. Cluster C includes dependent, avoidant, and OC (obsessive compulsive) PDs. A psychiatric assessment is needed to differentiate between dependent (below) and borderline PD (p.105), because the two share some symptoms.

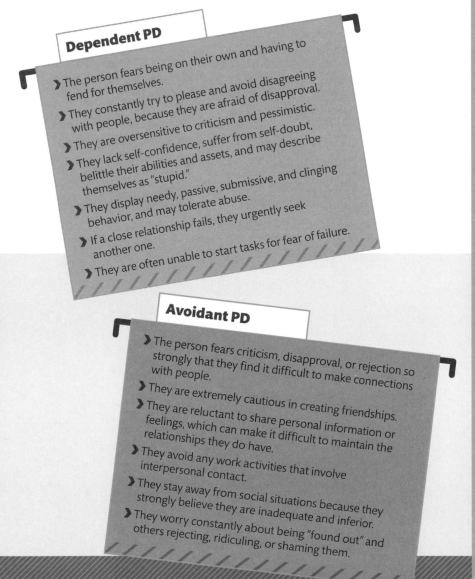

Dependent PD

> The person fears being on their own and having to fend for themselves.

> They constantly try to please and avoid disagreeing with people, because they are afraid of disapproval.

> They are oversensitive to criticism and pessimistic.

> They lack self-confidence, suffer from self-doubt, belittle their abilities and assets, and may describe themselves as "stupid."

> They display needy, passive, submissive, and clinging behavior, and may tolerate abuse.

> If a close relationship fails, they urgently seek another one.

> They are often unable to start tasks for fear of failure.

Avoidant PD

> The person fears criticism, disapproval, or rejection so strongly that they find it difficult to make connections with people.

> They are extremely cautious in creating friendships.

> They are reluctant to share personal information or feelings, which can make it difficult to maintain the relationships they do have.

> They avoid any work activities that involve interpersonal contact.

> They stay away from social situations because they strongly believe they are inadequate and inferior.

> They worry constantly about being "found out" and others rejecting, ridiculing, or shaming them.

Cluster A

Cluster B

Cluster C

10%

the estimated percentage of the global population affected by some form of personality disorder

Obsessive compulsive PD

> The person is preoccupied with orderliness, perfectionism, and mental and interpersonal control.

> They are rigid and stubborn in pursuit of their principles.

> They are so devoted to work that they neglect friends and other activities, so they do not form or maintain meaningful social relationships.

> They are overconscientious and scrupulous and may miss work deadlines because they persistently aim for perfection.

> They are inflexible on matters of morality or ethics.

> They are unable to discard worn-out or worthless objects even when they have no sentimental value.

OCPD OR OCD?

The need to perform behavioral or thinking tasks to reduce the frequency and intensity of obsessional thoughts and compulsions that cause extreme anxiety characterizes both OCPD (obsessive compulsive personality disorder) and OCD (obsessive compulsive disorder, pp.56–57). However, OCPD begins in early adulthood, whereas OCD can develop at any life stage. OCPD is an exaggeration of a personality style, and becomes a problem that interferes with daily life, whereas OCD is underpinned by an inflated sense of responsibility for harm occurring to the self or others. People with OCPD believe their thinking is entirely rational. Those with OCD are aware that their thinking is disordered and that the cycle maintains their anxiety.

⊕ TREATMENT

> **Dependent PD** Psychotherapy, specifically assertiveness training to help with self-confidence, and cognitive behavioral therapy (p.125) to help develop more robust attitudes and perspectives about themselves relative to others. Long-term psychodynamic therapies (pp.118–121) to examine early developmental experiences and help rebuild personality.

> **Avoidant PD** Psychodynamic therapy (p.119) or cognitive behavioral therapy to help the person identify strongly held beliefs about themselves and how they think others see

them and to change behavioral and social skills to improve work and social life.

> **Obsessive compulsive PD** Counseling and psychotherapy tailored to address every aspect of a person's strongly held beliefs, in particular, their rigid view of the world and others. Cognitive behavioral therapy and psychodynamic therapy to help the person identify their feelings about a situation, then stop to think about why the control maintains, rather than solves, the problems.

Other disorders

There are a number of conditions with physiological, developmental, or cultural origins that can also have a negative effect on a person's cognitive and behavioral functioning.

What are they?

There are many physical conditions that affect a person's performance, limit function, and cause enough distress to trigger behavioral problems - as well as depression and anxiety. These include developmental problems (such as Down syndrome), physiological conditions (such as dyspraxia, which affects coordinated movement), and degenerative

NAME	WHAT IS IT?	SYMPTOMS
SOMATIC SYMPTOM DISORDER	An excessive focus on physical symptoms such as pain or fatigue that causes severe anxiety and problems with functioning	Has high levels of anxiety and panic about physical symptoms and believes they indicate serious illness
FACTITIOUS DISORDER	Fabricating symptoms or self-harming—or presenting others as ill, injured, or impaired—in order to gain medical attention	Person or caregiver deceptively mimics, causes, or exaggerates physical symptoms, and seeks treatment from many doctors
DOWN SYNDROME	A developmental disorder that has varying impact on intellectual, physical, and social functioning	May have generalized anxiety disorder, OCD, sleep disorders, ADHD in children, and autism spectrum disorder
GENDER DYSPHORIA	The conflict that results from a mismatch between a person's biological sex and the gender they identify with	Displays feelings and behaviors of the opposite sex, distressed by puberty, disgusted with own genitals
SEXUAL DYSFUNCTION	Physical or psychological difficulties experienced by men or women that prevent them from enjoying sexual activity	Men have erectile dysfunction, premature or retarded ejaculation. Women lack desire or have pain on intercourse (dyspareunia)
PARAPHILIC DISORDERS	Sexual arousal only in response to specific inanimate objects, acts, or nonconsenting people	Can achieve arousal and satisfaction only with specific paraphilia, feels contempt for the object of the sexual focus
ELIMINATION DISORDERS IN CHILDREN	The repeated passing of urine (enuresis) or feces (encopresis) in places other than the toilet, either voluntarily or involuntarily	Defecates or urinates in inappropriate places; has loss of appetite, abdominal pain, social withdrawal, and depression
KORO (GENITAL RETRACTION SYNDROME)	A delusional disorder in which a person has an irrational fear that their genitals are retracting or disappearing	Strongly believes that penis (nipples in women) is shrinking despite lack of evidence, and that this is a sign of death
AMOK SYNDROME	A rare culture-specific disorder observed in Malay people, in which a sudden frenzied outburst follows a period of brooding	Causes serious injury to self and others in sudden frenzied, often armed assault; has no memory of the event
TAIJIN KYOFUSHO	A behavior culturally specific to Japan in which a person fears embarrassing others by being in their presence	Believes themselves to be disgusting, overconspicuous, and attracting unwelcome and unfavorable attention

illnesses (such as Parkinsonism). Even though not of psychiatric origin, the impairment or distress can be severe enough to require treatment.

Some disturbances are culturally specific, such as Koro or Amok, or arise from a conflict between an individual and their society or culture. Some Western disorders have Eastern counterparts and vice versa; for instance, the Japanese condition Taijin Kyofusho is similar to social anxiety disorder (p.53).

10–20%
of Japanese people suffer from Taijin Kyofusho

POSSIBLE CAUSES	IMPACT	TREATMENT
Genetics; emotional sensitivity to pain; negative personality traits; learned behaviors; problems processing emotions	Obsession with negative causes; problems with relationships; poor health; depression; distrust of medical opinion	Cognitive behavioral therapy to examine unhelpful thoughts and behaviors that maintain concern
Combination of psychological factors, stressful experiences, or complex or traumatic relationships in childhood	Deception impacts social relationships; serious health-related problems from unnecessary medical interventions	Psychotherapy to build personal insights and find alternative ways to cope with stress and anxiety
Chromosomal abnormality in which all or some cells in the body contain an extra copy of chromosome 21	Mild to moderate cognitive impairment; short- and long-term memory loss; slow acquisition of physical and language skills	Parent support and training, together with early intervention with techniques that support child's development
Probably hormonal influences before birth and intersex conditions (reproductive anatomy not fully male or female)	Stress; depression and anxiety; self-harm; suicidal thoughts	Psychotherapy to support living in preferred gender identity; physical transitioning with surgical intervention
Physical causes including illness, medication, and substance abuse; stress; performance anxiety; and depression	Loss of confidence; social anxiety; low self-esteem; depression; anxiety; panic attacks	Specific interventions for physical problems; couple-based anxiety and stress management and sex therapy
Sexual abuse or trauma in childhood; can be linked with severe personality disorders such as antisocial PD or narcissistic PD	Negative effect on intimate relationships; adopting risky or illegal behaviors	Psychoanalysis; hypnotherapy; and behavioral therapy
Trauma and stress; developmental delay; digestive problems	Loss of social confidence; secretive behavior; isolation, bullying, and other problems at school	Behavior programs to encourage good toilet habits; psychotherapy to help with shame, guilt, or loss of self-esteem
Presence of other mental disorders; lack of psychosexual education in puberty	Deep shame; fear; secretive behavior; depression; anxiety	Psychotherapy and medication for associated depression, body dysmorphic disorder, or schizophrenia
Geographical isolation; spiritual practices fueling a self-fulfilling prophecy	Long-term physical damage; social isolation; incarceration in a psychiatric institution; imprisonment	Psychotherapy for associated mental or personality disorders; tolerance of psychosocial stressors
Linked with specific phobias of blushing, deformation, eye-to-eye contact, and foul body odor	Depression; anxiety; social isolation; low self-confidence	Cognitive behavioral therapy to help examine and reevaluate exaggerated beliefs

HEALING THERAPIES

There are as many types of therapy as there are approaches to psychology. Matching the therapy to the individual's particular experience of a disorder is central to restoring peace of mind.

Health and therapy

Psychologists working in the area of health aim to improve the mental and associated physical health of individuals, specific groups, and the wider population. This involves devising and delivering therapies to prevent and treat mental disorders, and to promote general wellness. They also play a role in evaluating how therapies improve health and which are the most effective. This influences the way psychological treatments are delivered at both the individual and public level.

Roles of a psychologist

Whether working independently, as part of an inter-disciplinary health-care team, or in a research institution, psychologists are concerned with improving mental health and general well-being. Their different roles reflect the varied ways of achieving this goal for individuals or groups.

WHO CAN PROVIDE TREATMENT?

Many mental health specialists can deliver psychological assessments, therapies, and counseling, but only some can prescribe medications to treat disorders.

Psychologists

These professionals perform psychological assessments and deliver a range of talking or behavioral therapies, depending on the needs of the individual or group.

Psychiatrists

These are medical doctors who specialize in the treatment of mental disorders. They are licensed to prescribe psychiatric drugs as part of a patient's treatment.

General medical professionals

Doctors (GPs and hospital consultants) and advanced psychiatric nurses can prescribe drugs or other therapies.

Other mental health specialists

Social workers, psychiatric nurses, and counselors may deliver therapy alone or as part of a mental health team.

Health psychologist

What do they specialize in?

These specialists look at how people deal with illness and the psychological factors that influence their health. They may research and deliver strategies to improve health and prevent disease, for example, promoting weight loss or stopping smoking, or may help individuals manage specific illnesses such as cancer or diabetes.

Who would benefit from their help?

> **Chronically ill patients** needing help adjusting to a serious illness or managing pain.

> **Population groups** needing lifestyle advice to prevent disease.

> **Health-care providers** wanting to know how to improve their services.

> **Patient groups** such as diabetics, who need advice to help them manage their condition.

Where would you find them?

Hospitals, community health settings, public health departments, local authorities, research institutions.

Qualifications

Doctoral level of education, followed by practical training, and continuing professional development.

More than **75**% of GP appointments in the US are attributed to issues related to stress and anxiety

PSYCHOEDUCATION

Increasing people's awareness of living with mental health issues has become a key part of the therapeutic process. Whether delivered individually, in groups, or electronically via the Internet, psychoeducation helps those with mental disorders better understand their condition and the treatments, and also helps their families, friends, and caregivers provide more effective support. Having detailed information allows people to take better control of their lives and take positive steps to deal with their symptoms. It also improves a person's compliance with treatment and can play a role in reducing the stigma often associated with mental health disorders.

Clinical psychologist

What do they specialize in?

These psychologists help people to deal with mental and physical health issues such as anxiety, addiction, depression, and relationship issues. After clinically assessing an individual using tests, discussion, or observation, they will provide appropriate therapy.

Who would benefit from their help?

> **People with anxiety** or depression in need of individual or group therapy sessions.

> **Children** with learning difficulties or behavior problems.

> **Substance abusers** who need help to tackle their addiction.

> **PTSD sufferers** in need of therapy to overcome past traumatic events and experiences.

Where would you find them?

Hospitals, community mental health teams, health centers, social services, schools, private practice.

Qualifications

Doctorate in clinical psychology.

Counseling psychologist

What do they specialize in?

These specialists help people facing difficult life issues, such as bereavement or domestic violence, as well as those with mental health disorders. They build a strong client relationship to effect change, and may also undergo therapy to inform their practice.

Who would benefit from their help?

> **Families** experiencing relationship difficulties.

> **Children** experiencing social, emotional, or behavioral problems, or who have suffered any type of abuse.

> **Sufferers of stress** who can be helped to address underlying problems.

> **Bereaved individuals** needing emotional support and guidance.

Where would you find them?

Hospitals, community mental health teams, health centers, social services, industry, prisons, schools.

Qualifications

Doctoral level of education, followed by practical training, and continuing professional development.

Physical and psychological health

Scientific research increasingly links our mental health with physical health, and psychologists in this field have developed tools for assessing, and improving, our mind-body connection.

Making the connection

Health psychologists explore how a person's state of mind (someone, for example, suffering from the day-to-day experience of stress) affects their body, and they find ways to improve a person's physical health by helping them change the way they think. This may involve changing their lifestyle, social network, and attitude and perceptions. Health psychologists work in a variety of roles—in the community to help vulnerable and sick people, advising public authorities on health policy, and in hospitals.

When assessing an individual, the psychologist looks at all the factors that may contribute to an illness or a problem, and devises a strategy for change. This might include identifying behaviors that damage a person's health, such as smoking or poor diet; encouraging positive behavior such as exercise, a healthy diet, oral hygiene, health checks, and self-examination; improving sleep practices; and scheduling preventive medical screenings. Health psychologists may also promote cognitive behavior changes that give the person more control over their life.

Biopsychosocial model

Health psychologists use this model to assess three different forces meshing like a honeycomb in a person's life: biological (the impact of physical traits); psychological (thought patterns and attitudes); and social (the influence of life events and other people). Psychologists recognize that these three forces can have either a positive effect or a negative effect on health and well-being.

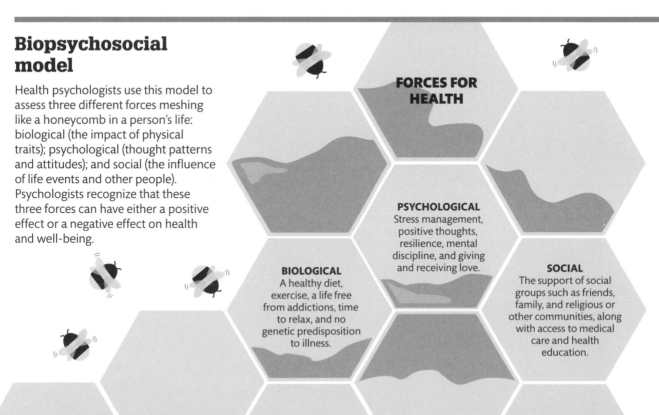

FORCES FOR HEALTH

PSYCHOLOGICAL
Stress management, positive thoughts, resilience, mental discipline, and giving and receiving love.

BIOLOGICAL
A healthy diet, exercise, a life free from addictions, time to relax, and no genetic predisposition to illness.

SOCIAL
The support of social groups such as friends, family, and religious or other communities, along with access to medical care and health education.

Managing health conditions

Health psychologists can help when people are diagnosed with conditions that require hospitalization or prolonged treatment, such as cancer, or alcohol or drug addiction. The psychologist will assess what can be changed to help improve the person's ability to cope mentally with physical pain or discomfort and the potentially life-changing impact of their condition.

A diverse range of strategies are also employed to aid rehabilitation. On the psychological front, health psychologists work to build and maintain a patient's self-esteem and motivation, training them to think more positively. Rallying the support of friends, family, and other health professionals is part of this process. On the physical side, they may implement alternative therapies, such as yoga and acupuncture, to enhance a patient's well-being, help control cravings, or overcome depression. They may also recommend regular exercise, a nutrition program, or vitamin therapy.

RATING MENTAL HEALTH

When a formal assessment is needed, psychologists use a questionnaire to rate or measure an individual's state of mind, differentiating between psychological health and emotional well-being.

Psychological health questions

> **Mood** Is your mood generally positive?
> **Positive relationships** Do you have friends or positive emotional ties?
> **Cognitive function** Can you properly think and process information?

Emotional well-being questions

> **Anxiety** Do you suffer from anxiety?
> **Depression** Are you depressed?
> **Control** Do you feel you have lost control or cannot control your feelings?

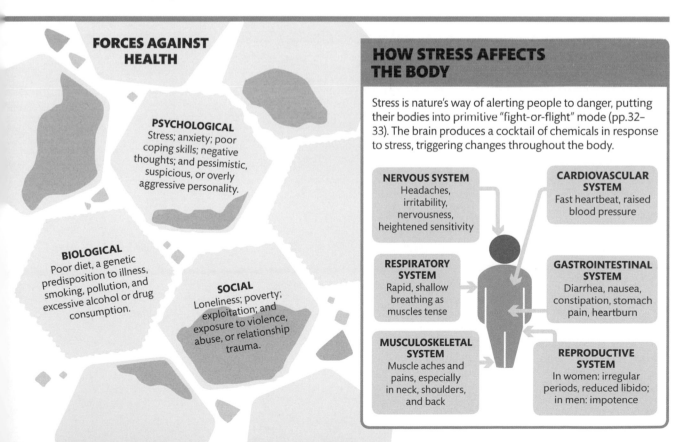

FORCES AGAINST HEALTH

PSYCHOLOGICAL
Stress; anxiety; poor coping skills; negative thoughts; and pessimistic, suspicious, or overly aggressive personality.

BIOLOGICAL
Poor diet, a genetic predisposition to illness, smoking, pollution, and excessive alcohol or drug consumption.

SOCIAL
Loneliness; poverty; exploitation; and exposure to violence, abuse, or relationship trauma.

HOW STRESS AFFECTS THE BODY

Stress is nature's way of alerting people to danger, putting their bodies into primitive "fight-or-flight" mode (pp.32–33). The brain produces a cocktail of chemicals in response to stress, triggering changes throughout the body.

NERVOUS SYSTEM
Headaches, irritability, nervousness, heightened sensitivity

CARDIOVASCULAR SYSTEM
Fast heartbeat, raised blood pressure

RESPIRATORY SYSTEM
Rapid, shallow breathing as muscles tense

GASTROINTESTINAL SYSTEM
Diarrhea, nausea, constipation, stomach pain, heartburn

MUSCULOSKELETAL SYSTEM
Muscle aches and pains, especially in neck, shoulders, and back

REPRODUCTIVE SYSTEM
In women: irregular periods, reduced libido; in men: impotence

The role of therapy

Psychotherapies use a range of strategies to help people modify the thoughts, actions, and emotions that are harmful to their physical or mental health, and also to promote improved self-awareness.

Therapeutic action

Psychotherapies are often referred to as "talking therapies" because communication with a therapist is the key agent for change. The aim is to manage adversity; maximize potential; clarify thought; provide support, encouragement, and accountability; and cultivate peace of mind and depth of consciousness. Therapy seeks to improve a client's understanding of themselves, others, and their relational dynamics. It may also be used to define personal goals and organize behavior into achievable systems.

Psychotherapy can uncover old wounds and help a client understand how past negative experiences currently affect them in unhealthy ways. It can also help them change the ways they react to external stimuli, and how they internally process and interpret experiences, allowing them to move beyond current states of thought and behavior. Therapy can empower a client to explore their psyche and spiritual self and to achieve more satisfaction in their lives. It is designed to increase self-acceptance and self-confidence, and to diminish unhelpful negative or critical thinking.

Types of therapy

Therapeutic approaches and methods are as diverse and creative as the mind itself, and psychological progress can be achieved in many ways. The main types of therapy are categorized according to the philosophy on which they are based. Methods of delivery vary and might comprise individual sessions, group therapy, or online guidance and task completion.

28%
of people in the UK have consulted a psychotherapist

PSYCHOANALYTICAL AND PSYCHODYNAMIC

These approaches are based on the concept that unconscious beliefs underlie maladaptive thoughts and behaviors. Gaining an insight into these beliefs can explain and relieve problems. The therapist and client also work to develop healthier ways of dealing with these previously repressed feelings, and to foster the client's inner resources and capability to manage their troubles.

COGNITIVE AND BEHAVIORAL

These therapies stem from the belief that it is not the things that happen to a person that upset them, but it is the way they think about the things that happen to them, and the meaning that they assign to their experience, that upsets them. Cognitive and behavioral therapies show people that they hold the power to change the way they think about things, and the way they react and behave as a result of these thoughts.

GROUP THERAPIES

12-step program

The 12-step model is a group therapy approach specifically used to tackle addictions (such as to drugs, alcohol, or sex), and compulsive behaviors like eating disorders. An essential part of overcoming addictions or compulsions is support from and connection to a community. Group therapy reduces isolation and associated shame, shows people that they are not alone in their struggle, and provides a network for support and accountability.

Self-help groups

These support groups focus on self-disclosure. Whereas some groups have a professional lead, others are peer-led. Shared experience is valued over professional knowledge.

SHARING EXPERIENCES in a group allows people to give and receive support and feedback, and to pool strategies for change.

HUMANISTIC

This approach prioritizes listening over observing. To this end, therapists use open-ended questions and qualitative tools to study personality and encourage the client to explore their own thoughts, emotions, and feelings. The therapist sees the client as inherently capable of and responsible for achieving personal growth, and not as a set of flawed unconscious drives.

SYSTEMIC

The "systems" approach enables people to work out issues arising from the interplay of relationships. Therapists can gain deeper understanding of problems by working with everyone in a system (family or group), hearing differing points of view, and watching people interact. This allows people to explore their identity as part of a larger group, and also has the advantage of strengthening their community network—useful for issues that worsen with isolation, such as addiction.

ROLE OF MEDICINE

The brain and behavior exert a continual reciprocal influence on one another. Medication can alter brain chemistry to improve mood, concentration, memory, and motivation; increase energy; and decrease anxiety. This improved functioning can alleviate the symptoms of mental illness and enable positive behavioral change.

Psychodynamic therapies

An umbrella term for all analytic therapies, psychodynamic therapy is also a method in itself. Analytic therapies follow the root aim of Sigmund Freud—to bring the unconscious mind into consciousness.

What are they?

The principle behind the psychodynamic approach is that the unconscious mind harbors feelings and memories, particularly from childhood, that shape thought patterns and behavior in adulthood. The therapist helps the client to talk about these often unwanted feelings and so draw them into the conscious mind. Burying unpleasant memories results in anxiety, depression, and phobias, and bringing them into the light of day gives the client the tools to resolve their psychological problems as an adult.

Acknowledging buried memories helps the client to identify, confront, and ultimately change the defense mechanisms they have developed to avoid experiencing painful realities or facing unpleasant facts and unwanted thoughts. These (usually unconscious) mental strategies include denial (refusal to accept reality), repression (burying an unwanted thought or feeling), compartmentalization (mentally separating conflicting emotions or beliefs), reaction formation (acting contrarily to how the person feels), and rationalization (self-justifying an unacceptable behavior).

In all psychodynamic therapies, the therapist listens to the client talking about their conscious problems while looking for patterns, behaviors, and emotions that hint at their subconscious feelings. The goal is to enable the client to deal positively with inner conflicts.

The session

All forms of psychodynamic therapy take place in a familiar, safe, respectful, non-judgmental environment. Sessions are usually one-on-one and last 50–60 minutes.

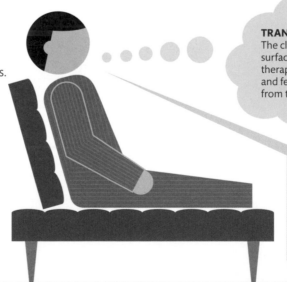

TRANSFERENCE
The client's unconscious conflicts surface in their relationship with the therapist. They redirect emotions and feelings, often from childhood, from themselves to the therapist.

DREAM ANALYSIS
A means of accessing the unconscious, analyzing dreams can reveal hidden emotions, motivations, and associations.

FREE ASSOCIATION
The client talks spontaneously about whatever comes to mind, without editing what they say or attempting to give a linear structure. True thoughts and feelings emerge.

RESISTANCE ANALYSIS
Showing the client what, how, and why they are resisting in thoughts, ideas, or emotions can explain defense mechanisms.

FREUDIAN SLIP
The client reveals what is really on their mind (their unconscious thought) by saying something they did not intend to.

THE CLIENT
In traditional Freudian analysis, the client lies on a couch and cannot see the therapist. In more interactive forms, the client can see the therapist.

Psychoanalysis

The purposes of psychoanalysis and psychodynamic therapy as specific methods are similar—to integrate the unconscious and conscious mind—but the depths of the processes differ.

What is it?

The founder of psychoanalysis, Sigmund Freud, developed his "talking therapy" after working in Paris with Jean-Martin Charcot, a neurologist who discovered that his patients' symptoms lessened after they talked about past traumas.

In the early 1900s, Freud established techniques such as free association, dream analysis, and resistance analysis, still widely used today. Silences in therapy are often as meaningful as what is said. All psychoanalysis assumes that psychological problems stem from the unconscious; that unresolved issues or repressed trauma hidden in the unconscious mind cause symptoms such as anxiety and depression; and that treatment can raise these conflicts to the surface so the client can resolve them.

Psychoanalysis often takes years, deconstructing and rebuilding the client's entire belief system. It benefits those who are robust of mind, with an outwardly successful life, but are aware of long-term worries or torments, such as an inability to stay in a relationship. Psychodynamic therapy is less intense and focuses on present-day problems, such as a phobia or anxiety.

INTERPRETATION
The therapist stays relatively quiet, reading between the lines of what the client says to help them overcome subconscious limitations.

THE THERAPIST
The analyst listens but does not judge so that the client need not fear saying something shocking, illogical, or silly.

	PSYCHOANALYSIS	PSYCHODYNAMIC THERAPY
Time	2–5 sessions a week	1–2 sessions a week
Duration	Long-term—several years	Short to mid-term—weeks, months
Delivery	The patient usually lies on a couch with the therapist behind, out of sight	The patient usually faces the therapist, who remains in sight
Relationship with therapist	The therapist is the expert—neutral and detached	The therapist is more interactive and acts as an agent for change
Focus	To promote deeper long-term change and happiness	To provide solutions for immediate problems

Jungian therapy

Carl Jung expanded Freud's ideas—he thought the unconscious mind went far deeper than the merely personal and was at the core of behavior patterns.

What is it?

Like his colleague Sigmund Freud, Jung considered that psychological distress occurs when the conscious and unconscious parts of the mind are unbalanced. But Jung thought that personal memories were part of a much larger whole.

Jung noticed that the same myths and symbols occur across the world, whatever the culture. He thought these must be the result of shared experience and knowledge of the human species, remembered by everyone as what he called the collective unconscious. These memories, in the deepest layer of the unconscious mind, take the form of archetypes—instantly recognizable symbols that shape behavioral patterns. The conscious ego is the public image that a

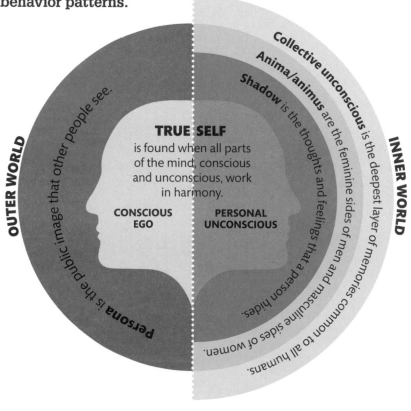

OUTER WORLD

Persona is the public image that other people see.

TRUE SELF is found when all parts of the mind, conscious and unconscious, work in harmony.

CONSCIOUS EGO

PERSONAL UNCONSCIOUS

INNER WORLD

Collective unconscious is the deepest layer of memories common to all humans.

Anima/animus are the feminine sides of men and masculine sides of women.

Shadow is the thoughts and feelings that a person hides.

NEED TO KNOW

> **Word association** The client says whatever comes into their mind when the therapist presents them with a word.

> **Extrovert** Someone whose attention is directed toward the outside world and other people; outgoing, responsive, active (even reckless), decisive.

> **Introvert** Someone whose attention is directed inward to their own thoughts and feelings; shy, contemplative, reserved, self-absorbed, indecisive.

---

person presents to the world. Its archetype is the persona, identifiable as a person being on their best behavior. The darker aspects of the mind that most people hide Jung called the shadow. Further archetypes are the anima (female traits in men) and the animus (male traits in women), which often clash with the conscious ego and the shadow. To find the true self, all the layers of a person's personality need to work in harmony.

Whereas psychoanalysis delves into the top layer of the client's unconscious, Jungian therapists

explore all the layers. Their role is to help the client use the archetypes to understand and change their own behavior.

Jungian therapists use techniques such as dream analysis and word association to reveal where the inner archetypes collide with outer-world experiences. This process of analysis enables the client to understand which layers of their mind are in conflict, and then make positive changes to restore the balance. Like psychoanalysis, this therapy is a fascinating journey into the mind and can take years.

Self psychology and object relations

Both of these therapies are offshoots of Freudian psychoanalysis. The therapist uses empathy to understand the client's unique perspective of life and create patterns of behavior that improve relationships.

What are they?

Both self psychology and object relations focus on experiences in a client's early life as a way to understand and improve their adult relationships. The premise of self psychology is that children deprived of empathy and support in their early years cannot develop self-sufficiency and self-love as adults. The therapist fulfills the client's urge to look to others to meet their needs, giving them the self-worth and self-awareness to carry into their own relationships. In object relations—the name for childhood relationships that the adult is repeating inappropriately—the aim is to use the empathy with the therapist as a platform for analyzing past interactions and emotions and applying new positive models of behavior.

IN OBJECT RELATIONS, the therapist helps the client relinquish relationships from childhood and replace them with models of behavior appropriate to their adult life.

Transactional analysis

Instead of exploring the unconscious to shed light on the conscious mind, transactional analysis focuses on the three "ego states" of an individual's personality.

What is it?

Rather than asking the client questions about themselves, the therapist observes and analyzes how they interact. Then they help the client develop a strategy for operating from the adult ego state, rather than copying how their caregiver treated them when they were young (the parent ego state) or acting out how that treatment made them feel and behave as a child (the child ego state).

Conflict occurs when a person operates simultaneously from different states, for instance, one part of their personality giving orders from their parent state and another part reacting defensively from their child state.

Transactional analysis helps the client to recognize these three states and guides them toward using their adult state in all interactions. It helps the client communicate as they wish to, unhindered by patterns formed in childhood. The adult state is based in the present, and evaluates data from the child and parent states to draw a logical, intelligent conclusion that directs behavior.

PARENT
Can be controlling and critical or nurturing and supportive

ADULT
Makes rational choices in response to the present time

CHILD
Uses feelings and behavior from childhood

**EGO STATES
(COMPONENTS OF A
SINGLE PERSONALITY)**

Cognitive and behavioral therapies

What an individual thinks affects how they feel and behave. This group of therapies focuses on how thoughts affect behavior and aims to help people change negative patterns.

What are they?

These therapies stem from the belief that it is not what happens to people but how they *think* about what happen to them that upsets them. These thoughts can lead an individual to behavior based on a false premise. Cognitive-based therapy seeks to change patterns of negative thought. Behavior-based therapy aims to replace unhelpful behaviors with positive actions that then change underlying feelings. Many therapies take elements from both cognitive and behavioral theories. The therapist helps the client challenge automatic thoughts and practice new ways of reacting. Once the client can change their viewpoint, they can alter how they feel and behave.

IRRATIONAL THOUGHTS AND BEHAVIOR

While reality feels absolute, it is subjective and influenced by individual thought patterns—two people in the same situation may feel and react very differently. Many people automatically make incorrect assumptions and act on them. Therapy helps people to challenge these assumptions.

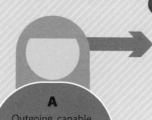

A

Outgoing, capable, and confident with a strong social network.

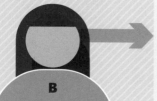

B

Unconfident, shy with low self-esteem and a poor support network.

Emotional stimuli

Two people (A and B) find out that a mutual friend is having a party, but has not invited either of them. Despite the identical emotional stimuli, A and B process the information in vastly different ways based on their respective cognitive patterns. Person A might analyze the rational possibilities why she has not been invited or diplomatically confront the friend, whereas person B automatically jumps to the conclusion that she has been deliberately excluded.

Rational thoughts

> **Technical error** Perhaps the invitation went astray.

> **Work function** Perhaps it is a party only for work colleagues and limited to those in the same industry.

> **Limited guest list** Perhaps it is just a small gathering for an old group of friends she is not part of who have not seen each other for a while.

Irrational thoughts

> **Negative personal feelings** The lack of an invitation reflects what the friend feels toward her.

> **Deliberate exclusion** The friend did not want to invite her because she is bad at socializing in groups.

> **Self-destructive patterns** She deserves not to be invited because good things do not happen to her.

Collaborative approach

Cognitive and behavioral therapies require clients to be actively involved in the therapeutic process. Rather than the therapist taking a leadership role, the client and therapist work in partnership to resolve issues. Intimacy and honesty are integral to progress.

In many types of psychotherapy, the therapist leads the process, actively diagnosing the client and directing the course of sessions and dialogues. This authoritarian approach can feel alienating to some clients, especially those who do not respond well to feeling directed or controlled, those who are sensitive to being judged or evaluated, those with issues around medical or authority figures, and those who have had negative past experiences in therapy.

In collaborative therapy, however, the relationship between client and therapist is equal, reciprocal, and flexible. Both the client and the therapist make observations, direct conversations, and evaluate progress. Discussion helps the client to view their problems from a new perspective, and then encourages them to take actions that change their patterns of behavior. The process is one of trial and error, so if one course of action only serves to increase the client's distress, client and therapist can discuss alternative behaviors and reinforce those that work for the individual. The client remains actively engaged and equally responsible for their part in the healing process throughout the therapy sessions.

Rational behaviors

> **Make contact** Phones or meets the friend having the party to have a casual conversation.

> **Collect answers** Asks thoughtful and diplomatic questions, without making assumptions, to ascertain the real reason for not being invited.

Irrational behaviors

> **Avoid** Does not confront the friend or situation because it is too difficult.

> **Confront angrily** Feels overly defensive, engages the friend in an angry confrontation and accuses her of being thoughtless, not caring, or being deliberately unkind.

> **Act defensively** Treats the friend badly in retaliation.

Therapy

Regardless of the real situation, person B's negative thought patterns created a specific illusion of reality based on her perceptions. Therapy can help with:

> **Recognizing emotional habits** In this case, tending to feel left out and to attribute self-blame and criticism.

> **Self-awareness** Understanding how emotional habits—such as poor self-esteem or anxiety—form and what situations trigger irrational thoughts.

> **Behavioral strategies** Using assertiveness training or working on communication skills.

> **Practice** Learning to challenge and contradict irrational and negative thought patterns and to recognize that other possibilities are more likely to be true.

> **Change** Practicing behavioral and cognitive strategies to create a toolkit for positive outcomes in the future.

Behavioral therapy

If behavior can be learned, it can also be unlearned. Based on this idea, this action-based approach aims to replace unwanted behaviors with positive ones.

What is it?

This approach is based on the concepts of classical conditioning (learning by association) and operant conditioning (learning through reinforcement) (pp.16–17).

Classical conditioning works by linking a neutral stimulus with an unconditioned response to modify a person's behavior. Over time, the stimulus invokes a new conditioned response. For example, a child who falls over and hurts themselves at the same time as hearing a dog bark (the neutral stimulus) may develop a fear of dogs. Behavioral therapy can reverse the process and desensitize the child. Operant conditioning uses reward-based systems that develop and reinforce desirable behaviors, and discourage and punish unwanted ones. Strategies include issuing tokens for good behavior and giving a child "time-out" to defuse a tantrum.

Repeating tasks that invoke positive behaviors allows a client to relearn responses. Behavioral therapy is useful for overcoming phobias (pp.48–51), OCD (pp.56–57 and below), ADHD (pp.66–67), and substance use disorder (pp.80–81).

Cognitive therapy

Developed in the 1960s by psychiatrist Aaron Beck, this therapy aims to change the negative thought processes and beliefs that lead to problematic behaviors.

What is it?

Beck proposed that negative or inaccurate thoughts and beliefs about ourselves, others, or the world have an adverse effect on our emotions and behaviors. This can create a vicious cycle whereby behaviors reinforce an individual's distorted thought processes.

Therapy focuses on breaking this pattern by helping people identify and replace negative thoughts with more flexible and positive ways of thinking. The therapist teaches the person how to observe and monitor their own thoughts and to evaluate whether they represent reality or are irrational. Setting tasks to be completed at home, such as diary keeping, can help the client to identify their negative beliefs and then prove them wrong. Changing the underlying beliefs leads to changes in connected behaviors. Cognitive therapy is especially suitable for depression (pp.38–39) and anxiety (pp.52–53).

THERAPY IN PRACTICE

With a disorder such as OCD, which has both cognitive and behavioral elements, therapy that aims to change either the thoughts that lead to the disorder or what the person does in response to those thoughts, or both, can help.

Behavioral therapy

❯ Suitable for those who carry out compulsive behavior to reduce fear.

❯ Helps client break the link between a certain object or situation and fear.

❯ Client learns to confront their anxiety without performing rituals.

❯ This decreases their anxiety so unhealthy behaviors can stop.

Cognitive therapy

❯ Suitable for those who carry out internal checks, practicing avoidance and rituals in the mind and physically.

❯ Helps client unlearn beliefs and restructure their thought patterns.

❯ Challenging the meaning the client assigns to these thoughts makes them lose their power.

❯ Client has no need to perform rituals.

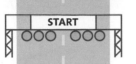

START

PHASE 1

Get to know client,
build trust,
explain cycle:

THOUGHT,
FEELING,
BEHAVIOR
CYCLE

Negative
thoughts
create
feelings

Behavior
reinforces
thoughts

Feelings create
unwanted behavior

PHASE 2

Aim to break
this cycle

Explore client's
problematic
thoughts and
behaviors

Analyze the effect
these have on the
client and on
others

Together develop
a plan to alter these
thoughts and actions

PHASE 3

Use a range of
tools to break
the cycle:
relaxation
techniques,
problem-solving
with client,
exposure therapy
(p.128)

Monitor which
activities help client

PHASE 4

Encourage client
to practice
techniques after
therapy

CBT (cognitive behavioral therapy)

This therapy helps people to identify, understand, and correct the distorted thoughts that can have a negative effect on feelings and behavior.

What is it?

This practical, structured, problem-solving approach employs theories first used in cognitive therapy (left) to reshape how a client thinks, and strategies from behavioral therapy (left) to alter how they act. The aim is to change the negative thought and behavioral cycles that make the client unhappy.

In order to understand the link between thoughts and behaviors, the therapist breaks problems down into separate parts, analyzing the person's actions, thoughts, feelings, and physical sensations. The therapist can then understand how the client's internal dialogue, their automatic thoughts (usually negative and unrealistic), affects their behavior. The therapist helps the client to recognize what experiences or situations trigger these unhelpful thoughts, and gives them the skills to change their automatic reactions.

Learning and practicing these skills is key to the effectiveness of the therapy. The therapist sets tasks for the individual to practice at home. By implementing new strategies repeatedly in their daily life, the client creates new patterns of positive behavior and realistic thinking and learns to apply them in the future.

ACTION
PLAN

Complete tasks between
sessions, such as thought
log, recording anxiety
levels, diary of enjoyable
activities

CBT

❯ Suitable for those who link situations with fear and exaggerate thoughts.

❯ Helps client stop their compulsions in the mind and in behavior.

❯ Client learns nothing bad happens if they stop performing compulsions.

❯ Their anxiety decreases and they break the thought cycle, so the behaviors can stop.

Road to change

The therapist helps the client to follow and practice small structured steps and gain the skills to tackle new problems independently.

Third wave CBT

This group of evolving methods both extend CBT approaches and change the aim. Rather than focusing on reducing symptoms—though this is a benefit—they help the client step away from unhelpful thoughts.

What are they?

Two therapies that come under the third wave CBT umbrella are ACT (acceptance and commitment therapy) and DBT (dialectical behavior therapy).

ACT aims to change the client's relationship with their thoughts. Rather than trying to alter or stop unwanted thoughts, the client learns to accept and observe them. Instead of thinking, "I never do anything right," the client switches to, "I am having the thought that I never do anything right." Becoming an observer of their thoughts diminishes the power which that thought has over their state of mind and being. The thought no longer has to guide reaction or behavior, and the person can instead choose actions based on their values.

Some people experience intense emotional reactions and have little ability to cope with their strong feelings. This may lead to damaging behaviors such as self-harm or substance abuse. DBT teaches the skills to accept and tolerate distress and to manage disturbing or provocative emotional stimulation. The process involves gaining behavioral control, then experiencing rather than silencing emotional stress—discussing and accepting past traumatic experiences, and tackling self-blame and dysfunctional thoughts.

Mindfulness (p.129) skills such as visualization help the client to maintain emotional regularity in everyday life, to build confidence to deal with problems calmly, and to expand their capacity for joy.

THE ACT METHOD

ACT therapists teach the client to defuse the power of their negative self-judgments.

> **Values** Define what is most important to you.

> **Acceptance** Instead of trying to control or change thoughts, accept them without judgment.

> **Cognitive defusion** Distance yourself from the interpretations of your mind—just observe.

> **The observing self** Maintain a stable state of inner consciousness and awareness regardless of external stimuli.

> **Commitment** Set goals for behavioral change and commit to them, regardless of any sabotaging thoughts or emotions.

MINDFULNESS
Become aware of the emotional experience—observe rather than react.

INTERPERSONAL EFFECTIVENESS
Stay calm and pay respectful attention to other people.

DISTRESS TOLERANCE
Use self-soothing encouragement in stressful situations.

EMOTIONAL REGULATION
Choose to behave in a positive way despite negative emotions.

The four skills of DBT

Skills training teaches people who feel at the mercy of their emotions to accept themselves and their thoughts and to replace dysfunctional behaviors with positive actions.

CPT (cognitive processing therapy)

This therapy helps people to address and change negative, fear-based thoughts—referred to as stuck points—that recur after traumatic events so that they feel calmer and safer.

What is it?

CPT is particularly effective for people with PTSD (p.62). Sufferers often experience biased, upsetting thoughts that delay recovery, including feelings of helplessness; loss of trust, control, and self-worth or deservedness; blame; and guilt. These "stuck points" keep the person stuck with the symptoms of PTSD, and are usually not based on what actually happened.

CPT aims to help the individual evaluate these stuck points and ask the question "Do the facts support my thoughts?" Clients reexamine the trauma, and are helped to recognize acquired distortions and rewrite their negative post-traumatic view. This cognitive restructuring helps them to accurately differentiate between what is truly dangerous and what is safe, and to modify unhelpful thoughts in the future.

STAGES

The stages of CPT are designed to help the individual understand how trauma has affected their brain.

PSYCHO-EDUCATION
Discuss symptoms of PTSD, thoughts, and emotions.

FORMAL PROCESSING OF TRAUMA
Recall trauma to gain awareness of thoughts.

USING NEW SKILLS
Learn and practice skills to challenge thoughts and modify behaviors.

REBT (rational emotive behavior therapy)

Through this therapy clients come to understand that how they think about events is more significant than the events themselves.

What is it?

REBT works to replace the irrational beliefs that cause misery and self-defeating behaviors with more productive, rational thoughts. It breaks a client's rigid thought patterns—often governed by words like "should," "ought," and "must"—such as dwelling harshly and solely on the negative; thinking in black-and-white absolutisms, especially about themselves; and global-rating ("total idiot"). Understanding the ABC framework (right), clients learn to accept themselves and other people, to distinguish an irritation from a crisis, and to meet the challenges of life with tolerance and assertiveness. REBT is useful for anxiety and shyness disorders (pp.52–53) and phobias (pp.48–51).

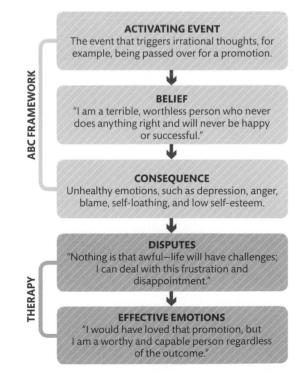

ABC FRAMEWORK

ACTIVATING EVENT
The event that triggers irrational thoughts, for example, being passed over for a promotion.

BELIEF
"I am a terrible, worthless person who never does anything right and will never be happy or successful."

CONSEQUENCE
Unhealthy emotions, such as depression, anger, blame, self-loathing, and low self-esteem.

THERAPY

DISPUTES
"Nothing is that awful—life will have challenges; I can deal with this frustration and disappointment."

EFFECTIVE EMOTIONS
"I would have loved that promotion, but I am a worthy and capable person regardless of the outcome."

Methods used in CBTs

People often make their stress or fear worse through poor coping mechanisms. Two methods that offer practical strategies are SIT (stress inoculation therapy) and exposure therapy.

What are they?

SIT helps people to recognize the triggers and distorted thought processes that incite a stress response. Many clients overestimate the threat level of a situation and underestimate their ability to deal with it.

The therapist presents anxiety-provoking situations that cue stress through role-playing, visualization, or recordings of stressors. In response, the client learns and practices new coping mechanisms, such as relaxation and mindfulness techniques and assertiveness. Gradually the client learns how to change their reaction to stress and cope with it instead of engaging the previous unhelpful response.

People who have undergone traumatic experiences, or who have phobias, tend to avoid exposure to situations, objects, or places ("triggers") that might cause fear. This avoidance often makes the problem worse, allowing the fear to grow. In exposure therapy, the therapist deliberately exposes the client to anxiety-provoking stimuli to erode their fears.

Exposure is incremental and starts with "imaginal" exposure—imagining the feared thing, or recollecting the traumatic memory. The intensity of exposure increases with "in vivo" exposure—real exposure in settings that provoke anxiety but are not truly dangerous. Various models can be used (right).

EXPOSURE METHODS

❭ **Flooding** Intense exposure to the person's worst fears to extinguish the fear response.

❭ **Systematic desensitization** Gradual exposure to fears to eliminate them.

❭ **Graded exposure** Grading anxiety-provoking situations to create a hierarchy of fears; the person progresses up the list, tackling the most feared last.

❭ **Exposure and response prevention** Exposing OCD sufferers to a trigger while not letting them engage in their usual rituals; for example, a compulsive hand washer is not allowed to wash their hands and finds there are no disastrous consequences, so the compulsion subsides.

❭ **Aversion therapy** Pairing an unpleasant stimulus with the unwanted behavior to change it.

Exposure therapy in practice

Therapists find that exposure is particularly effective for treating phobias.

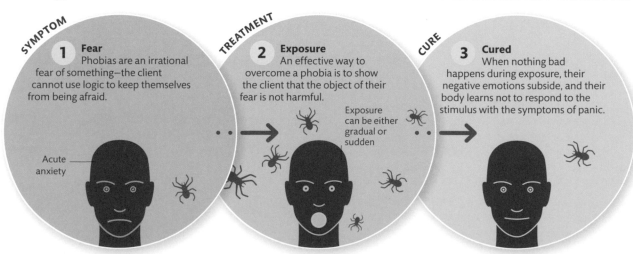

SYMPTOM

1 Fear
Phobias are an irrational fear of something—the client cannot use logic to keep themselves from being afraid.

Acute anxiety

TREATMENT

2 Exposure
An effective way to overcome a phobia is to show the client that the object of their fear is not harmful.

Exposure can be either gradual or sudden

CURE

3 Cured
When nothing bad happens during exposure, their negative emotions subside, and their body learns not to respond to the stimulus with the symptoms of panic.

Mindfulness

Learning to focus awareness on the present—to observe what their thoughts, feelings, and body are experiencing at any one moment—can help people understand and manage unhelpful responses.

What is it?

Mindfulness techniques help people to give their full attention to what is happening around them and to them. Observing and accepting these experiences and sensations in a detached and nonjudgmental way gives people the space to evaluate whether thoughts and behaviors are dysfunctional, and then to modify their responses. Practices to promote mindfulness include breathing, visualization, and listening exercises; yoga; tai chi; and meditation.

Benefits of mindfulness

Learning to observe rather than be controlled by their thoughts allows people to anticipate and deal more effectively with stressful experiences and anxiety, and to replace negative thought patterns. Mindfulness exercises also have a calming effect—switching off the regions of the brain that stress turns on, and activating the parts that deal with awareness and decision-making. This allows people to focus on positive actions to promote well-being.

"... refuge to the mind is mindfulness."

Buddha

STRATEGIES FOR MINDFULNESS

MINDFUL WALKING
Focusing your awareness on what you see, hear, and smell; your thoughts; and the physical sensation of walking allows you to connect with the present.

MINDFUL EATING
Slowing down, taking the time to bring full attention to the process and sensation of eating, focuses your mind and can change your responses.

MINDFUL BODY AWARENESS
Practicing yoga or doing a "body scan"—bringing your attention to each part of the body in turn, and noting how it feels—focuses mind and body.

MINDFUL BREATHING
Learning to concentrate on the flow of your breath is a useful, calming meditation technique to relieve stress, anxiety, and negative emotions.

POSITIVE PSYCHOLOGY

Traditional psychotherapy concentrates on tackling disorders and problem behaviors; positive psychology, like humanistic therapies, focuses on the goals of self-fulfillment and well-being as a catalyst for change. Learning to think positively and to focus on what brings happiness encourages people to pursue positive actions—to develop their strengths, improve their relationships, and achieve goals—on a personal and societal level. Mindfulness techniques are often used to help people focus their mind and behaviors on positive action.

PERMA model

Developed by psychologist Martin Seligman, this model for change defines the elements that promote well-being: (P) positive emotion; (E) engagement; (R) positive relationships; (M) meaning; and (A) accomplishments. Understanding the importance of these elements and then taking steps to pursue them through everyday thoughts and actions allows people to build on their own strengths and resources to achieve future happiness.

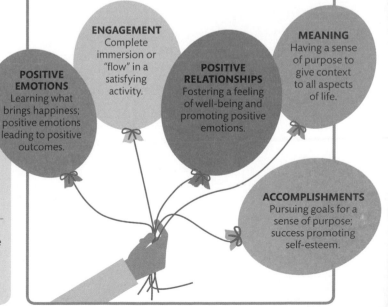

ENGAGEMENT
Complete immersion or "flow" in a satisfying activity.

MEANING
Having a sense of purpose to give context to all aspects of life.

POSITIVE EMOTIONS
Learning what brings happiness; positive emotions leading to positive outcomes.

POSITIVE RELATIONSHIPS
Fostering a feeling of well-being and promoting positive emotions.

ACCOMPLISHMENTS
Pursuing goals for a sense of purpose; success promoting self-esteem.

Humanistic therapies

This group of therapies encourages an individual to resolve their problems and issues and achieve greater fulfillment by recognizing, understanding, and using their own capacity to develop.

What are they?

Before humanism developed in the late 1950s, psychological issues were viewed as flaws within a person that required intensive behavioral or psychoanalytic treatment. Psychological theories relied on measurements of behavior and other scientific, quantitative (statistical) studies to evaluate and categorize people.

Humanists viewed these concrete, methodical approaches as too limited in scope to capture the broad, colorful, and individualistic human experience. In contrast with psychoanalysis, humanistic therapies view the person as a whole being able to exercise free will and make active choices, rather than as a set of predetermined drives, urges, and behaviors.

Therapists emphasize the individual's inner strengths, resources, and potential as the foundation for working through issues. Life may be filled with challenges and heartbreak, but humans are essentially good, resilient, and capable of enduring and overcoming difficulties.

Humanists also expanded the concept of therapy as a

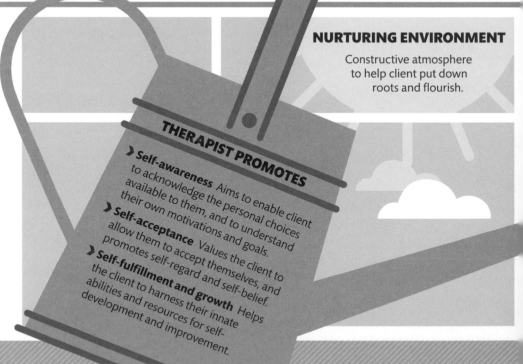

Therapeutic relationship

Humanistic therapists aim to cultivate a positive and constructive relationship by valuing their client, and showing genuine, unconditional, positive regard. This environment nurtures the client's self-knowledge, confidence in their own choices, and emotional development so that they can self-actualize (fulfill their own potential).

THERAPIST PROMOTES

> Self-awareness Aims to enable client to acknowledge the personal choices available to them, and to understand their own motivations and goals.

> Self-acceptance Values the client to allow them to accept themselves, and promotes self-regard and self-belief.

> Self-fulfillment and growth Helps the client to harness their innate abilities and resources for self-development and improvement.

NURTURING ENVIRONMENT

Constructive atmosphere to help client put down roots and flourish.

treatment for severe neuroses to a broadly applicable approach for anyone wanting to self-improve. They recognized people's natural desire to overcome problems, seek happiness, improve the world, and live a satisfying and fulfilling life as the primary, central human motivation. An individual's need to realize their potential and fulfill their goals and dreams is called self-actualization.

Humanists believe that not only is a person capable of making changes and achieving personal growth but it is their responsibility to do so. This idea places the individual fully in control of their choices and goals.

Humanistic approaches for getting to know a client are as creative and diverse as people themselves, but all are based on talking and trust. In a session, rather than relying on their own observations, the therapist asks open-ended questions and listens to what the client makes of their own behavior and personality. All humanistic therapists use their empathy and understanding to help the client accept themselves.

✓ NEED TO KNOW

> **Therapist/client relationship** In close and collaborative counseling, the therapist encourages the client to use their own resources to find solutions.

> **Qualitative methods** Rather than evaluating behavior with a questionnaire (a quantitative method), listening is the basis of therapy, as the client is seen as the expert in their own experiences. The therapist guides the client toward greater self-awareness.

"[A person is] a continuing constellation of potentialities, not a fixed quantity of traits."

Carl Rogers, American humanistic psychologist

CLIENT ACHIEVES

Self-actualization Attains their goal or wishes, realizes their potential, and becomes their ideal self.

CLIENT ENGAGES WITH THE PROCESS

Responsibility Takes active role to make the changes needed for personal growth; therapist helps the individual take responsibility for their choices, behaviors, and self-development.

Person-centered therapy

In this approach, the accepting, supportive relationship between therapist and client promotes self-belief, confidence, and personal growth.

What is it?

True to humanism, person-centered therapy holds that all people possess the resources they need to gain insight, experience personal growth, and change their attitudes and behaviors to reach their full potential—self-actualization.

Therapy sessions focus on the present and future, rather than on the past, and the client leads the conversation. The therapist listens intently to the client's experiences, responding without judgment.

The authenticity and depth (congruence) of this relationship encourages clients to express their thoughts and emotions freely. The therapist's unconditional positive regard validates the client's feelings, attitudes, and perspective, and the therapist's acceptance allows the client to truly accept themselves. Self-esteem, self-understanding, and confidence improve; guilt and defensive reactions lessen.

Self-acceptance allows clients to have more faith in their abilities, express themselves better, and improve their relationships, and can also help with body perception in people with dysmorphic disorders.

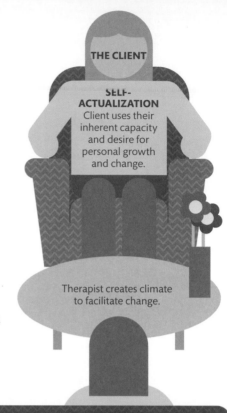

THE CLIENT

SELF-ACTUALIZATION
Client uses their inherent capacity and desire for personal growth and change.

Therapist creates climate to facilitate change.

THE THERAPIST

CLIENT/THERAPIST RELATIONSHIP
The therapist is the vehicle for the client's self-improvement.

CONGRUENCE
The therapist is positive, optimistic, and genuine.

UNCONDITIONAL REGARD
The therapist sees the client in a positive light, enabling the client to do the same.

EMPATHY
The therapist understands and experiences the world through the eyes of the client.

Reality therapy

This problem-solving therapy seeks to help the client evaluate and change their current behaviors and thought processes. It is especially useful for relationship issues.

What is it?

In reality therapy, the therapist helps a client change how they act, then how they think, as both behaviors are easier to control than how they feel or react. The therapy holds that the only behavior an individual can control is their own, which is motivated by the five basic needs (right). Focus is on the present. The therapist discourages criticizing, blaming, complaining, and excuses, all of which harm relationships. Instead, client and therapist together identify and monitor behavior patterns and create a workable plan of change.

FIVE BASIC NEEDS

Fun
Pleasure, fulfillment, and joy

Physiological (survival)
Food, shelter, and safety

Love and belonging
Part of a family, network of friends, or community

Power
To succeed, provide, feel competent, and be recognized for accomplishments

Freedom
Autonomy and control over own life

Existential therapy

This philosophical therapy helps people come to terms with the specific, inherent challenges of simply existing by making choices and taking responsibility for their actions.

What is it?

Existential therapy is based on the premise that if people make peace with the givens of existence (right), they can lead a more fulfilling and enjoyable life, free from anxiety. Existentialism holds that people have free will and are active participants in their own lives. Therapy focuses on increasing self-awareness by exploring the meaning, purpose, and value in the client's life, and by helping them understand that they are in charge and not just a passive victim of drives and impulses. A session may address questions such as "Why are we here?" and "How can life be good if it involves suffering?" and "Why do I feel so alone?"

By learning to accept responsibility for decisions in the past that led to emotional disruption, the client gains the power to take control of their experiences. The therapist helps the client find individual, nuanced solutions; and acceptance, growth, and welcoming future possibilities are key themes.

THE GIVENS OF EXISTENCE

❯ **The inevitability of death** The natural drive to exist conflicts with awareness that death is inevitable.

❯ **Existential isolation** Everyone enters the world alone and leaves it alone. Regardless of any relationships or connections, people are innately alone.

❯ **Attendant isolation** People are alone, yet seek connection.

❯ **Meaninglessness** People seek purpose, yet finding a path and understanding the meaning of existence often eludes them.

❯ **Freedom and responsibility** All have a responsibility to create their own purpose and structure, as existence inherently has none.

Gestalt therapy

This lively and spontaneous therapy liberates clients and helps them become more aware of their thoughts, feelings, and behavior and their effect on their surroundings.

What is it?

The German word gestalt roughly translates as "whole," reflecting the belief that the individual is more than the sum of their parts and has a unique experience of the external world. Gestalt therapists believe that discussion alone cannot alleviate guilt, unresolved anger, resentment, or sadness. The client must evoke and experience negative feelings in the present to resolve them. The therapist may use role-play, fantasy, visualization, or other stimuli to arouse negative feelings from the past so that the client gains insight into how they react to certain situations. This increased self-awareness allows the client to identify patterns and see the true, rather than perceived, effect of their behavior. Gestalt was developed to treat addiction but helps depression, grief, trauma, and bipolar disorder, too.

EMPTY-CHAIR TECHNIQUE
The client addresses a chair as if it is an important figure in their life, then changes roles to understand the opposing view. Releasing feelings and emotions increases self-awareness.

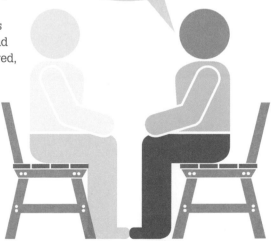

ENACTMENT LEADS TO SELF-AWARENESS

Emotion-focused therapy

This approach attempts to help people understand their emotions better and acknowledge them, and to use this newfound self-awareness to guide their behavior.

What is it?

This therapy is based on the premise that emotions form the foundation of people's identity and govern their decision-making and behavior. With this approach, the client is encouraged to discuss and analyze how they feel or have felt in past situations to identify which emotions are helpful or unhelpful to them and to make sense of their emotional responses.

Increasing awareness allows the client to describe their emotions more clearly, to assess whether the feelings are appropriate to the situation, and to learn to use positive emotions to guide their actions. Recognizing how unhelpful emotions, including those linked to traumatic experiences, negatively impact choices and behavior also helps the client to regulate these feelings and to develop strategies to change their emotional state.

Strategies may include using breathing techniques, using imagery and visualization, repeating positive phrases, or using new experiences to elicit positive emotions.

EMOTIONALLY FOCUSED THERAPY

Although its title is similar, emotionally focused therapy is different from emotion-focused therapy. It is a relationship therapy for couples and families to help them understand the emotions that govern their interactions. Because negative patterns of behavior and conflict can occur when emotional needs are not met, the therapist helps clients recognize their own feelings and acknowledge those of family members or partners. Learning how to express and regulate emotions, listen to others, and positively use emotion tightens bonds with partners or family members, resolves past issues, and offers strategies for the future.

Solution-focused brief therapy

This forward-looking therapy encourages individuals to focus on their strengths and to work positively toward achievable goals rather than dwelling on or analyzing the past.

What is it?

This therapy is based on the belief that everyone has the resources to improve their lives but may need help in structuring plans. The so-called miracle question ("How is life different if ...?") is often asked so the person envisions what life will be like when their issue is resolved. From here, the individual can define a goal, create possible solutions, and outline specific steps to achieve their goal. Coping questions, such as "How have you handled this in the past?" also encourage the person to focus on previous successes, showing them that they already have the skills, resourcefulness, and resilience to achieve a positive outcome.

Therapy usually involves about five sessions. While the therapist provides accountability and support, the client is always considered to be the expert on their own problems. It is a particularly effective method for young people, who may prefer a short, structured approach rather than a probing analysis of their past.

REACH GOAL/ DESIRED SITUATION

ASSESS WHAT HAS ALREADY BEEN ACHIEVED

SCALE HOW CLOSE THE GOAL IS AND DECIDE ON SMALL REALISTIC STEPS

DESCRIBE THE GOAL IN DETAIL AND PICTURE A SOLUTION

DECIDE ON A CLEAR AND REALISTIC GOAL

Somatic therapies

These therapies—based on the idea that unresolved emotional issues are stored physiologically as well as psychologically—act on the body to release negative tension and restore mental health.

What are they?

Sometimes psychological healing occurs through methods that cannot be entirely explained, yet are still effective. This is true of many mind-body healing therapies, sometimes called energy psychology, which deal holistically with the body and mind.

Somatic therapies consider that the integration of mind and body is essential for mental health. Massage, body work, breath work, yoga, tai chi, and the use of essential oils or flower essences are all examples of somatic therapies that may relieve physical and emotional tension.

Certain body parts are associated with psychological issues. Many people carry stress in their shoulders, for instance, and emotional trauma may create physical pain or digestive problems. Changing body posture can change the psychological experience—a broken heart, for example, often leads to a shoulders-forward, heart-protected slouch, and a sense of defeat results in a downward gaze. Encouraging the client to thrust their shoulders back, sit up straight, and lift their chin to the sky can help them to feel powerful, more optimistic, and more open to facing the world.

Trauma destabilizes the autonomic nervous system. Psychological issues are stored in body and mind.

Yoga and other somatic therapies restore balance by releasing negative emotions held in the body.

The healing power improves the person's state of mind and reduces physical symptoms of pain.

EMOTIONAL FREEDOM TECHNIQUE

This holistic therapy works on the same meridians (energy channels) as acupuncture and acupressure. The theory is that traumatic experiences can block these channels, causing continuing distress. The therapist uses their fingertips to tap meridian points on the body, while the client thinks about a specific problem, image, or negative feeling, and voices positive affirmations.

Tapping these points appears to calm the amygdala—the part of the brain that processes emotions and controls the fight-or-flight response. Over time, this process reprograms the individual's thoughts, removing negative emotions and replacing them with new, positive feelings and behaviors. Individuals can also learn to perform the tapping sequence themselves.

TAPPING POINTS
After the karate-chop points are tapped, meridian points are tapped from the head downward, 1–8.

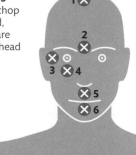

Karate-chop point

80% of individuals report a positive effect from **EFT**

EMDR (eye movement desensitization and reprocessing)

This therapy stimulates the brain using eye movement, reprocesses traumatic memories so that they lose their power to disturb, and teaches the client techniques to deal with emotional disturbances.

DURING BILATERAL STIMULATION, side-to-side eye movements help the brain to digest traumatic memories, and reorganize how they are mentally stored.

What is it?

In this therapy, the client recalls a picture, scene, or feeling from a past trauma while tracking bilateral stimulation, such as the therapist's hand moving back and forth across their field of vision. The client thinks of a negative statement linked to the trauma (for example, "I am unworthy," from a childhood marred by a disapproving parent) and replaces it with a positive, preferred self-statement.

Based on the idea that the negative belief system has been trapped in the client's nervous system, even though the actual danger has long since passed, the combination of eye movement and psychological recall neurologically releases the traumatic memory and its negative effects. This allows the memory to be stored neutrally, and helps install a new healthy belief system.

The process mimics the memory processing and physical movement thought to occur during REM (rapid eye movement) dream sleep. The therapy is particularly effective in treating individuals with PTSD (p.62) and symptoms can be significantly reduced in as few as three 90-minute sessions.

Hypnotherapy

During hypnotherapy, the client enters a deep, trancelike state of relaxation that suppresses the conscious mind, allowing the subconscious to become more alert and receptive.

What is it?

The therapist uses the power of hypnotic suggestion to quiet the analytical parts of the brain and fully focus the client's attention on the subconscious mind. Once the client is deeply relaxed, the therapist makes suggestions that instill different brain patterns, changing the client's perceptions, thought processes, and behavior.

Hypnotherapy is particularly useful for helping clients to overcome unwanted habits such as smoking or overeating. It can also be used to reduce pain in future situations that the client anticipates will be painful such as childbirth or surgical or dental procedures. Another use is to allow suppressed or hidden memories to surface so that the related issues and emotions can be addressed.

Clients practice deep relaxation, often using a recording taped by the therapist between sessions to consolidate the work.

Arts-based therapies

These approaches use the alternative languages of art and music to promote self-discovery, self-expression, and well-being. They can help people articulate thoughts and feelings and regulate their emotions.

What are they?

It can be difficult for some people to find words to express emotions and perceptions. Art therapy provides a way for them to describe their inner life, investigate and validate thoughts and feelings, and increase self-awareness. The physical act of producing art can be therapeutic in itself too, as it concentrates body and mind on a single creative goal.

The focus in art therapy is not on the skill of the artist, but on the creative process as a form of communication.

Displaying their art in public can help individuals overcome their self-consciousness and self-criticism and lead to greater acceptance of themselves and improved self-esteem.

Music therapy plays a different role. When music stimulates the brain (left), it activates a myriad of sensory connections, which can change the individual's physical and emotional states. Music acts on neural pathways throughout the brain to alter how a person processes information, experiences and expresses emotions, uses language, relates to others, and moves.

Music can promote long-term behavioral and emotional changes, including decreasing symptoms of depression and anxiety. Its physiological effects include triggering the release of mood-enhancing chemicals, such as dopamine, and lowering heart rate.

All styles of music can be used, and sessions may involve listening to music, using instruments, singing, improvising, or composing.

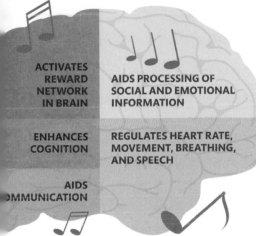

ACTIVATES REWARD NETWORK IN BRAIN

AIDS PROCESSING OF SOCIAL AND EMOTIONAL INFORMATION

ENHANCES COGNITION

REGULATES HEART RATE, MOVEMENT, BREATHING, AND SPEECH

AIDS COMMUNICATION

Animal-assisted therapy

This approach uses the bond between people and animals to improve communication skills, emotional control, and independence, and to decrease feelings of loneliness and isolation.

What is it?

Interacting with animals increases levels of oxytocin, a hormone that promotes intimacy and trust, and mood-enhancing endorphins. Learning how to handle animals also improves behavioral and social skills and boosts self-esteem.

Stroking cats, looking after dogs or horses on a regular basis, and swimming with dolphins are some of the ways vulnerable people can learn about boundaries, respect, and trust and develop self-reliance and independence.

In anger-management and substance-abuse group therapy, the presence of animals can encourage participants to open up and talk about lost innocence and violent pasts, leading to greater self-acceptance and forgiveness.

"A pet is a medication without side effects."

Dr. Edward Creagan, American oncologist

Systemic therapies

These approaches recognize that people are part of a network of relationships that shape their behaviors, feelings, and beliefs. The therapies seek to influence the whole system, not just the individual.

What are they?

Systemic therapies make use of the concepts of systems theory, which hold that any individual object is just one part of a larger and more complex system. In human terms, this might be a family, workplace, organization, or social community.

Disruption in one part of the system may affect or unbalance other parts of the network. For example, a person experiencing depression may find that it disrupts their relationships with family members, but it may also affect interactions with work colleagues and friends. Rather than treating the problems of the individual in isolation, systemic therapies therefore tackle them in the context of the system as a whole—looking for solutions that work for everybody. Making a change to one part of the system—such as providing better support for the individual at work—can benefit all members of the network.

As well as viewing the system as a whole, these therapies address system dynamics, attempting to identify deeply entrenched patterns and trends. The dynamics of many families, for example, are governed by a series of unwritten rules and unconscious behaviors.

By making individuals aware of the ways in which they interact and influence one another, these therapies help people to make positive changes that benefit the dynamics of the group. This involves considering the perspectives, expectations, needs, and personalities of all the people involved, and encouraging dialogue to enable each person to gain an insight into the roles and needs of others in the group.

To resolve issues, all members of the group have to accept that change is needed and recognize how their actions influence others. In many cases, small individual changes can lead to large shifts in group behavior.

Looking at problems systemically also reveals how seemingly unrelated issues can be closely linked. Solving one issue may therefore bring the bonus of a beneficial effect on other parts of the system.

> "The **family** crucible **must have a shape, a form, a discipline** of sorts, and the **therapist** has **to provide it.**"
>
> Augustus Napier, American author and family therapist

Balancing relationships

When conflict occurs between two people, they may focus on a third person as a way to stabilize their relationship, rather than resolving the issue between themselves, so emotional relationships can be seen to be triangular. Adding a third person into an existing relationship (for example, the arrival of a baby) is not always beneficial and may cause friction between the original two.

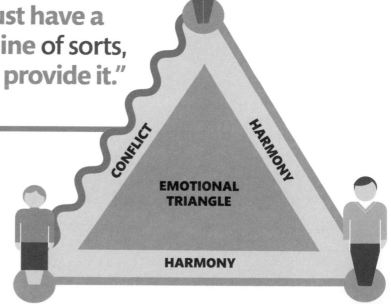

Family systems therapy

Relationships within the family unit are regarded as both the underlying cause of issues and the means by which they can be solved in this therapeutic approach that focuses on group dynamics.

What is it?

This therapy is based on the theories of psychiatrist Murray Bowen. Bowen used eight interlocking concepts to find out how birth order, a person's role within the family, personality, and inherited traits all affect how individuals relate to each other in a family system. He defined the family by both the people within it and the way in which they interact.

Viewing the family as an emotional unit in this way enables individuals to work together to solve problems—these might be emotional issues affecting the whole family, such as death or divorce, or specific issues related to an individual member that have an impact on the rest of the unit.

Therapists explore how family members see their roles and express them. This exploration allows each person to understand better how their actions affect other members of the group, and how they are affected in turn.

Understanding how external factors impact relationships within the family, and how patterns can be repeated over generations, is also key. For example, children with a poorly defined sense of their own individuality (perhaps due to overbearing parents) may seek out a partner with a similarly low level of differentiation. The two of them then pass on conflicts or problems associated with these traits to their own children. Improving communication, self-awareness, and empathy can help individuals to break these generational patterns, and enable the family unit to build on its strengths and to use its interdependence to make positive changes.

BOWEN'S EIGHT INTERLOCKING CONCEPTS

Differentiation of self
How a person maintains their own sense of individuality, while still functioning in the group.

Emotional triangle
How the smallest network in a human relations system, in many cases formed by two parents and a child, operates.

Family projection process
How parents' emotions, conflict, or difficulties are passed on to their children.

Emotional cutoff
How individuals manage conflict within the family network by distancing themselves.

Sibling position
How birth order influences the way children are treated—differences in expectation lead them to take on different roles.

Multigenerational transmission
How people seek partners with similar differentiation, so patterns repeat down the generations.

Societal emotional process
How family emotional systems go on to influence wider systems in society, like the workplace.

Nuclear family emotional process
How any tensions in the family affect the relationship patterns within the unit.

Strategic family therapy

The therapist plays a key role in this approach, helping families to identify the problems affecting their relationships and to develop structured plans and targeted interventions to solve them.

What is it?

This solution-focused technique, based on the theories of therapist Jay Haley, uses strategies specific to each family's structure and dynamics to achieve an agreed-on outcome. The focus is always on current problems and solutions rather than analyzing past causes and events.

The therapist plays an active role in helping the family to identify their problems. Together they agree on a goal achievable in a relatively short time frame. The therapist develops a strategic plan to help family members adopt new ways of interacting that they might not have considered before. Individuals might be encouraged to replay common family interactions or conversations, with the aim of increasing the family's awareness of how they operate and how problems arise.

Strategies for change are based on the strengths of family members. This allows the family to use their own resources to support each other in making positive changes to behavior, and to successfully achieve their goal as a unit.

> "[In strategic therapy] the therapist takes responsibility for directly influencing people."
>
> Jay Haley, American psychotherapist

STRATEGIC ROLE OF THERAPIST

> **Identify solvable problem**
> Observes the family and identifies a problem, such as teenage son Tom not communicating.

> **Goal setting** Helps the family decide on a clear goal—Tom must tell parents where he is.

> **Design an intervention** Develops a plan that targets the problem within the family—Tom will phone in regularly.

> **Implement plan** Devises and reviews role-playing, discussions, and homework to help the family understand why Tom is reluctant to keep in touch.

> **Examine the outcome** Ensures parents as well as Tom have made positive changes.

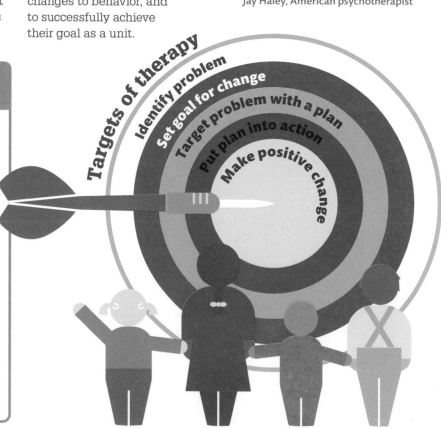

Targets of therapy

Identify problem
Set goal for change
Target problem with a plan
Put plan into action
Make positive change

Dyadic developmental therapy

This therapy aims to give children who have experienced emotional trauma a firm base from which they can form stable attachments and loving relationships with parents or caregivers.

What is it?

Children who are neglected, abused, or not properly cared for may be prone to rule-breaking and aggressive behavior; thought, attention, and personality disorders; anxiety; depression; and difficulties in forming healthy attachments.

Dyadic therapy aims to establish a safe, empathetic, and protective environment for children with such a background, where they can learn new patterns of communication and behavior. The therapist needs to build a collaborative relationship with both the child and the caregiver as a basis for promoting a strong bond between the child and the parent or caregiver. They use the principles of PACE—a Playful, Accepting, Curious, and Empathetic approach—to govern interactions with the child. This allows the child to feel valued, safe, and understood, and to be open to receiving nurture and support in their relationships.

THERAPIST IS:
PLAYFUL,
ACCEPTING,
CURIOUS,
EMPATHETIC

CLIENT FEELS:
SAFE, INCLUDED,
HEALTHY, ACTIVE,
NURTURED,
RESPONSIBLE,
RESPECTED

Contextual therapy

The aim of this approach is to restore balance within a family so that everyone's emotional needs are met fully, fairly, and in a reciprocal manner.

What is it?

Imbalances in family relationships can occur when members feel others are treating them unfairly, ignoring their needs, or not reciprocating feelings.

Contextual therapy uses a concept of fairness and equal rights and responsibilities, called relational ethics (right), as a starting point for understanding the problems in family relationships. Relational ethics is also the basis for developing strategies to restore balance and harmony. The ages, backgrounds, and psychological characteristics of the members in the family unit provide context for grievances. The therapist encourages each member to express their side of the conflict, and to listen to the views of others in the family group. They are helped to acknowledge the positive efforts made by others in the family, and also to accept responsibility for their own behaviors.

Understanding that each person in the family deserves to have their needs met, and learning to take mutual responsibility for this, allows families to develop new patterns of behavior that balance give-and-take.

FACTORS GOVERNING FAMILY DYNAMICS

> **Background** Age, social and cultural factors, and experiences that make each person individual.

> **Individual psychology** The personality and psychological makeup of each person.

> **Systemic transactions** How family members relate to one another—the emotional triangles, alignments, and power struggles, including relationships across generations and inherited patterns of behavior.

> **Relational ethics** The balance of give-and-take and the emotional need and fulfillment that governs family dynamics; to be balanced, everyone must take responsibility for their actions and transactions with other family members.

Biotherapies

These therapies are based around the idea that biological or physical factors strongly influence mental disorders. They aim to change the structure of the brain, or how it functions, in order to alleviate symptoms.

What are they?

Unlike psychotherapies, which focus on environmental and behavioral factors and use the client–psychologist relationship as an agent for treatment, biotherapies are prescribed by a psychiatrist and target how the brain functions mechanically. They are usually delivered in the form of medication or, in extreme cases, with interventions such as ECT (electroconvulsive therapy), TMS (transcranial magnetic stimulation), or psychosurgery. Some of these therapies attempt to correct the biological irregularities that are linked with the symptoms of mental illnesses such as bipolar disorder and schizophrenia. These irregularities may result from genetics, abnormalities in brain structure, or dysfunction in how parts of the brain interact.

Biotherapies are often used to bring symptoms under control and work alongside nonbiological approaches, such as behavioral or cognitive therapies, which help people manage their symptoms and the factors that contribute to their condition.

Drug therapy

Medication can be used to reduce specific symptoms such as hallucinations, low mood, anxiety, or mood swings. While psychiatric drugs do not change the underlying mental health problem, they can help people to cope better and function more effectively.

CATEGORY	USED FOR	DRUG TYPES
ANTIDEPRESSANTS	Depression, including despondent mood; anhedonia (inability to experience pleasure); hopelessness. Sometimes given for anxiety.	SSRIs (selective serotonin reuptake inhibitors); monoamine oxidase inhibitors; seratonin-norepinephrine reuptake inhibitors; tricyclics.
ANTIPSYCHOTICS	Bipolar disorder; schizophrenia; and for symptoms such as hallucinations, delusions, difficulty thinking clearly, and mood swings.	A group of drugs that block dopamine. Older versions are called "typical"; newer drugs, "atypical."
ANTI-ANXIETY DRUGS	GAD (generalized anxiety disorder); panic disorder; social anxiety disorder; PTSD; OCD; and phobias.	Benzodiazepines; buspirone; beta blockers; SSRIs; seratonin-norepinephrine reuptake inhibitors.
MOOD STABILIZERS	Bipolar disorder; may also be used to treat mood issues related to schizophrenia, depression, and seizure disorders.	Lithium (for mania); anticonvulsants (such as carbamazepine, used for depression); antipsychotics (such as asenapine).
STIMULANTS	Narcolepsy and ADHD.	Amphetamines; caffeine; nicotine.
SLEEPING DRUGS	Sleep disorders.	Antihistamines; sedative hypnotics; benzodiazepines; sleep-wake cycle modifiers.
DRUGS FOR DEMENTIA	Improving the associated symptoms of dementia and slowing disease progression (not able to cure the underlying cause).	Cholinesterase inhibitors.

Treatments

Psychiatric drug therapies act on neurotransmitters, such as dopamine and norepinephrine (both associated with reward and pleasure), and serotonin (which regulates mood and anxiety) (pp.28–29). They can be very effective in reducing symptoms but may have side effects, including drowsiness, nausea, or headaches.

Treatments that physically disrupt or stimulate the brain's electrical signals are sometimes used when drug therapy has been ineffective. In ECT and TMS, low electrical currents are passed through the brain. Very occasionally, psychosurgery is used to alter brain functioning. This involves making small lesions in the brain to disrupt connections in the limbic system (pp.26–27).

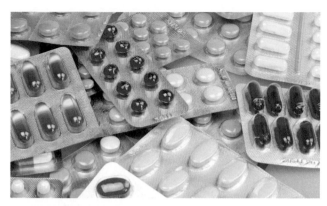

MEDICATIONS block or enhance the activity of different chemical neurotransmitters in the brain. They may increase the production of a particular neurotransmitter, interfere with how neurotransmitters are absorbed by receptors in the brain, or act directly on receptors.

Antidepressant use increased nearly 65% from 1999 to 2014

US Centers for Disease Control and Prevention, 2017

HOW THEY WORK	EFFECT ON PERSON TAKING THEM	SIDE EFFECTS
"Feel-good" neurotransmitters (serotonin, dopamine, and norepinephrine) are made increasingly available for the brain to absorb.	Improve mood and sense of well-being; increase motivation and optimism; raise energy levels; improve sleep patterns.	Weight gain; drowsiness; inhibited libido and ability to achieve orgasm; sleep disturbance; dry mouth; nausea; headaches.
Block the uptake of dopamine by the brain, as overactivity of the dopamine system causes psychotic symptoms.	Decrease auditory and visual hallucinations; stabilize mood; improve clarity of thought.	Emotional effects such as irritability and moodiness; neuromuscular effects; body temperature problems; dizziness.
Vary greatly in their action—some modify neurotransmitters; others (beta blockers) address physical symptoms.	Improve ability to manage stress and face challenges; decrease muscle tension; lower reaction to psychological triggers.	Dizziness; poor balance or coordination; slurred speech; memory issues; difficulty concentrating; withdrawal symptoms.
Vary in their action—some modify neurotransmitters, such as dopamine; others increase calming chemicals.	Reduce mania; prevent cycle of manic and depressive episodes; alleviate depression.	Weight gain; flat affect (little emotional reaction); dry mouth; acne; restlessness; sexual dysfunction; sun sensitivity.
Increase the availability of neurotransmitters such as dopamine and norepinephrine to the brain, enhancing activity.	Improve alertness and concentration; increase clarity and organization of thoughts; raise energy levels.	Anxiety; insomnia; loss of appetite; weight loss; increased heart rate; jaw tremors.
Block histamines (antihistamines); enhance GABA (p.29) (hypnotics, benzodiazepines); act on melatonin (cycle modifiers).	Induce ability to fall asleep and/or remain asleep.	Memory loss; daytime drowsiness; increased risk of falling; risk of tolerance and dependence.
Inhibit the action of cholinesterases—enzymes that break down acetylcholine, a neurotransmitter important for memory.	Prevent successive strokes; delay further decline of cognitive function.	Weight loss; nausea; vomiting; diarrhea.

PSYCHOLOGY IN THE REAL WORLD

Specialist psychologists study all aspects of society. Their aim is to understand how people interact as children and adults, at work and play, and ultimately to improve everyone's experience of the world.

Psychology of self-identity

A person's concept of who they are and how they relate to the real world forms their self-identity and is expressed through their personality. Psychologists in this field of individual differences start from the premise that people have enough self-esteem to want to develop their awareness of themselves and how they relate to the world. Over time, a person's identity may change or evolve, and they may develop a stronger sense of self, even reaching the pinnacle of self-actualization.

The web of identity

Part of a person's sense of who they are comes from their social or group identity. The groups they belong to reinforce their beliefs and values, and give them validation and self-esteem. As a person goes through life, they add to this web of identities as they accumulate experiences, meet new people, change jobs, and make choices and commitments. Social media and new technologies are changing how people shape their identity, as the distinction between private and public self blurs.

SOCIALIZATION
People see themselves in relation to friends and other social groups, who may share views or interests.

INDIVIDUAL IDENTITY

RELIGION
Belonging to a religious group can inform a person's cultural and social identity, as well as their private belief system.

SUBCULTURE
Identifying with a particular clique or club can be a way of self-defining within a wider society or culture.

PEERS
A peer group, especially during adolescence, plays a formative role in establishing values and identity.

EDUCATION
How a person is educated, where, and to what level informs personal identity and acquired values.

HOBBIES
Belonging to a group of people with the same interests fosters self-esteem and identity.

REGION
Where a person is born, or chooses to live, can feed certain characteristics into identity.

STATUS
Social and economic status influences how a person feels about themselves, and how they feel others view them.

SELF-ESTEEM AND AWARENESS

❯ **Self-esteem** Sense of self-worth, based on a person's appraisal of their own thoughts, beliefs, emotions, choices, behaviors, and appearance; seen in psychology as a personality trait, which means that it is stable and enduring.

❯ **Private self-awareness** A person's thoughts, emotions, and feelings (which cannot be seen), including the way they view themselves and others, how they would like to be, and their self-esteem.

❯ **Public self-awareness** Linked to a person's physical attributes, including their concepts of beauty, body language, physical abilities, public actions, and material possessions; also how far a person chooses to conform to cultural and social norms relating to public self-expression.

> "The **reward for conformity is** that **everybody likes** you **except yourself.**"
>
> Rita Mae Brown, American writer and activist

NORMS
Whether a person strives to follow or to flout cultural or social norms defines who they are.

POLITICS
Political affiliations reflect a sense of community, and are a public expression of personal values and beliefs.

CULTURE
The prevailing culture influences self-identity through imagery, values, beliefs, and social codes.

CLASS
The social categorization of either belonging to or being excluded from a class group is part of identity.

FAMILY
Family provides the genetic identity and also a set of values and social network within which to play a part.

AGE
A person's age group reflects how they think about themselves, and how others see them.

ROLES
The different public roles a person plays—child, brother, lawyer, wife, tennis captain—feed into a sense of self.

SOCIAL MEDIA
Technology allows people to connect with subgroups that reflect their personal interests and beliefs.

GENDER
A person's gender governs how they view themselves, their relations with others, and their place in society.

VALUES
Children take on the values of their parents; later they may adopt the value systems of other groups.

WORK
Workplace and colleagues can define a person in terms of status, self-esteem, interests, and choices.

Identity formation

Beginning in childhood, individuation (the formation of identity) is tested in adolescence as young people explore their sense of themselves and their role in the world, and develops in adulthood.

What is it?

Questions such as "Who am I?" and "What makes me special?" underpin the development of personal identity. For infants, how their caregivers treat them answers these questions. By the age of three, children develop a view of themselves and their place in the world according to their personal attributes and abilities, as well as factors such as their age, gender, cultural or religious background, and interests. Children who are supported during this period develop a strong and positive sense of identity that fosters confidence and self-esteem. A secure identity also encourages tolerance—the willingness to accept difference and not feel threatened by it.

As children establish a more detailed idea of who they are, they start to compare themselves with others (in personality, looks, and ability), and also internalize how they are viewed by others.

Adolescents may question their previous notions of identity, which can cause a period of confusion. New external influences as well as physical and mental changes encourage teenagers to redefine their sense of self. Their self-identity is strengthened by increasing independence, and a move from attachments to family to relationships with friends.

By adulthood, identity or sense of self may be fixed in some respects, but it can continue to evolve in others. In addition to unique characteristics, internal or external factors may alter people's attitudes, goals, and professional and social networks, modifying aspects of their personal and public identities.

Stages of identity development

Psychologist Erik Erikson argued that identity develops in eight distinct stages, influenced by a person's interactions with the environment. During each stage some form of psychosocial crisis (conflict) occurs. Personal development (the achievement of a "virtue") rests on how this conflict is resolved.

Early years

Children develop a "self-concept"—the abilities, attributes, and values that they believe define them. Interactions with caregivers, peers, and, later, teachers influence this self-concept and the development of confidence and self-esteem.

3–6 YEARS
INITIATIVE VS. GUILT
"PURPOSE"

Children begin to assert control, but feel guilt if this is stifled by caregivers.

1–3 YEARS
AUTONOMY VS. SHAME
"WILL"

Children begin to practice being independent, but are afraid of failure.

1. Age
2. Conflict
3. "Virtue"

0–18 MONTHS
TRUST VS. MISTRUST
"HOPE"

Infants are uncertain about the world. Trust replaces fear if they have good care.

Adolescent years

During this crucial stage of identity formation, adolescents explore who they are and often experiment with different roles, activities, and behaviors. This may lead to confusion—an identity crisis—as they work through different choices. Resolving this crisis helps adolescents to establish a strong sense of self as adults.

65–DEATH

INTEGRITY VS. DESPAIR

"WISDOM"

People may become depressed if they feel that they have not achieved their goals.

26–64 YEARS

GENERATIVITY VS. STAGNATION

"CARE"

Adults feel unproductive if they are not contributing to wider society.

20–25 YEARS

INTIMACY VS. ISOLATION

"LOVE"

Young adults start to worry about finding the right partner, fearing isolation.

12–19 YEARS

IDENTITY VS. CONFUSION

"FIDELITY"

Adolescents search for a sense of self, exploring a range of beliefs and values.

6–12 YEARS

INDUSTRY VS. INFERIORITY

"COMPETENCE"

Children compare their abilities to those of their peers, and may feel inadequate.

IDENTITY STATUS THEORY

Building on Erikson's theories about adolescence, psychologist James Marcia proposed that identity develops when young people resolve crises (evaluate their choices) in domains such as school, relationships, and values, and when they commit (choose specific roles or values). Marcia envisaged four statuses along the continuum of identity development:

❯ **Identity diffusion** Adolescents have not committed to a particular identity or set a life direction or goals.

❯ **Identity foreclosure** They commit to an identity prematurely, adopting traditional or imposed values without exploring their own views.

❯ **Identity moratorium** Young people actively explore different roles and options but have not yet committed to a particular identity.

❯ **Identity achievement** Adolescents explore a range of choices and solve their identity issues by committing to a set of goals, values, and beliefs.

Personality

Psychologists have long sought to understand how personality—how someone expresses their identity—develops. Genetics, life experiences, and environment are just some of the factors involved.

What is it?

Personality is the characteristic patterns of thoughts, feelings, motivations, and behaviors that impact how people see themselves, others, and the world around them. It drives how people feel, how they think, what they want, and how they behave. Personality is what makes each person unique and it influences everything from relationships to careers.

Major approaches to personality

These approaches attempt to understand and explain the complex issues around personality. Some focus on how personality develops, whereas others are concerned with explaining individual differences in personality.

Biological

Psychologists such as Hans Eysenck have emphasized the role of genetic and biological factors in the formation of personality. This approach suggests that characteristics and traits are determined by brain structure and function, and that they can be inherited—that nature plays more of a role than nurture.

Behaviorist

According to this approach, personality develops through a person's interaction with the environment, and continues to evolve throughout their lives. New experiences, meeting new people, and new situations all influence responses and traits.

Psychodynamic

Encompassing the theories of Freud and Erik Erikson, this approach indicates that an individual's personality is shaped by unconscious drives and how successfully they resolve a series of psycho-social conflicts that occur at defined stages of life.

Humanistic

Humanists believe that people's innate desire to realize their potential by exercising free will, and the personal experiences they accrue as a result of free will, shape personality. Their view suggests that people can take responsibility for who they want to be.

Evolutionary

This approach takes the line that different personality traits evolve at the genetic level in response to environmental factors. Different traits are therefore evolved adaptations as a result of natural selection or sexual selection. These are traits that in a particular environment increase the chances of reproduction and survival.

Social learning

Related to behaviorist theory, the social learning view is that social interaction and environment mold personality. Traits develop from observing behavior modeled by others and through conditioning. People internalize actions and responses that feed into their personality. For example, a child who is consistently told that they are naughty internalizes this message and gradually assumes this personality.

Dispositional (trait)

Trait theory proposes that personality is made up of different broad dispositions or traits. How these traits combine and interact is unique to each person (their "central traits"), although common traits (such as extroversion) may be shared by many people from the same culture. "Cardinal" traits are those that are so dominant that they come to define a person—for example, altruism and Nelson Mandela.

A number of prevailing theories attempt to understand how people's individual personalities develop, and to classify personality traits or types. Whereas the biological outlook implies that personality traits are fixed, other approaches, such as the humanistic and behaviorist theories, indicate that environmental factors and experiences modify personality over time. Research using studies of twins suggests that both nature (biological) and nurture (environmental) play a role in personality. The Big Five personality theory (below) is now widely used to categorize and measure the different characteristics or traits that make up an individual's personality. It implies that personality can be malleable—while some traits remain stable and consistent, others may change how they manifest themselves or take greater prominence, depending on the type of situation the individual finds themselves in.

The Big Five personality theory

The most popular and widely accepted model of personality, the Big Five suggests that personality comprises five broad dimensions. Each individual's personality lies somewhere along the spectrum of these five traits.

LOW SCORE	TRAIT	HIGH SCORE
Practical; inflexible; prefers routine; conventional	**O** — **Openness** Includes imagination, insight, feelings, and ideas	Curious; creative; adventurous; open to abstract concepts
Impulsive; disorganized; dislikes structure; careless	**C** — **Conscientiousness** Includes thoughtfulness, competence, impulse control, and goal setting	Dependable; hard-working; organized; detail-driven
Quiet; withdrawn; reserved; prefers solitude	**E** — **Extroversion** Includes sociability, assertiveness, and expressiveness	Outgoing; articulate; affectionate; friendly; talkative
Critical; suspicious; uncooperative; insulting; manipulative	**A** — **Agreeableness** Includes cooperativeness, trustworthiness, altruism, and kindheartedness	Helpful; empathetic; trusting; caring; polite; amiable
Calm; secure; emotionally stable; relaxed	**N** — **Neuroticism** Includes levels of calmness and emotional stability	Anxious; easily upset; unhappy; stressed; moody

CASE STUDY: STANFORD PRISON EXPERIMENT

In 1971 at Stanford University, psychologists set up a simulation of prison life. A group of young men took on the roles of guards; others, those of prisoners. The experiment was terminated after six days because the guards behaved so abusively and brutally and the prisoners took their extreme suffering so submissively. The study implies not only that all people harbor ugly traits, but also that environment and circumstances can shape behavior and attitudes—effectively altering personality.

"I practically considered the prisoners cattle."

Stanford University "prison guard"

Self-actualization

This concept attempts to describe what motivates people. It explains the different goals in life that shape behavior, and how individuals can realize their full potential.

What is it?

Associated with the theories of humanist psychology (pp.18–19), self-actualization means an individual's desire to realize their full potential. In 1943 psychologist Abraham Maslow proposed that self-actualization formed the pinnacle of a "hierarchy of needs" that all people strive to fulfill. At the bottom of the hierarchy are basic survival needs; once these are satisfied, individuals aspire to fulfill more abstract concrete goals. These include social needs (for love and belonging), the need for esteem and respect, and finally a sense of purpose that is achieved only when people fulfill their true potential—creatively, spiritually, professionally—in whatever realm is meaningful to them.

Hierarchy of needs

Maslow thought that people's behavior is motivated by their desire to fulfill a set of needs. Once lower needs have been met, people are motivated not by deficiencies, but by a desire for fulfillment and growth. "Peak" experiences are possible when people have reached the highest state of personal growth.

Self-actualization

Fulfillment
When a person achieves a self-actualized state, they are doing all that they are capable of.

LOSS OF STANDING

Esteem
The individual strives for recognition from others, prestige, and a sense of achievement, which gives them confidence in their abilities and boosts self-esteem.

Psychological

DIVORCE

Belonging and love
An individual strives to satisfy their psychological need for love and belonging through close relationships, family, friends, and within their community.

FAMILY

JOB LOSS

Safety
A person's need for stability, physical security, foreseeable employment, resources, health, and property must be met in order for them to feel safe and free of fear.

ENOUGH MONEY

HOME

Basic

Physiological
A person must satisfy their basic needs for air, food, drink, shelter, warmth, and rest. These needs are usually met in childhood, and must be a given in adulthood before an individual can start seeking higher needs that make life meaningful.

FOOD/WATER

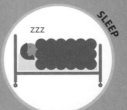
zzz
SLEEP

Barriers to personal growth

Maslow believed that every person desires and is capable of self-actualization, but only 1 percent of people ever achieve it. Lower-level needs often resurface throughout life, which make progression to self-actualization impossible. Life experiences such as divorce, bereavement, or losing a job mean that people struggle to meet their needs for financial security, safety, love, or esteem, and cannot fulfill their psychological, creative, and personal potential. The pressures of today's hypercompetitive, information-driven society also mitigate against self-actualization. People receive constant messages that they should be doing more, working harder, earning more, or socializing more, depriving them of the quiet reflection time necessary for personal growth.

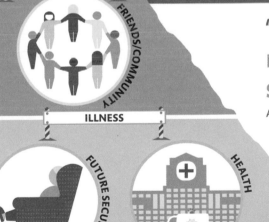

PRESTIGE/RESPECT

BEREAVEMENT

FRIENDS/COMMUNITY

ILLNESS

FUTURE SECURITY

HEALTH

SHELTER/WARMTH

CLOTHING

STEPS TOWARD SELF-ACTUALIZATION

❯ **Do not compare** Instead of measuring yourself against others, concentrate on your own personal progress.

❯ **Accept** Rather than being self-critical, accept and understand your strengths and weaknesses.

❯ **Let go of defense mechanisms** Denying unpleasant facts or feelings or regressing into childlike behavior are examples of mechanisms that hold you back. Find new and more creative ways to react to situations.

❯ **Make honest choices** Examine your true motives so you make genuine choices and act with integrity.

❯ **Experience life fully** Immerse yourself in the moment to truly enjoy experiences.

❯ **Trust your personal abilities** Adopt a positive outlook so you feel in control and can deal with life's challenges.

❯ **Keep growing** Self-actualization is a continuous process, so seek new challenges.

"What a man **can be**, he **must be**. This **need** we call self-actualization."

Abraham Maslow, American psychologist

✓ NEED TO KNOW

❯ **Peak experience** Moment of transcendence or true fulfillment that reflects self-actualization.

❯ **Purpose** A sense of meaning that self-actualization brings.

❯ **"Deficit" needs** Lower-hierarchy survival needs that are missing.

❯ **"Being"/growth needs** Needs linked to personal development.

The psychology of relationships

Psychologists who specialize in relationships are primarily concerned with how relationships work and why they either flourish or break down. The modern approach to relationship psychology is based on the premise that people choose their partners through a combination of biological, social, and environmental factors, and that a key impetus for individuals to build romantic liaisons and families is their genetic drive to form and maintain relationships.

Theories of attachment

Psychologist John Bowlby first developed attachment theory in 1958, backed by research into both human relationships and those of other species. According to Bowlby, a child's earliest experiences dictate what kind of relationships they form as adults. Multiple studies support this theory, including Harry Harlow's experiments with rhesus monkeys in the 1950s and 1960s. His findings showed that monkeys who were denied the affection of their own mother grew up to be more timid, less sure of how to behave with other monkeys, and less able to mate. In the 1970s, Mary Ainsworth built on previous experiments, observing interactions between human mothers and infants through a one-way mirror. She concluded that children with mothers who were highly responsive to their needs developed a sense of security in their attachment that children with less sensitive mothers lacked. This security, or lack of it, forms the foundation of adult relationships (pp.156–157).

> "The quality of your life is ... the quality of your relationships."
>
> Anthony Robbins, American author and life coach

COUPLES THERAPY

When it emerged as a psychological tool in the 1990s, couples therapy was aimed at getting two individuals to agree to bury their differences. However, based on extensive research by John Gottman at the University of Seattle, therapists now recognize that conflict in a relationship is inevitable. Couples therefore should try to:

> **Accept conflict** and repair rifts.

> **Improve communication** rather than burying their feelings and growing emotionally distant.

> **Be emotionally open** and overcome fears of expressing a need for closeness.

COUPLES THAT PLAY TOGETHER STAY TOGETHER by enjoying small moments of daily life together, which helps to build a strong relationship.

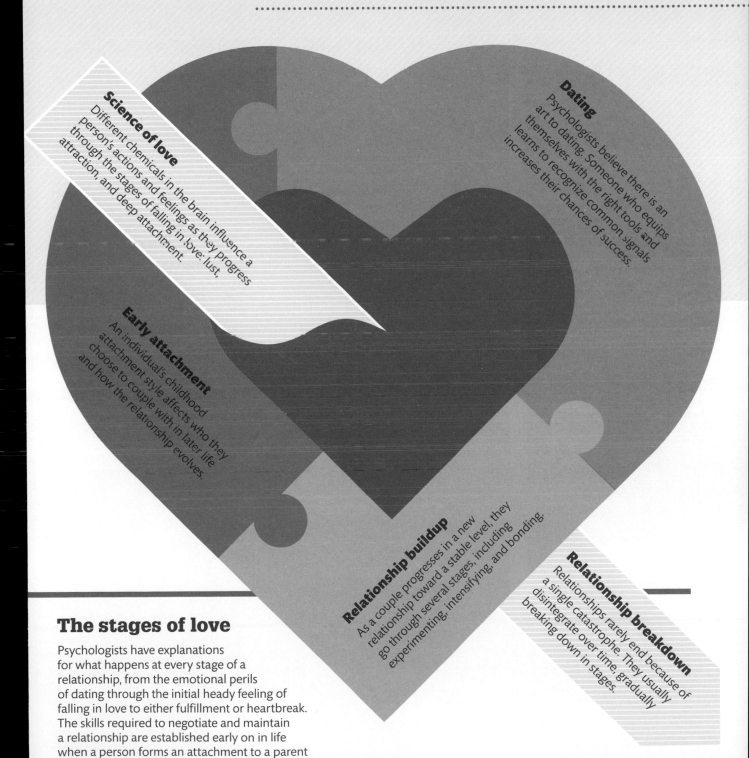

Science of love
Different chemicals in the brain influence a person's actions and feelings as they progress through the stages of falling in love: lust, attraction, and deep attachment.

Dating
Psychologists believe there is an art to dating. Someone who equips themselves with the right tools and learns to recognize common signals increases their chances of success.

Early attachment
An individual's childhood attachment style affects who they choose to couple with in later life and how the relationship evolves.

Relationship buildup
As a couple progresses in a new relationship toward a stable level, they go through several stages, including experimenting, intensifying, and bonding.

Relationship breakdown
Relationships rarely end because of a single catastrophe. They usually disintegrate over time, gradually breaking down in stages.

The stages of love

Psychologists have explanations for what happens at every stage of a relationship, from the emotional perils of dating through the initial heady feeling of falling in love to either fulfillment or heartbreak. The skills required to negotiate and maintain a relationship are established early on in life when a person forms an attachment to a parent or caregiver, although they can still be refined and built on in adulthood.

Psychology and attachment

One of the dominant theories in relationship psychology is that a person's childhood experience of attachment, and in particular, that formed with a caregiver, influences how they behave with a partner as an adult.

Bonding as a baby

The principle that the way in which a person bonds as a baby can dictate how they bond as an adult grew out of the pioneering work of John Bowlby. Like psychoanalyst Sigmund Freud, he was interested in how early childhood experience affects later life. Bowlby, whose theories were published in the 1950s and 1960s, believed that everyone is born with an instinctive need to form attachments in order to survive; that everyone needs to have one close, continuous bond for the first two years of their life; and that failure in this process may cause depression, heightened aggression, suppressed intelligence, and difficulty showing affection as a child and later in life.

Over the ensuing decades, psychologists expanded and refined Bowlby's hypothesis, creating experiments

ATTACHMENT STYLES

Childhood attachment		Adulthood attachment
SECURE When a child feels sure that their needs are met, they develop a secure attachment. The caregiver is sensitive to the child's needs, responding quickly and regularly. The child is happy enough to explore their environment and feels secure.	LEADS TO	**SECURE** As an adult, they feel confident in relationships and are willing to ask for help from a partner, as well as offer support and comfort to their partner when necessary. They retain independence but are loving toward their partner.
AMBIVALENT The child does not believe the caregiver can be relied on to meet their needs. The caregiver's behavior is inconsistent—they are sometimes sensitive but other times neglectful. The child becomes anxious, insecure, and angry.	LEADS TO	**ANXIOUS-PREOCCUPIED** Constant fear of rejection drives this adult to be clingy, demanding, and bordering on obsessive, not wanting to be separated from their partner at all. Their relationships are driven by emotional hunger rather than real love and trust.
AVOIDANT If the caregiver is distant and somewhat unresponsive to the child's needs, that child also becomes emotionally distant, subconsciously detecting that their needs are unlikely to be met. The child does not develop a secure attachment.	LEADS TO	**DISMISSIVE-AVOIDANT** Emotionally distant, the adult appears self-focused and independent. The independence is an illusion, a result of denying the importance of loved ones. If their partner is upset and threatens to end the relationship, they appear not to care.
DISORGANIZED The unpredictable caregiver scares the child, either by being abusive or because of their own passive, frightened state. The distressed child grows withdrawn, unresponsive, and confused, with no strategy for having their needs met.	LEADS TO	**FEARFUL-AVOIDANT** The adult swings from one extreme to another, is emotionally unpredictable, and may end up in an abusive relationship. They are torn between seeking comfort from their partner and being afraid to get too close for fear of being hurt.

to observe how infants behave with their mothers or other caregivers. This research revealed that the key in developing attachment is not who feeds or changes the infant but who communicates and plays with them. It also showed that individuals develop different ways of attaching to other people. These styles of attachment emerge during early childhood and go on to shape relationship choices and behavior in adulthood. Today psychologists have recognized four attachment styles in childhood and four linked attachments in adulthood.

ROMANTIC ATTACHMENTS

To form a successful romantic relationship, it helps to understand how the different adult attachment styles work in partnerships. People with secure attachment styles generally have the most stable relationships; those with less secure styles need to work harder at cementing a romantic partnership. The pairings below are based on the original three attachment styles that psychologist Mary Ainsworth's 1970s psychological experiments (p.154) revealed. A minority of people can have both anxious and avoidant qualities, in which case they should learn about how both anxious-preoccupied and dismissive-avoidant types behave in different pairings.

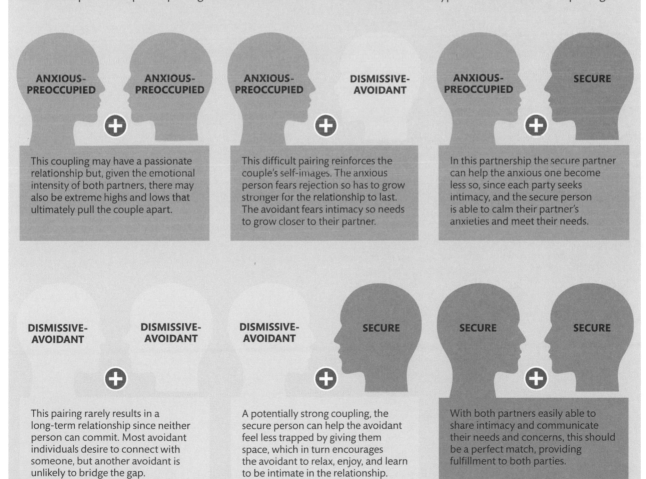

ANXIOUS-PREOCCUPIED + **ANXIOUS-PREOCCUPIED**

This coupling may have a passionate relationship but, given the emotional intensity of both partners, there may also be extreme highs and lows that ultimately pull the couple apart.

ANXIOUS-PREOCCUPIED + **DISMISSIVE-AVOIDANT**

This difficult pairing reinforces the couple's self-images. The anxious person fears rejection so has to grow stronger for the relationship to last. The avoidant fears intimacy so needs to grow closer to their partner.

ANXIOUS-PREOCCUPIED + **SECURE**

In this partnership the secure partner can help the anxious one become less so, since each party seeks intimacy, and the secure person is able to calm their partner's anxieties and meet their needs.

DISMISSIVE-AVOIDANT + **DISMISSIVE-AVOIDANT**

This pairing rarely results in a long-term relationship since neither person can commit. Most avoidant individuals desire to connect with someone, but another avoidant is unlikely to bridge the gap.

DISMISSIVE-AVOIDANT + **SECURE**

A potentially strong coupling, the secure person can help the avoidant feel less trapped by giving them space, which in turn encourages the avoidant to relax, enjoy, and learn to be intimate in the relationship.

SECURE + **SECURE**

With both partners easily able to share intimacy and communicate their needs and concerns, this should be a perfect match, providing fulfillment to both parties.

The science of love

Psychologists have carried out numerous scientific studies as they attempt to understand the process of falling in love and analyze how a person's mind works when they are in love.

The rewards of romance

A scientific approach to the reason that people fall in love or commit to a relationship may seem contrary to the idea of romance, but psychologists have proposed some interesting explanations.

In the 1960s Robert Zajonc put forward a theory called the Mere Exposure Effect, which was based on observations of people in the same apartment building.

The theory proposed that one of the main reasons one person becomes attracted to another is due to regular close physical proximity. In another study in the 1980s, Caryl Rusbult observed the relationships of college students and came up with a mathematical explanation as to why people chose to commit or not, and why they may stay in an unhappy relationship. Her Investment Model put forward an equation that

Sternberg's Triangular Theory of Love

According to psychologist Robert Sternberg, the ideal form of love combines intimacy, passion, and commitment to create consummate love. Sternberg imagined the three components as the interactive sides of a triangle. For example, greater commitment may lead to greater intimacy, while greater intimacy may lead to greater passion. Relationships can have a combination of any of the three components, resulting in one of eight different types of love.

Commitment
A short-term decision to love a particular person and a long-term promise to maintain that love are key to fulfilling a partner, but commitment by itself is an empty form of love.

Companionate Love

Fatuous Love

Consummate Love
The ideal love has all three components: intimacy, commitment, and passion.

Passion
The physical attraction that may have ignited the relationship is a prime component in keeping love alive, but on its own is just infatuation.

Intimacy
Feeling close and connected is part of a loving relationship, but if this is the only component it results in liking rather than true intimacy.

Romantic Love

Nonlove
No components are present.

suggested that Commitment = Investment + (Rewards – Costs) – Attractive Alternatives.

More recently, anthropologist Helen Fisher and her colleagues identified three stages of falling in love—lust, attraction, and attachment—which are in part governed by humans' innate need to reproduce for species survival, though people are usually unaware of this deep-seated urge. Each stage of love is driven by chemicals that affect both emotions and behavior.

The chemistry of love

Many studies point to the role played by the brain's chemical reactions when a person falls in love. Scientists believe that neurotransmitters flood the brain with chemicals, such as adrenaline, dopamine, and serotonin, that make the person feel on a high, and cause them to constantly think about their partner. This physical reaction is reflected in their behavior. According to research, desire in the first few minutes of meeting is displayed through body language and the tone and speed of voice rather than what is said.

In a study in Italy, psychologists took blood samples from newly infatuated couples and revealed that their serotonin levels were similar to those found in people with OCD (pp.56–57). Scent plays a part, too—a Swiss study found that women preferred the smell of men whose immune systems were genetically different from their own. Though not a conscious preference, their choice of men who had genetically different immune systems would, if translated into a real-life pairing, produce the healthiest offspring.

CHEMICAL ATTRACTION

By taking blood samples from research subjects in different stages of a relationship, scientists have measured the changes that take place in hormone levels at each stage of a relationship, from the first rush of desire through deep attraction to commitment.

❯ **Lust** The sex hormones—testosterone in men and estrogen in women—drive this first stage of love.

❯ **Attraction** Adrenaline provides a rush of excitement, quickening the pulse; dopamine gives more energy and less need for sleep and food; and serotonin fuels a happy feeling as well as sexual desire.

❯ **Attachment** Oxytocin, which is released during orgasm, makes a person feel closer to their partner after sex; vasopressin is also released after sex and is thought to promote an individual's sense of devotion to their partner.

THE SENSE OF SMELL and chemical reactions in the brain are two invisible factors in the mating game and can start a rapid reaction—it takes between 90 seconds and 4 minutes for a person to decide whether they are attracted to someone.

"Romantic **love** is ... a drive. It comes **from** the motor of the mind, the **wanting part** of the mind, the **craving part** of the mind."

Helen Fisher, American anthropologist and researcher

How dating works

Most relationships begin with a date, but this process can often be an anxious one. Understanding the psychology behind dating can help people succeed and help them determine a good match.

The quest for love

Advice on dating may seem the domain of pop psychology, but research into the science of relationships has yielded useful insights into how people behave during dates, and how to improve the chances of romance.

Psychologists advise adopting the same approach whether finding a partner through traditional or online dating. Dating is a numbers game, and so the chances of finding a compatible partner are slim. The first date should therefore be short—an initial screening—since most serious relationships

start to bloom around the second- or third-date stage. While there is no fail-safe formula for dating success, psychologists emphasize the importance of keeping an open mind. Physical attraction is usually apparent within the first few minutes of meeting someone, yet according to research, around 20 percent of spouses did not wholly like their partners at first, and only warmed to them on later dates.

For a person who is looking for a serious relationship, there is a simple psychological strategy to employ: a person should gradually reveal their likes and hopes, and

observe how the date responds and behaves in order to evaluate how good a potential match they would make. However, miscommunication and heightened sensitivity can undermine the dating process by causing people to jump to incorrect conclusions—for example, that a delayed response to a text signals a lack of interest, or the fact that someone who is not ready to say "I love you" means that they do not wish to continue the relationship.

Signs that dates like each other

There are some obvious cues to look for on a first date, while others are so unconscious that they may go unnoticed. As well as body language and speech, there are various theories about what draws people to one partner rather than another.

THE BODY LANGUAGE OF ATTRACTION

> **Dilating** pupils
> **Tilting** the head slightly
> **Looking at** eyes-lips-eyes (the "flirty triangle")
> **Smiling** to project positive vibes
> **Mirroring** body language
> **Stroking hair,** fiddling with necklace, blushing

> **Leaning in** toward date
> **Pulling sleeves up** to show wrist
> **Touching** accidentally
> **Pointing feet** at date
> **Changing the volume** or pitch of voice (women)
> **Laughing,** interrupting, and varying volume of speech (men)

Matching hypothesis

According to the matching theory developed by Elaine Hatfield and her colleagues, people are likely to form relationships with those who resemble them and hold a similar social position and level of intelligence. Such individuals are more attainable than someone "out of a person's league."

Filter modeling

According to Alan Kerckhoff and Keith Davis, relationships go through three filtering stages. The first involves assessing similarities in background, education, and location; the second, looking for similar beliefs and attitudes; and the third, complementing each other's needs. People who are too different are filtered out.

Reward/need theory

Donn Byrne and Gerald Clore's theory shows that people are most attracted to potential partners who meet their needs for friendship, sex, love, and feeling good.

Social exchange

Caryl Rusbult's theory (p.158) indicates that people stay in a relationship if the benefits, such as gifts, outweigh costs, including time and money invested in it.

First-date self-disclosure

People expect that when they reveal information about themselves on a first date it will be reciprocated. If their date does not follow suit, the person may be revealing too much, or their date may not be interested. If a date does like the person who discloses first, however, they will probably like them even more for sharing.

DATING COACHING

For those who are having trouble attracting a long-term partner or feel they are attracting the wrong kind of person, a psychologically qualified dating coach may be able to help. Dating coaches train their clients to communicate more confidently and to hone important dating skills such as flirting, body language, personal presentation, and how to pace the rate of self-disclosure. A dating coach can also explore any psychological barriers that a client may be putting up; can help the client to develop a realistic profile of the kind of person they want to meet; and can advise them on strategies for meeting more compatible prospects.

Psychology and the stages of relationships

Psychologists have developed frameworks that explain how relationships grow and break down, and help people recognize the phases and navigate between them.

The stages of a relationship

After decades of study, psychologists have determined what most people experience in life but are often too blinded by love to see. Relationships are built in stages, and each stage brings its own developments, along with challenges that both parties have to meet before moving on to the next level.

One of the most cited relationship models is that of psychologist Mark Knapp, who visualized a flight of stairs going up to explain how a partnership builds, a plateau where the two maintain the bond, and a flight of stairs down

Knapp's relationship model

Envisaged as a metaphor for relationships building and breaking down, Knapp's staircase has five steps up as a relationship builds step by step—and five steps back down in the event of a couple breaking up. His model provides an insight into where things can go wrong and the different challenges that couples may face.

Tools for maintaining

> **Forgive** minor transgressions, downplay faults, and emphasize each other's virtues to keep closeness in the relationship.

> **Spend time** together as a couple.

Bonding

The couple's lives are fully intertwined. They make their love public and may discuss marriage or some other permanent bond.

Integrating

The relationship becomes much closer, and the couple integrates aspects of their lives. Both are willing to be vulnerable, including making declarations of love.

Intensifying

Both parties start to reveal more personal information and let their guard down. Feelings intensify as they nurture the relationship, and both sides start to expect commitment.

Experimenting

The two parties discover more about each other, probing for information and common interests so that they can make a decision as to whether to continue in the relationship.

Initiating

Usually a very short stage, this is when first impressions count. Dates express an interest and size each other up, taking into account appearance, dress, body language, and voice.

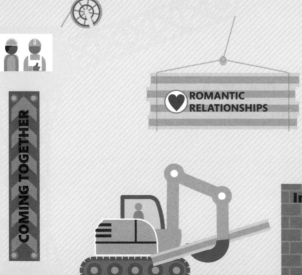

ROMANTIC RELATIONSHIPS

COMING TOGETHER

if a relationship deteriorates. By segmenting these processes into clear steps, Knapp's model offers couples the tools to work out where they are in a relationship at any given time, predict where it may be going, and make necessary changes. The speed at which partners negotiate these steps may vary. They may also skip whole steps if the relationship is either progressing or unraveling rapidly.

Progress and decline

After analyzing her own marriage, psychologist Anne Levinson developed a simple five-stage model for how relationships progress and decline. She applied this not only to romantic partnerships but also to consumer relationships, and likened the rapport between sexual partners as similar to that between a brand and shoppers, who are seduced, are won over, commit for a time, and then either stay committed or move on for a range of reasons. The first stage of her model is Attraction, followed by Build-up and Commitment, before Deterioration if the partnership is not working, and finally Ending.

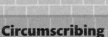

the relationship
> **Merge** friendship networks.
> **Do favors** for one another; be willing to put own needs on hold to help partner.
> **Maintain** mutual affection levels.

Differing
As the pressures of life cause stress, both people see themselves less as a couple and more as individuals. Their bond seems to be broken.

Circumscribing
Brewing resentment creates barriers and reduces levels of communication. The couple may even stop meaningful communication for fear of an argument.

Stagnating
The relationship declines rapidly and is unlikely to improve. Communication is even more limited. But some couples may stay together for their children.

Avoiding
Communication is nonexistent and the pair lead separate lives, even if under the same roof. They may be tempted to get back together to avoid the painful reality of a permanent split.

Terminating
The relationship is over. Married couples finalize divorce. Both parties move to separate homes, if they have not already done so, and lead their own separate lives.

48% of **men fall in love at first sight** compared to **28% of women**

COMING APART

Talking to each other

The way in which a couple communicates can have a dramatic effect on their relationship, and awareness of conversational patterns can make the difference between a relationship growing and falling apart. Psychologists maintain that a person can improve their partner choices from the outset as well as the quality of their relationships by understanding the mechanisms of communication and looking for warning signs.

From the opening moments of meeting a potential partner, how much an individual reveals about themselves—what psychologists call self-disclosure—has a significant impact on what happens next. Early on, most couples share as much information as possible with each other, starting with superficial topics and moving on to more personal details such as hopes for the future. However, if one partner reveals much more information than the other, they may feel that the other is less invested in the relationship. Revealing intimate information too early on can also be intimidating when neither person feels ready to commit.

Good communication is crucial to keep a relationship from declining, but sometimes this is still not enough. Social psychologist Steve Duck identifies four ways in which a relationship breaks down: "preexisting doom" due to a basic mismatch; "mechanical failure" because of poor communication; "process loss" from not reaching its full potential, again because of a lack of communication; and "sudden death" due to a violation of trust. Relationship expert John Gottman also explains breakups as a direct consequence of poor communication (below and right).

The finish line

Negative communication can kill a couple's love in four stages, according to research by John Gottman and fellow psychologists Coan, Carrere, and Swanson. Their explanation for how this happens is called The Four Horsemen of the Apocalypse after the biblical harbingers of doom because each stage is an omen of the death of a relationship.

65%
of **divorces** stem from communication problems

COMMUNICATION IN RELATIONSHIPS

American professor of psychology John Gottman is renowned for his research into family systems and marriage. His ideas have been hugely influential in relationship psychology and in couples therapy, and form the basis of The Gottman Method Couple's Therapy. After observing thousands of couples, Gottman maintains that a gentle communication style—which involves active, not reactive, listening—enables couples to recover and repair the damage after a serious argument.

Reactive listening

Taking things personally and feeling defensive about what a partner is saying is almost guaranteed to inflame the conversation. Instead of instantly denying what is being said, with replies such as "That's not true" and "No, I don't," the key, according to Gottman, is for a person to be realistic and reflect on whether their own behavior may have been annoying. Turning the tables on a partner to deflect self-indignation, with comments along the lines of "At least I'm not ..." or "You're overreacting," is to be avoided.

Active listening

The person should focus on expressing how they feel about a situation rather than making sweeping statements. When responding, Gottman recommends starting sentences with "I" instead of "You"—for example, "I feel you are not listening to me," rather than "You're not listening"—to diffuse a potentially volatile conversation. Controlling tone of voice and volume reinforces this conciliatory and constructive approach to resolving differences.

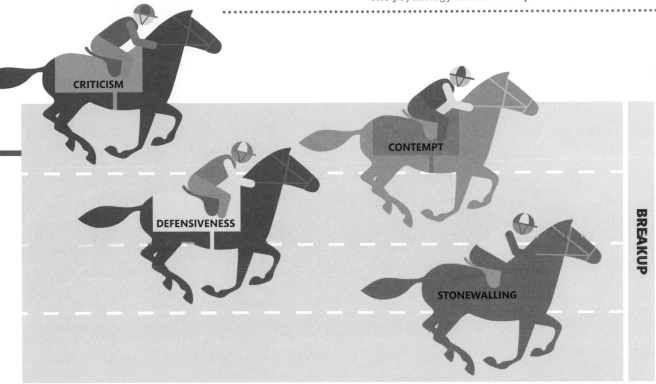

CRITICISM

Stage 1 Verbally attacking a partner's character or personality rather than tackling the annoying behavior together. This can make the other person feel negatively about themselves.

Constructive alternative

Actively listen to your partner, and express your feelings about them rather than attacking them directly. Focus on explaining why their behavior annoys you rather than their personal qualities.

DEFENSIVENESS

Stage 2 Reacting negatively to criticism by making excuses and blaming the other person, rather than taking responsibility for a part in the conflict. This increases feelings of dissatisfaction.

Constructive alternative

Be prepared to apologize for your own behavior and to take responsibility for it if appropriate. Listen to your partner and try to understand their dissatisfaction; try not to take it personally.

CONTEMPT

Stage 3 Being rude and showing open disrespect through facial expressions such as rolling the eyes. Both parties have to work hard to regain respect from one another.

Constructive alternative

Think about causes of your own behavior and why it is hard to express upset feelings in a constructive way. Focus on your partner's positive attributes instead of keeping score of their flaws.

STONEWALLING

Stage 4 Withdrawing by cutting off physical and emotional contact with a partner, who feels abandoned and rejected. Stonewalling can happen when the first three stages are overwhelming.

Constructive alternative

Let your partner know when you need time to yourself to think, and resume conversation when you are ready. This way, your partner will understand that your aim is not to reject them.

psychology in education

The primary aim of educational psychology is to identify the most effective ways of learning. Educational psychologists research and observe how the brain processes information and solves problems, how memory works, and how external factors such as peers and even classroom layouts can affect learners. Their research can then be applied to help children and adults as they learn and to help those with behavioral and learning issues, too.

Strategies to improve learning

Educational psychologists can suggest a range of strategies to help learners improve how they acquire and retain information. Encouraging students to work alone to achieve their own goals can be beneficial, but it is also important to share knowledge and work together to improve group solidarity and foster confidence.

"The **principal goal** of education in the **schools** should be creating **men and women** ... capable of doing **new things.**"

Jean Piaget, Swiss clinical psychologist

HOW WE LEARN

Individuals retain information best when they are motivated to learn and are committed to improving their skills. Working alone fosters independence and a sense of individual achievement.

WHERE EDUCATIONAL PSYCHOLOGISTS WORK

❯ **Schools** The most common employment settings for educational psychologists are schools and educational institutions. Here they advise on how to improve teaching effectiveness by offering analysis and programs. They instruct on better ways to manage classrooms, train teachers, and identify problem learners and instigate special education when needed.

❯ **Businesses** In the corporate setting, educational psychologists may work in-house or as consultants for companies wanting to improve the effectiveness of their staff. They develop and administer psychometric testing to screen new recruits for ability and honesty, and run specialist training for staff to improve employee motivation and performance.

❯ **Government** Here psychologists provide vital support as they advise on educational policy. They develop curriculums and learning strategies for teachers in the state school system, advise on ways to help children with learning difficulties, and train the staff who provide such support. Their role also involves helping to train specialist personnel, especially for military roles.

CLASSROOM STRUCTURE

Activities in small groups encourage questions and build confidence. If a learning environment is emotionally and physically safe, individuals are more likely to test ideas.

TEACHING METHODS

Teachers can use a range of tools to reinforce learning, such as using more than one way to explain each concept, breaking down information into chunks, and encouraging active participation.

Educational theories

The complex methods by which people process, memorize, and retrieve information—and then develop independent thought—can be interpreted through a range of theories.

In the classroom

As science and research techniques have advanced, so have ideas about how the mind receives new information and retains it. Applying these ideas in the classroom can be beneficial. An early, but still dominant, idea is cognitive learning theory (CLT), based on the work of influential psychologist Jean Piaget. CLT proposes that learning is the result

Piaget's theory of cognitive development

Jean Piaget believed that as people develop from babies to adults, they build a vast series of knowledge units that shape the way they understand the world. Every time they encounter something new, they draw on their previous knowledge to assimilate it. When they cannot, they are forced to learn and accommodate new information.

SENSORIMOTOR STAGE (0–2 YEARS)
The first knowledge to develop is understanding that an object can exist even when it cannot be seen, known as object permanence—for example, knowing that a toy is simply hidden under a blanket.

PREOPERATIONAL STAGE (2–7 YEARS)
Children begin to develop language abilities but do not yet grasp logic. However, they are starting to use symbols and understand that an object can represent something else—pretending a doll is a person, for example.

Kolb's experiential learning cycle

EXPERIENCE

TESTING IDEAS IN PRACTICE

OBSERVATIONS/REPETITIONS

David Kolb built on Piaget's work, publishing his four-part theory in 1984. His cycle of learning has four connected stages that form a continuing process. Initially, concrete experiences lead to reflective observations about what has been experienced. These observations are then translated into abstract concepts—in other words, ideas are developed. The fourth stage is putting these ideas into practice, which Kolb called "active experimentation."

DEVELOPMENT OF IDEAS

Race's ripple theory

Devised by Professor Phil Race, the ripple model offers an alternative to Kolb's cycle. It involves four integrated processes that intersect like ripples on a pond, with a basic need or desire at its core.

> **1. Motivation** Learning starts with an aspiration.

> **2. Practice** Trial and error drives action and discovery.

> **3. Making sense** Discoveries are digested.

> **4. Seeing results** Feedback affects motivation.

4-FEEDBACK
3-DIGESTING
2-DOING
1-NEEDING/WANTING

of mental processes, which are influenced by internal and external factors. An example of an internal factor would be a person's belief about their own ability—students who believe they can improve their capability will be more likely to progress in their learning, whereas those who believe they are stuck with a certain level of intellect are unlikely to learn as effectively. External factors might be a teacher who is supportive or a safe learning environment.

Under these influences, an individual learns through a number of mechanisms. One is observing and copying other people. Another is being encouraged by teachers or parents to put what they have learned into action, which reinforces it. Practice or repetition is also a critical part of learning, as is reproduction—the replication of newly learned behavior and adjustment, if necessary, based on the feedback given by others.

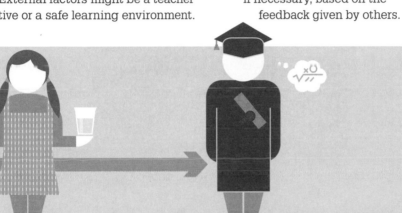

CONCRETE OPERATIONAL STAGE (7–11 YEARS)
Now children start to think logically. For example, they understand that a portion remains the same even though it may change in appearance, such as a quantity of water poured from one glass into two glasses.

FORMAL OPERATIONAL STAGE (ADOLESCENCE–ADULTHOOD)
As young teenagers progress to adulthood, they acquire the ability to think abstractly and to logically test hypotheses. They can imagine potential outcomes to situations, which allows them to problem solve and plan.

ADULTS CONTINUE TO LEARN
Using everything they have acquired during the development stages, adults go on to expand their learning. Moving beyond Piaget's theory and continuing to learn new skills throughout adulthood can strengthen cognition and memory.

SOCIAL LEARNING THEORY

Developed by Albert Bandura, social learning theory centers on how behavior is learned, and combines the cognitive approach (where internal mental processes influence learning) and the behavioral approach (where learning is a result of environmental stimuli). It argues that children learn by copying other people who serve as models, and who can influence a child's behavior positively or negatively. The theory posits four requirements for learning positive behavior:

 Attention
The individual must take notice of the behaviors they are exposed to. If the behavior is novel or different in some way it is more likely to focus an individual's attention.

 Retention
A memory of the behavior or attitude that has been observed needs to form so that it can be referred to and acted on later in a situation similar to that in which it was learned.

 Reproduction
Mental and physical practice of what has been observed is key to improving and changing behavior. With practice, an individual can reproduce learned behavior when required.

 Motivation
The individual must have a reason to reproduce what they observe. If they know that they will be punished or rewarded for acting in a certain way, they are more likely to alter their conduct.

How learning works

The field of neuroscience has increasingly overlapped with psychology as discoveries about the chemistry of the brain have helped psychologists understand how we process information. New technologies such as fMRI (functional magnetic resonance imaging) have enabled scientists to map brain activity, revealing how it changes when we learn.

Research pioneered by neuroscientist Nathan Spreng has revealed that practicing a task can change brain structure. The area of the brain required for paying close attention is used when learning something new (the conscious area), but with repeated training of a particular task, activity switches to the unconscious area of the brain. Neurons also begin to fire more frequently when a skill is repeatedly practiced correctly, thus making the messages passing between them stronger.

Studies have also shown that lifestyle changes, such as diet and stress control, affect the performance of the brain, and the way in which people learn can significantly enhance the brain's ability to absorb and retain new information, too (right).

Exercise

Physical activity stimulates the production of neurotransmitter chemicals (pp.28–29), such as dopamine, which the brain uses to make, interpret, and transfer signals within it and the body.

"… imagining particular behaviors can change brain structure."

John B. Arden, American author and director of mental health programs

GAGNE'S HIERARCHY OF LEARNING

American educational psychologist Robert Gagne devised a classification system for different types of learning, increasing in complexity from 1 to 8. If each step is completed in order, learners build on their skills and their engagement and retention increase.

1 SIGNAL LEARNING
Individuals can be conditioned to respond in a desired way to a stimulus that would not normally produce that response. For example, on seeing a hot object they automatically withdraw their hand (see classical conditioning, pp.16–17).

2 STIMULUS RESPONSE LEARNING
A system of rewards and punishments is used to reinforce a desired response. For example, a child learns to say thank you when prompted by their mother, and is praised in reward (see operant conditioning, pp.16–17).

3 CHAINING
People learn to string together several previously learned nonverbal stimulus response actions—for example, picking up a ruler, lining it up against two points on a piece of paper, and drawing a line between them.

4 VERBAL ASSOCIATION
The next step in Gagne's system is being able to put together separate, previously learned verbal skills—for example, a child describing "my fluffy teddy bear" instead of just "bear." This is key for developing language skills.

5 DISCRIMINATION LEARNING
Individuals learn to differentiate, or discriminate, among chains of information, both physical and conceptual. An example of this is a Spanish speaker learning Italian, which has many similar words.

6 CONCEPT LEARNING
In this stage, people learn relationships between different concepts and learn to differentiate between them. Individuals grasp the skills of learning by example and by being able to generalize and categorize.

7 RULE LEARNING
The main type of learning required for basic day-to-day functioning, rule learning shapes behavior so that people can speak, write, and carry out routine activities, all of which are governed by basic rules.

8 PROBLEM-SOLVING
The most complex learning task, this requires individuals to select and organize previously learned sets of rules, chain them into a new set of rules, test them, and decide on the best solution to a new challenge.

Plenty of sleep

Research has shown a direct link between hours slept and grades achieved at school. For teenagers the optimum number is 9 hours 15 minutes, according to sleep expert Dr. James Maas.

Repetition and practice

Neuroscience has shown that the more a person practices something—with feedback to correct their practice—the stronger and faster their nerve impulses become due to increased production of a special neuron coating called myelin.

Slow introduction of material

New material should be learned in small chunks to maximize the ability to process and retain it— 15 minutes of learning content is advised, followed by a short period of resting time before introducing the next chunk.

Visualization

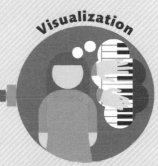

The more senses that are used for remembering information, the better the brain can absorb it. For example, imagining your hands on a piano while reading the notes when learning a new composition can enhance memorization.

Changing the brain

Psychologists with a special interest in education have researched how the brain can be reprogrammed to improve the outcomes of learning. A few simple strategies can make a big difference, but it is only in the past few decades that hypotheses have been backed by experiments.

The psychology of teaching

An important niche for educational psychologists is teacher training, and a large body of research has resulted from developing and testing ideas to help teachers become more effective in the classroom.

What teachers can do

Teachers can help their students fundamentally improve how they learn by refocusing them on the idea of competence instead of a belief in innate intelligence. By increasing a student's belief in their ability to do well, known as self-efficacy, educational psychologists believe that a student's cognitive functioning and motivation improve. Students with high self-efficacy are more likely to take on challenges and make an effort to perform well at these if they believe they can succeed. With low self-efficacy, students see any failure as a setback and will therefore not set themselves high aspirations going forward. This in turn leads to poor academic performance, which continues the student's cycle of self-doubt. If teachers can help students to grasp that success or failure in a task is not related to ability but to the amount of practice and effort applied, then it keeps students motivated rather than feeling demoralized.

Learning goals

There are two types of learning goals that teachers can set: performance goals and mastery goals. Performance goals rely on the student's own competence in order to achieve a specific level—for example, getting an A in French. Mastery goals emphasize the student's perseverance and desire to learn—for example, becoming fluent in French. Mastery goals are better than performance goals in that learners focus on honing and improving their skills, whereas performance goals emphasize competition as a motivator for performing well and rely on an individual's level of intelligence.

THE LEARNING PYRAMID

Research from the US National Training Laboratories Institute has shown that some teaching methods are more effective than others. A learning activity that requires students to actively participate results in better retention levels, whereas activities requiring less involvement result in lower retention levels.

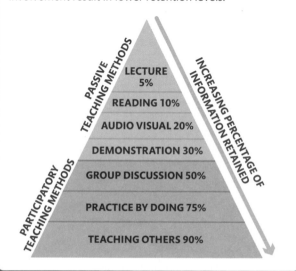

PASSIVE TEACHING METHODS

PARTICIPATORY TEACHING METHODS

INCREASING PERCENTAGE OF INFORMATION RETAINED

LECTURE 5%

READING 10%

AUDIO VISUAL 20%

DEMONSTRATION 30%

GROUP DISCUSSION 50%

PRACTICE BY DOING 75%

TEACHING OTHERS 90%

Building blocks for successful teaching

There are a number of practical tools that teachers can use to encourage student confidence and a love of learning. Teachers should ensure that these methods are working together to create a progressive learning environment.

"People's **beliefs about** their **abilities** have ... [an] **effect** on those **abilities**."

Albert Bandura, Canadian social cognitive psychologist

Make positive connections

Offer support for students; nurture personal relationships and encourage positive relations with other students and teachers; and set clear expectations about appropriate classroom conduct.

Teach specific skills

Help students understand how to transfer one learned idea to another context, and give them practice activities such as sample tests, activities, and problems to encode learning into long-term memory.

Foster student creativity

Ask students to design their own research projects, demonstrate tasks, and build models to explain concepts. Allow them to explore and struggle while providing support.

Give students timely feedback

Monitor students in every lesson and redirect them when they need it. Ensure that praise and constructive criticism are related to their degree of practice and effort.

Set students short-term goals

Instead of overwhelming students with a big task, give them incremental goals, allowing them to successfully complete each stage of the task.

Control student stress level

Run an organized classroom with a daily schedule; have enough breaks for students to process each chunk of learning; and maintain a safe environment.

Promote group teaching and discussion

Encourage other students to voice their concerns, questions, and ideas to give the group a sense of solidarity and allow individuals to feel confident in expressing themselves.

Encourage motivation

Set high but realistic expectations for your students; reinforce the value of practice and effort over innate intelligence; encourage self-evaluation; and adopt a caring attitude.

Assessing problems

In order to help people learn more effectively, educational psychologists must first identify any problems a person is facing, how these have developed, and the ways in which they are affecting the learning process.

How it works

Through their research, educational psychologists understand that the learning process is affected by a variety of factors, including emotional and social issues and specific physiological disorders. It can be clear from an early age if a child has learning problems, and parents may seek the help of an educational psychologist at this stage. However, a learning problem may not emerge until the child is in preschool, in which case teachers play a key role in noticing any difficulties in how the child plays and undertakes basic tasks. In some cases, problems may not be identified until adulthood, often because they were missed when the individual was at school.

Uncovering difficulties

Identifying a learning problem early on often originates with the teacher who suspects issues after daily observation of the student. An educational psychologist can then make a full assessment and develop a plan for helping the student.

HOW PSYCHOLOGISTS ASSESS PROBLEMS

Talk to teachers
Those with concrete, firsthand experience of a student's difficulties are usually current or previous teachers. Talking to teachers is normally a first step.

Talk to parents
Talking with a child's parents can shed light on how the child performs certain tasks at home and how the child relates to family members.

Observe child in classroom
This can flag key indicators such as how the child controls implements such as pens, how they cope with buttons, and how well they follow directions.

Talk to child
The child does not always need to be involved in the assessment, but talking to them might reveal how they comprehend and pronounce words, for example.

Learning problems

It is difficult to pinpoint the exact cause of a learning disability, whether it is environmental, biological, or a combination of both, but it is possible to identify it by its symptoms. The four examples outlined here all begin with the Latin prefix "dys," meaning difficulty.

DYSLEXIA
Difficulties with reading, writing, and spelling. Often good at creative thinking.

DYSGRAPHIA
Trouble with writing and processing letters in words, and difficulty coordinating.

DYSCALCULIA
Impairments in basic arithmetic and making calculations.

DYSPRAXIA
Poor coordination causing clumsy movements, and a lack of the basic ability needed to coordinate daily activities.

Taking action

It is crucial for psychologists to fully understand the nature of an individual's problem, so they employ a variety of strategies to build up an accurate picture of how the person behaves and processes information in an educational setting. Previously, this would have involved a written or oral intelligence test. Today, although formal testing can still play a part when educational psychologists assess a student—especially when a particular disability such as dyslexia is suspected—the current approach is more holistic.

Educational psychologists often work together with psychiatrists, social workers, speech therapists, and teachers, applying ideas of behavioral, cognitive, and social psychology to the classroom. These applications are integral to understanding why a student may behave in a certain way in a classroom setting, how their brain processes and retains information, and how family and peers may affect learning. Psychologists can apply these approaches to any educational environment, from preschools and primary schools to adult learning centers and corporate training schemes.

Analyze schoolwork

A selection of the child's schoolwork may uncover patterns in the way a child writes their answers, and whether their problem is in one particular area, such as mathematics, or several areas.

Questionnaire or specific assessment

There are a number of standardized tests for measuring different aspects of learning problems, from those that are rooted in social or emotional issues to those that are neurological or developmental.

6.6 million
children in the US have a special education need

National Center for Education Statistics, 2015

ASSESSMENT TYPES

By utilizing different types of tests, psychologists can get a well-balanced view of a student's problems and begin to implement ways to address these.

> **Cognitive and developmental** tests measure a pupil's ability to process and interpret information, and compare results against the norms for that age group.

> **Social, emotional, and behavioral** tests identify problems that stem from underlying social and emotional issues. They reveal an individual's stress level, sense of self-esteem, and ability to overcome adversity.

> **Motivational** tests measure a student's incentive to learn—a vital element. Such tests include the Motivation Assessment Scale for Learning (EMAPRE) in higher education, which uses a questionnaire format.

> **Academic** tests are more formal types of testing that can identify whether a student is in the appropriate class for their academic level, and flag learning disabilities. IQ testing can also be undertaken, but results are limited.

Behavioral problems

Psychologists can help teachers deal with disruption in the classroom by assessing a child with behavior issues to try to uncover the triggers and how to resolve them. This often means getting parents on board and examining lifestyle issues such as diet, stress, and social pressure.

Psychology in the workplace

Industrial/organizational psychology explores the behavior of people in the workplace, and applies psychological principles to understanding organizations and improving the lives of employees. It addresses the human elements underlying the structures and processes of professional life, and can advise on hiring, goal setting, team development, motivation, performance appraisal, organizational change, and effective leadership.

Making organizations great

Organizations require the shared vision and coordinated efforts of many people. Psychology plays a big role in helping managers to hire effective employees, set appropriate goals, develop successful teams, ensure good leadership, and cope with the challenges of organizational change.

Appraisal

Offering regular feedback allows employees to develop their strengths and address areas that need improvement and growth.

Hiring

Choosing the right person for the job is a vitally important process as the success of an organization is directly related to the success of its employees.

Interview

Assessing potential employees through interviews is a widely used method because they allow for lengthy, open-ended responses.

Motivation

Promoting enthusiasm helps companies achieve success, as employees must be motivated (both within themselves and by external rewards) to reach their goals.

90,000
the **approximate** number of **hours** an average **person** spends at **work** in a **lifetime**

BRANCHES OF PSYCHOLOGY

Industrial and organizational psychology both cover psychology in the workplace. Industrial psychology is the older of the two branches and is concerned with how to manage people in order to achieve maximum organizational efficiency. It looks at job design, talent selection, employee training, and performance appraisal, trying to tap the potential of people working within an organization.

The second branch, organizational psychology, developed from the human relations movement and concentrates on enhancing the experience and well-being of employees. It is focused on understanding and managing employee attitudes and behavior, reducing job stress, and designing effective supervisory practices.

Team development

Encouraging employees to work together increases team coordination and benefits company performance.

Goal setting

Setting goals that are challenging but realistic strongly influences motivation, which in turn influences effectiveness and achievement.

Leadership

Defining an organization's culture and goals gives leaders the responsibility of motivating their employees to meet those goals.

POSITIVE WORKPLACE PSYCHOLOGY

The humanitarian work psychology movement encourages industrial/organizational (I/O) psychologists to apply their skills, talents, and training with the mission of reducing poverty and promoting well-being in workplaces around the world. I/O psychologists can help people develop marketable skills, design programs to train the unemployed to return to the workforce, promote humanitarian aid for the communities most in need, and devise environmental sustainability initiatives.

Change

Achieving goals often necessitates a change to an organization's structures and policies, and psychologists can help companies do this well.

Selecting the best candidate

Employee performance determines an organization's success, so it is vital to choose the right person for the job. Psychologists have come up with various tools to analyze job requirements and assess applicants.

Job analysis

Before assessing applicants for selection, an analysis of the job to be filled is completed. This analysis consists of a comprehensive job description, including the experience and attributes necessary to fulfill the required tasks and responsibilities. Industrial/organizational psychologists and human resources specialists collect information from various sources, including job analysts, job incumbents, supervisors, and trained observers. They watch people performing the job (or even perform the job themselves), conduct interviews, and use questionnaires.

There are two general categories of job analyses: job-oriented analysis, which focuses on the specific tasks performed on the job, and person-oriented analysis, which focuses on the personal characteristics required. Person-oriented job analysis provides a list of the KSAOs (knowledge, skills, abilities, and other characteristics) necessary to perform a job successfully. A list of KSAOs for a particular job will usually include characteristics that applicants are expected to have already, and others that they will be expected to develop on the job through training.

Job analysis is also helpful for mapping out career development by identifying key competencies on every rung of the career ladder. It can also serve as the basis for performance evaluation, setting standards against which to measure employee performance.

BEST JOBS FOR DIFFERENT PERSONALITY TYPES

The Myers-Briggs Type Indicator (MBTI), based on Carl Jung's theories of personality, is a personality test widely used in the hiring process, but it can also be used by students to choose a suitable career. The MBTI evaluates people according to four sets of opposite traits: extroversion or introversion, sensing or intuition, thinking or feeling, and judgment or perception. This results in 16 possible personality types, each with general tendencies, strengths, and weaknesses that lend themselves to specific jobs.

SPECIFIC OCCUPATION
An ESTJ might make a successful lawyer or pharmacist, whereas an ISFP could be a great fashion designer or physical therapist.

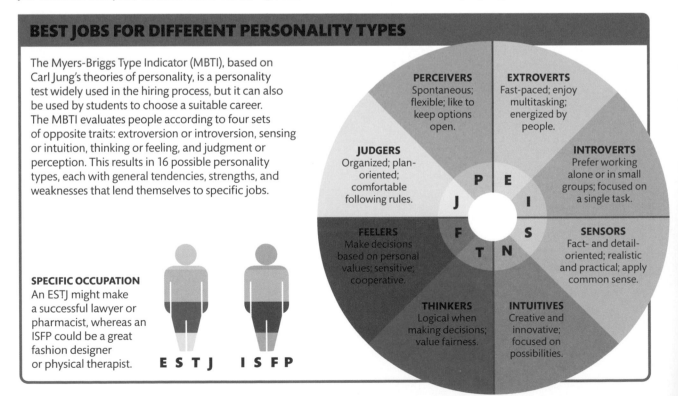

PERCEIVERS
Spontaneous; flexible; like to keep options open.

EXTROVERTS
Fast-paced; enjoy multitasking; energized by people.

JUDGERS
Organized; plan-oriented; comfortable following rules.

INTROVERTS
Prefer working alone or in small groups; focused on a single task.

FEELERS
Make decisions based on personal values; sensitive; cooperative.

SENSORS
Fact- and detail-oriented; realistic and practical; apply common sense.

THINKERS
Logical when making decisions; value fairness.

INTUITIVES
Creative and innovative; focused on possibilities.

P E
J   I
F   S
T N

ESTJ   ISFP

Talent selection

The ability to attract and retain the right people helps to make an organization great. If employees are well matched to their positions, they are more likely to be excited by what they are doing and the environment in which they are working. Talent selection involves a set of procedures to determine how well job applicants fit the job requirements. These are used alongside a standard job application, which asks questions about education, job skills, characteristics, and work history.

Assessment types

Five main techniques are commonly used for evaluating candidates, and often several of these are used together. These procedures reveal an applicant's strengths and weaknesses in different areas, giving an organization valuable information about how a person might perform once employed.

WORK SAMPLE

A work sample is a simulation in which candidates perform part of a job, showing how well they can do relevant tasks under standardized conditions. They receive the necessary materials and tools, and instructions on how to complete the task. Work samples are good predictors of future performance because of the similarities between the assessment situation and the job.

BIOGRAPHICAL INFORMATION

A biographical questionnaire asks for information about relevant prior professional and educational experiences. The questions are more detailed than those in a standard job application, and may include questions about specific experiences at school or work. There may also be questions about verifiable facts and subjective experiences.

INTERVIEW

The candidate's answers and behavior in an interview both provide important information about their suitability for the job, as well as their ability to communicate and relate. Even eye contact or the firmness of a handshake can affect ratings. Most organizations use interviews because they allow candidates to give detailed responses and indicate their interpersonal skills.

ASSESSMENT CENTERS

In an assessment center, exercises and task simulations are used to measure how well a person can perform the job. Exercises are varied and can take several days to complete. Assessment centers evaluate candidates on the basis of oral and written communication, problem-solving, interpersonal relations, and planning. Candidates are scored on various dimensions and then given an overall score, which is useful for hiring decisions.

PSYCHOMETRIC TESTS

Candidates are often asked to take psychometric tests (pp.246–247) under controlled conditions, involving problem-solving, answering questions, or tests of manual dexterity. They can evaluate personality, cognitive ability, knowledge and skills, emotional intelligence, or vocational interests. Questions can be closed-ended, with several possible responses to choose from, or open-ended, in which test takers must generate their own responses.

INTERVIEW RELIABILITY

Psychologists have found that interview accuracy is subject to the biases of the interviewer. Race, gender, and likability can all affect interview assessments and hiring decisions. Interviewers should:

❯ Be trained to conduct interviews.

❯ Ask standardized questions.

❯ Not evaluate the candidate until after the interview has ended.

❯ Rate candidates on individual elements, such as qualifications.

Managing talent

It is crucial for organizations to manage employee performance effectively to reach success. This can be achieved by implementing practices that increase motivation and regular feedback cycles.

Motivation

Often concerned with the desire to achieve a specific goal, motivation is an internal state that drives a person to carry out particular behaviors or tasks. People are motivated by many different things at work, including acquiring money, benefiting a social cause, and winning admiration. Employee motivation has been shown to be directly correlated with job satisfaction and job performance, and indirectly correlated with organizational success. If a person has the appropriate skill set, high levels of motivation generally lead to great performance at work, and this is essential to meeting an organization's major goals.

Psychological theories of work motivation are concerned with the reasons why some people are motivated to perform their jobs better than others, and they allow management to see what they need to provide to maximize motivation and

HAVING A CAREER PATH is more likely to motivate an employee to perform well due to feeling their efforts will be rewarded.

performance. Need hierarchy theories hold that a person's behavior is directed toward fulfilling their needs, and that their motivation is generated internally. Reinforcement theory assumes that behavior arises from the desire to earn rewards and reinforcements, and so is generated externally. Self-efficacy theory examines how people's belief in their own abilities can affect performance, and goal-setting theory explains how people's goals and the ways in which they are set can affect their motivation and performance.

Setting goals

In the 1960s, Dr. Edwin Locke pioneered the goal-setting theory of motivation, which states that working toward a goal increases motivation and performance. He found that specific and challenging goals work most effectively.

Clarity
Goals must be clear, specific, and measurable, with unambiguous deadlines, so employees know what is expected of them and when.

Challenge
Tougher goals are often more motivating because people anticipate greater rewards. However, the goal must not be so challenging that it is unrealistic.

Commitment
Goals must be understood and agreed upon by both employer and employee. This makes an employee more committed to achieving them.

Performance appraisal

Offering employees feedback on their performance helps motivate them to achieve their goals, allows for the acknowledgment of good work, and provides an opportunity to give them constructive criticism and guidance if their performance is low. A performance appraisal is a two-step process that includes first defining the criteria for good performance, and then implementing a performance appraisal procedure. It can benefit the organization as well as the employee, providing information that contributes to administrative decisions (such as hiring and firing) and employee development, which is necessary for improving and maintaining job performance over time. Organizations often have an annual appraisal structure that includes goal setting and periodic feedback sessions between the employee and the supervisor.

OVERCOMING RATING BIASES AND ERRORS

Human judgment is imperfect, and when supervisors make performance ratings, they often unintentionally exhibit biases and errors. Studies have found that ratings can be affected by how well a supervisor knows and likes an employee, by the employee's overall mood, and by cultural and racial factors. Supervisors can also be subject to the halo effect, in which they give an individual the same rating across all appraisal dimensions, as well as the distributional error, in which they give the same ratings across all their supervisees. To overcome these problems, organizations can give supervisors rater training designed to show them the typical errors to avoid. In 360-degree feedback, more than one person rates an employee, to reduce the effects of individual biases.

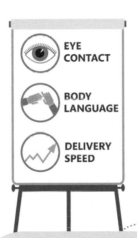

EYE CONTACT

BODY LANGUAGE

DELIVERY SPEED

GOAL ACHIEVED

60% **of employees would like their work to be praised more often**

Feedback
Regular progress reports are crucial for clarifying expectations, adjusting the difficulty of goals, and recognizing employee achievement.

Task complexity
Success depends on whether the goals can be completed in the time frame agreed upon. Employees need time to learn the skills required to meet their goals.

Achievement
The conditions for success are met when a goal is clear, challenging, and appropriately complex; commitment is high; and feedback is regular.

Team development

Work teams can be dynamic and powerful and help organizations thrive. There are many ways of developing the strengths, effectiveness, and potential of people working in groups and of groups as a whole.

How it works

Teamwork offers the advantages of group performance, which is often better than individual performance because the strengths of every team member combine to create something more effective than can be achieved alone. In a successful team—a group of surgeons performing a complex operation, for example—the actions of every member are coordinated and oriented toward achieving a common goal. Each member has a specific role, but all members are interdependent, relying on each other to perform their jobs well. This level of cooperation requires trust, which can be built through good communication, competence, commitment, and collaboration. However, not all teams perform as well as they should, an outcome that is called process loss. This may occur due to social loafing, when people expend less effort as part of a team than they would if working alone (pp.240–241), and impaired brainstorming, when a group generates fewer ideas than are produced by the same number of people on their own.

KEY CONCEPTS FOR TEAMS

> **Role** Every team member has a distinctive and discrete job within the team.

> **Norms** Certain unwritten rules of behavior (such as how late people work) are accepted by team members and strongly affect individual behavior.

> **Group cohesiveness** A sense of unity and trust, among other variables, brings team members together and enables them to continue working together.

> **Team commitment** An individual's acceptance of team goals and willingness to work hard reflect the strength of their involvement with the team.

> **Mental model** A good team has a shared understanding about the task, equipment, and situation.

> **Team conflict** Whether teams are cooperative or competitive as they attempt to deal with clashes determines how effective they are.

Five-stage model

Psychologist Bruce Tuckman presented five stages of team development necessary for growth. Progressing through these stages allows teams to face challenges and find solutions together.

The birds take off and establish their flying positions.

2. Storming

In the early stages of working together, team members compete with each other for status. Differing opinions about what should be done, and how, can cause conflict.

Migrating birds must work as a team to ensure they survive their long journey.

1. Forming

The team members meet each other. They share information about themselves, learn about the project and their roles in it, and establish ground rules for working together.

Improving teams

Several techniques can be used to improve teamwork. Creating autonomous work teams that are responsible for a particular product or process can improve efficiency. Some companies create quality circles, where groups of employees meet to discuss problems and propose solutions, giving them deeper insight into issues facing the group. Colleagues can also take part in team-building activities, which are often led by an expert consultant. Some activities aim to strengthen the team's ability to perform a task, while others focus on interpersonal skills, helping to improve trust, communication, and interaction. Team building aims to result in better team coordination and performance, enhanced skills for individual team members, and more positive attitudes within the team as a whole.

GROUPTHINK

When people work together in groups, their decision-making process can be compromised by groupthink, a phenomenon in which groups make decisions that individual members know are bad. Groupthink is likely to occur in highly cohesive groups with strong leaders and a strong pressure to conform. People put aside their own perceptions and rationalize their doubts in order to fit in with other members. If the group is isolated from outside influences, and no one in the room is willing to challenge the leader, the chance of groupthink increases. To prevent this, leaders should act as impartial moderators in group meetings.

The birds fly in a V formation with those at the top working hardest.

3. Norming

Members begin to feel part of the team. They are less focused on individual goals and more focused on working together effectively, creating processes and procedures.

The birds swap places regularly, taking turns at the front.

4. Performing

The team is functioning at a high level, with members collaborating and creating an open and trusting atmosphere. They rely on each other and are focused on achieving group goals.

On arrival, the birds scatter in search of food.

5−9

is the **ideal number** of members **for a successful team**

5. Adjourning

As a project nears completion, the team conducts an assessment of its work, celebrating successes and seeing what can be improved. Team members say goodbye and go on to new projects.

Leadership

Leaders are highly influential within their organization, and their approach can affect productivity and success. Good leaders use their knowledge and authority to inspire and motivate employees.

Types of leader

Leaders influence the attitudes, beliefs, behaviors, and feelings of other people, and their leadership style forms the basis of team dynamics. There are two main types of leader in the workplace: formal leaders who occupy supervisory roles, and informal leaders—often the more influential type—who emerge from groups through interactions with colleagues.

Informal leaders can possess expert power, based on perceived expertise, and referent power, which is granted because subordinates like and identify with the leader. Formal leaders may have additional types of powers. Legitimate power is inherent in a supervisor's job title, while reward power allows leaders to praise employees and grant pay increases and promotions. When leaders discipline employees through salary reduction or firing, they are using coercive power.

Good leaders use power appropriately, showing concern for the welfare of subordinates, and providing structure by setting clear expectations. They can be identified by psychologists and companies using the trait approach (pp.150–151) (specific traits make them natural leaders), the leader emergence approach (they are singled out from within groups for their leadership potential), or the leader behavior approach (what matters is not who they are, but what they do).

Path-goal theory

Developed by Robert House, this model is designed to help supervisors enhance their employees' job performance by making it easier for them to complete tasks and achieve goals. Leaders can adopt one of four different styles to match the employee, the environment, and the goal.

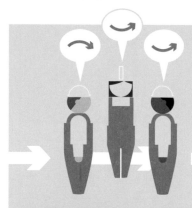

SETTING A CHALLENGE
Achievement-oriented leadership is the best approach for high-performing subordinates facing complex tasks.

Achievement

Achievement-oriented leaders set challenging goals, and both demonstrate and expect high standards. They show faith in their subordinates.

QUALITIES OF GREAT LEADERS

Strong ethics	Empowering others	Fostering a sense of belonging	Openness to new ideas	Nurturing growth
An ethical leader models and expects honesty across the company, and their strong ethics create a safe and trusting environment in which employees can do their best work.	No leader can do everything alone, and having external input is highly valuable; so it is important for leaders to delegate work and to distribute power.	People spend a lot of time at work, so need to feel connected to the organization and to coworkers in order to improve emotional well-being and productivity.	Progress requires innovation and a willingness to solve problems. A leader who is open to new ideas creates an environment in which progress is possible.	People are most motivated when they are encouraged to develop. Leaders who commit to fostering growth end up with more motivated and loyal employees.

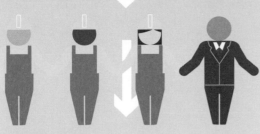

Supportive

Supportive leadership is characterized by considering employees' needs, showing concern, and creating an encouraging work environment.

HAND-HOLDING
Supportive leadership is the best approach when the task is dangerous, tedious, stressful, or boring.

"The key to successful leadership today is influence, not authority."

Ken Blanchard, American management expert

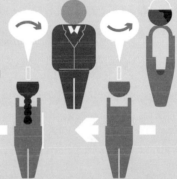

ASKING ADVICE
Participative leadership is the best approach to use when advice from experienced subordinates is needed.

Participative

Participative leaders consult with subordinates, and take their ideas and suggestions into account when making decisions.

Directive

Directive leaders tell subordinates what must be done and offer appropriate guidance, such as schedules and deadlines for them to work toward.

GIVING ORDERS
Directive leadership is the best approach for inexperienced subordinates, especially if they are carrying out unstructured tasks.

TRANSFORMATIONAL LEADERSHIP

Some leaders are unusually effective at motivating others to join a cause, adopt a set of goals, and work persistently toward high achievement. These leaders are charismatic and capable of great influence. They inspire others with their creativity, power, innovative spirit, trustworthiness, and shared vision. They earn trust by prioritizing employees' development and well-being, and in this way, they build a loyal, motivated, and high-performing team. As with political leaders and activists such as Martin Luther King Jr., charisma and vision are important qualities that an individual needs to become a transformational leader.

Organizational culture and change

One of the most important building blocks for a thriving organization, culture consists of shared beliefs and behavior. To be productive it may need to change to accommodate new people, ideas, and technologies.

Culture

Organizational culture is how employees make sense of their workplace and one another, and it contributes to the organization's unique social and psychological environment. Culture is defined by the values and rituals that unite work teams, and by consistent and observable patterns of behavior. It encompasses the organization's norms, systems, language, assumptions, visions, and beliefs, and directly influences how organizations treat people, make decisions, and ensure commitment to projects. Culture is also shaped by leadership, and the incentive and compensation structures that are in place.

Organizational change is not easy to implement because of people's ties to culture, but it becomes necessary when existing structures and processes no longer effectively meet requirements or achieve goals. Attachments to psychological contracts (the unspoken expectations of employees) can also cause resistance to change because it remolds these expectations.

Making changes

Successful change takes place in several stages and needs to be presented with compelling arguments. Helping anxious employees understand why change is needed can reduce their resistance during implementation and speed their acceptance of the new structure and processes.

1. Evaluate

Carrying out an evaluation of the organization's current status is the first step toward change. This will help determine which systems and processes are not performing well, and so establish the main areas for improvement.

2. Assess

An assessment will examine the overall scope of the change, such as how many employees will be affected, as well as the type of change that is needed. Success relies on the participation of the people whose daily work lives will change.

THE PROBLEM
Assessment is vital in planning change. A new bridge must be strong enough to withstand both the river and the traffic.

AFTER CHANGE
Managers should assess continually how well a new structure is working, and make repairs as necessary.

5. Manage change

Leaders should be attuned to how employees react to change, addressing issues as they arise and assessing how successful implementation has been.

4. Implement

Applying change in stages will make the transition smoother for employees who will often resist change. An organization should communicate well and make people feel involved so that the new ways of operating will eventually become accepted.

TOOLS
The right tools are needed to build a new structure. Training programs, financial incentives, and even threats can be used to get employees to cooperate.

3. Design

A structure that meets the requirements of the organization's new strategies and goals will be designed. This design will identify key activities, create new departments, and establish interdepartmental relationships.

PROCESS
It takes time to design a new structure, and change does not happen all at once. The process takes place in several stages, usually with the help of an external change agent.

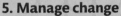

GUIDELINES TO FACILITATE CHANGE

Various steps can be taken to help employees cope with organizational change.

❯ **Strong leadership** Managers should show their support for the change to bolster the enthusiasm of subordinates.

❯ **Employee involvement** Members of staff should be included in the decision process to feel a greater sense of ownership.

❯ **Communication** The specific nature of the change should be communicated in a systematic and structured way, as should its implementation and timeline.

❯ **Celebration** Every success should be celebrated throughout the process to build positivity.

✓ NEED TO KNOW

❯ **Kaizen** A common organizational goal is to establish kaizen, a system that originated in Japan, in which continuous improvement is possible. Employees at all levels are asked on a daily basis to suggest improvements, the aim being to get rid of unnecessary tasks and increase productivity.

HFE psychology

HFE (human factors and engineering) psychology is devoted to helping people cope better in their work environment, making it safer, more productive, and more user-friendly. At its essence is the study of how people interact with machines and technology, and the formulation of ways to improve these interactions by designing better systems, products, and devices. Positioned at the crossroads of psychology and technology, HFE psychology is primarily focused on safety.

HFE in practice

On a practical level, HFE psychologists use their knowledge of how people interact with machines to design more effective work practices and products. This entails studying how a person's mind, reflexes, vision, and other senses function in particular settings, from the factory floor to a hospital operating theater. By studying people's workplace behaviors, HFE psychologists can advise business decision-makers, industrialists, and governments on strategies for avoiding accidents and enhancing productivity.

One key application of this psychology is commercial aviation, an industry that has been using HFE since the 1960s to improve airline safety statistics. Eliminating mortality due to human error in hospitals is another focus, as is reducing risk in critical operations such as the supply of nuclear power. Even the humble bicycle has benefited, becoming faster, easier to use, and more comfortable thanks to HFE psychology.

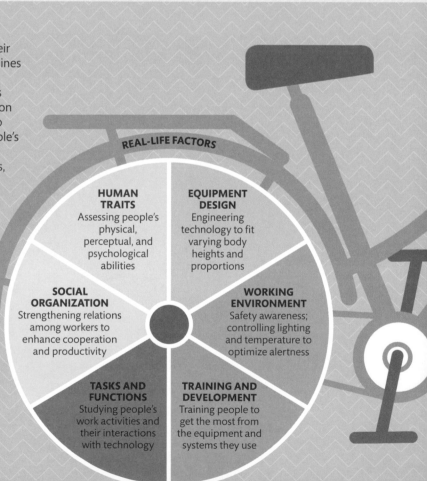

REAL-LIFE FACTORS

HUMAN TRAITS
Assessing people's physical, perceptual, and psychological abilities

EQUIPMENT DESIGN
Engineering technology to fit varying body heights and proportions

SOCIAL ORGANIZATION
Strengthening relations among workers to enhance cooperation and productivity

WORKING ENVIRONMENT
Safety awareness; controlling lighting and temperature to optimize alertness

TASKS AND FUNCTIONS
Studying people's work activities and their interactions with technology

TRAINING AND DEVELOPMENT
Training people to get the most from the equipment and systems they use

70%
or more of **aircraft accidents** are due to **human error**

Two important fields within HFE are anthropometry—the science of measuring the human body and its proportions—and ergonomics—engineering products to fit the human body. Both are essential in creating user-friendly technology. Products such as office chairs designed with a full set of measurements, taking proportions into account, promote worker efficiency and protect from short- and long-term physical harm. Measurements include both obvious ones, such as eye height when sitting, and proportional distances, for instance, between the sitter's buttocks and toes.

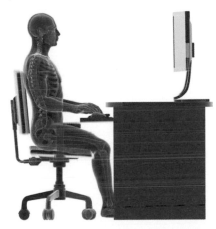

ERGONOMIC SEATING takes into account the sitter's elbow height, seat height, thigh clearance, eye level, and back support.

PSYCHOLOGICAL FACTORS

DECISION-MAKING
Addressing each step in the decision-making process to fix operator glitches

STRESS AND ANXIETY
Using well-designed equipment to avoid workers' frustration

SITUATION AWARENESS
Training staff to assess work situations objectively

WORKLOAD
Balancing employees' workload so that they are alert, are focused, and exercise good judgment

HUMAN ERROR AND SAFETY
Analyzing the causes of mistakes and making changes to improve safety

TEAMWORK
Fostering work relations to ensure team members cooperate

Two-way process

HFE psychologists apply a scientific approach to understanding how humans behave in their interactions with technology. This is a two-way process—people's efficiency can be undermined by poorly designed equipment, and flaws in people's behavior undermine the efficiency of the technology they use. To confront these issues and predict future performance, psychologists study how individuals perceive stimuli and events, assess these to determine a course of action, and make an appropriate response.

Engineering displays

Drawing on their understanding of how people's minds process information, psychologists work with product designers to engineer better machines.

User-friendly technology

A key role of HFE psychologists is designing machines, signs, and systems that can be operated more effectively by their human users. Three interlinked considerations are vital in technology design: how easy the displays are to see and understand; how easy the controls are to use; and how to reduce or eliminate room for error.

Displays are a prime component of technology because they are the interface between machines and their human users. People receive the information they need to operate any particular machine, and also get feedback, via dials, lights, or screens. This applies to a vast array of technological products and systems, including industrial and office equipment, traffic signs, aviation controls, and medical devices.

Display perception

Psychologists provide valuable input during the design process, using their in-depth knowledge of exactly how the mind sees and interprets color, outlines, background and foreground, sound, and touch. The aim is to achieve a "natural design" that makes use of perceptual cues instantly recognizable by the human brain, without the need for further explanation. Using the color red to indicate "stop" is a classic example, since humans associate it with danger because it is the color of fire and blood.

ALERTING DISPLAYS

Within display design, psychologists have developed a hierarchy of color and sound combinations to convey clear priorities to users. These are based on research into how the eyes, ears, and brain respond to specific cues. They are also based on the knowledge that people pay more attention to messages communicated via more than one sense. For warnings, red is used alongside an audible alert, whereas advisory messages may be signaled with only a visual cue.

Organizing controls

Well-engineered displays take into account the way in which people see, hear, and touch stimuli and process them as information. These stimuli—lights, colors, contrast, sound, touch, and so on—should be arranged to ensure that the brain can react quickly and respond accurately. Four principles govern display engineering: perception, mental mode, attention, and memory.

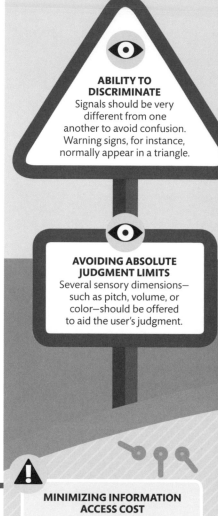

ABILITY TO DISCRIMINATE
Signals should be very different from one another to avoid confusion. Warning signs, for instance, normally appear in a triangle.

AVOIDING ABSOLUTE JUDGMENT LIMITS
Several sensory dimensions—such as pitch, volume, or color—should be offered to aid the user's judgment.

MINIMIZING INFORMATION ACCESS COST
Information that is accessed most often should be at hand so that the user does not have to spend too much time finding it.

MOVING PARTS
Any parts that move should synchronize with the user's expectation—a forward button, for instance, should move in the same direction as the moving part.

Perception
How users first perceive the information in front of them—it must be presented in an unambiguous way.

Mental model
How the design aligns with the mental model of its user—people usually interpret a display based on their experience of similar systems.

Attention
How accessible and easy to process the information is, even in a distracting environment.

Memory
How it reinforces a user's preexisting memory, acting as an aid to recall rather than forcing the user to store information within reach in their working memory.

REDUNDANCY GAIN
Presenting a message in more than one way (such as an extra brake light) enhances its impact.

CONSISTENCY
Information should be presented consistently to ensure a user knows how to interpret it—for example, on traffic lights, red always means "stop."

PROXIMITY COMPATIBILITY
Relevant or linked information, like three brake lights, should be displayed close together.

PICTORIAL REALISM
A display should convey information graphically—for example, if the level of fuel has gone down, the fuel gauge should also go down.

LEGIBLE DISPLAY
Dials and backlit information must be clear, with contrasting colors and a large enough font size for the information to be read easily.

MULTIPLE RESOURCES
Information should be delivered through more than one medium—satellite navigation systems use a voice as well as a screen.

KNOWLEDGE OF THE WORLD
Showing information means the user does not have to rely as much on memory.

PREDICTIVE AIDING
Users should be helped to predict a course of movement, such as where a traffic jam is expected to be, so they can be proactive.

TOP-DOWN PROCESSING
The expectations of the user based on past experience should be met—for example, a user expects to press a button to turn something on.

Human error and prevention

The most important aspect of HFE psychology is minimizing the role of human error to improve safety in the workplace and reduce the risk of accidents and fatalities.

What is it?

Eliminating human error may be an impossible goal, but HFE psychology is dedicated to reducing it as much as possible through strategic changes to the design of workplace machines and displays and the way in which people handle information. Error reduction is especially relevant for situations in which the risk of death is high, such as road-traffic control centers, nuclear power facilities, hospitals, airplane flights, and war zones.

What went wrong?

Most accidents in these industries result from human error. In commercial aviation, for example, failure to load the aircraft correctly, air traffic control mistakes, and errors pilots make in operating the

---

Inadvertent error

Skill-based error (action error)

Trained worker who loses concentration or is distracted making an unintentional error during a routine task carried out perfectly many times before

Mistake

Worker inadequately trained for the situation making a poor decision: doing the wrong thing while believing it to be right

Slip of action

> Executes steps in the wrong order
> Mistimes an action
> Transposes digits—0.56, not 0.65
> Presses the wrong button
> Turns a control the wrong way

Memory lapse

> Forgets to do something
> Skips an important step
> Repeats a step
> Fails to switch off a machine
> Gets distracted; loses their place

Rule-based mistake

> Uses the wrong set of rules
> Ignores a genuine alarm after numerous false ones
> Fails to initiate a rule in time
> Applies a poorly conceived rule

Control measures

> Improve the design of equipment to reduce skill-based errors
> Analyze error incidents and update work conditions accordingly

airplane's controls or assessing weather conditions are the most likely causes of accidents.

In studying past errors and the sequence of human action leading up to them, psychologists have concluded that wrong decision-making is usually because of a lack of situation awareness. Therefore, a primary aim of HFE psychologists is to enhance such awareness. This includes a person's ability to perceive his or her environment accurately, comprehend what is happening, and predict an outcome.

TRAFFIC PSYCHOLOGY

Some HFE psychologists specialize in the study of how drivers behave on the road and respond to traffic management. The areas this covers include behavior and accident research, which looks at age and personality as accident risk factors; traffic enforcement strategies; and driver rehabilitation programs. Studying the role played by stress, tiredness, phone use, alcohol, and other factors helps psychologists understand what causes accidents.

TRAFFIC SAFETY TRAINING and education helps to keep people safe on the roads.

HUMAN ERROR

→ ### Deliberate noncompliant violation

Routine
Commonplace rule breaking, such as using the fire escape stairs instead of the elevator between office levels

Situational
Rule breaking due to time pressure, poor equipment, or work-place design, such as using untrained staff to help meet an urgent deadline

Exceptional
Rule breaking with little choice in a rare situation, such as a bus driver letting off a frail passenger between stops when paths are icy

Knowledge-based mistake
❯ Lacks the knowledge to deal with the task
❯ Develops a solution that does not work
❯ Applies trial and error to a task

Preventing violations
❯ Ensure rules are relevant; explain reasons behind them
❯ Offer adequate supervision and training for emergencies
❯ Encourage open communication

Control measures
❯ Train staff to be prepared for nonroutine, high-risk tasks
❯ Supervise inexperienced staff and provide them with diagrams to explain procedures

Forensic psychology

This rapidly expanding field concerns the application of psychology within a legal context. Its primary goals are the collection, examination, and presentation of evidence for judicial purposes, and the treatment and rehabilitation of criminals once they have entered the prison system. Psychologists are becoming increasingly influential in court proceedings across the world, bringing their expertise to a wide range of criminal, family, and civil cases.

IN THE POLICE FORCE

Real-world contributions from forensic psychologists who help track down criminals are less dramatic than they appear on TV, but they have helped open the door to a kind of investigative psychology that serves many aspects of the criminal investigation process.

Selecting police candidates

Psychologists perform evaluations of prospective police officers to see if they have the qualities needed for the job. They use psychological tests and interviews and can offer recommendations.

Managing information systems

They help to establish effective systems for collecting, organizing, and making sense of the vast quantities of information and paperwork associated with a criminal case.

Conducting interviews

They use their expert knowledge of the human mind and patterns of behavior to refine interview processes. They can detect when people are lying or hiding the truth by analyzing and interpreting words, facial expressions, intonation, and body language.

Linking crimes to suspects

Their analysis of police evidence can be used to identify patterns that link offenses to culprits.

IN THE COURTROOM

Forensic psychologists can be an invaluable help in the courtroom. They can assist legal proceedings in a number of ways in both criminal and civil courts.

Giving expert testimony

Psychologists can present not just the facts of the case in court, but also their specialized opinions and interpretations of those facts. Such opinions can greatly influence the verdict.

Providing guidance for lawyers

They can advise lawyers at every stage of the judicial process, from helping them to prepare a case for court to advising about jury selection and lines of questioning for witnesses and defendants.

Offering opinions to judge and jury

They help judges and juries make educated decisions by offering their expert opinions about human behavior, and by interpreting defendants' behavior throughout the legal proceedings.

> "**Punishment** is not for **revenge**, but to **lessen crime** and **reform** the **criminal.**"
>
> Elizabeth Fry, British prison reformer

IN THE PRISON SYSTEM

Prisons are ideally correctional facilities in which offenders are rehabilitated. However, in reality they are harsh and unnatural environments that present many challenges to the psychologists who work there. Their role is to help rehabilitate offenders and to aid staff in the preparation of case files and reports.

Working with offenders

Psychologists aim to identify which aspects of an offender's life are most in need of treatment to reduce the risk of their relapsing in the future. They provide a mixture of group therapy sessions and one-on-one counseling. Treatment can also involve mitigating the ill effects of being in prison, where childhood traumas are often reactivated, feelings of being dehumanized are rife, and distrust among prisoners frequently leads to violence.

Working with staff

They keep the prison authorities informed of their patients' progress, and communicate directly with parole boards. Their assessment plays a vital role in whether parole is granted.

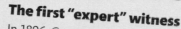

The first "expert" witness

In 1896, German psychologist Albert von Schrenck-Notzing became the first recorded expert witness when he testified at the trial of a man who had murdered three women. Von Schrenck-Notzing argued that witnesses could not distinguish between pretrial press coverage and what they had seen.

CYBERCRIME

In recent decades, psychologists have had to extend their expertise to cover the increasing occurrence of Internet-based crime.

Who is involved?

Terrorists, hackers, and malware developers thrive on the anonymity of the Internet. However, forensic psychologists are specifically trained to search for individuals whose identities are not known. To do so, they use psychological profiles of known perpetrators to narrow down their list of suspects—because certain crimes attract certain kinds of criminals.

> **Phishers,** who fake e-mail messages to access personal information, tend to be motivated by money only.

> **Political/religious hackers** are less interested in money than in disrupting the computers of their enemies.

> **Insiders** are typically individuals who have been fired from or demoted within an organization.

ASSESSING OFFENDERS

A psychologist studies an offender's background for sentencing and rehabilitation purposes, and to garner their profile for future cases.

> **Is there a family history** of abuse or criminality?

> **What types of crimes** are they thought to have committed, and who were their victims?

> **What is their attitude** toward the crime: do they justify or deny it?

> **What level of education** did the offender achieve, and how did they perform at school? What is their general level of intelligence?

> **Are they in a relationship** or have they ever been in one?

> **Are they employed,** or have they ever been financially responsible?

> **Do they show signs** of mental illness or personality disorder?

Psychology and criminal investigations

The process of investigating crimes and identifying offenders is often long and painstaking. Psychologists can help police during this process, chiefly in data analysis and victim and suspect interviews.

How are psychologists involved?

Books and films rarely depict the labor-intensive work involved in most criminal investigations. If there is no obvious suspect, detectives must review a vast amount of information from records of previous crimes or criminals to surveillance recordings; photographs of crime scenes; and interviews with victims, witnesses, and suspects. A forensic psychologist's understanding of criminal behavior and the motivation behind it can be invaluable in collating and analyzing this material.

If a crime scene does not yield specific evidence, psychologists can create a profile from the forensic data that is collected, which may link a person or their behavior to the crime (p.198). Their knowledge of psychological disorders and the behavior patterns associated with them can also assist in the identification of suspects. They can use incisive interview techniques to ascertain as much as possible from a witness or suspect. A psychologist can also use their understanding of human behavior and the fallibility of human memory to help ascertain whether a person is telling the truth or is covering for someone.

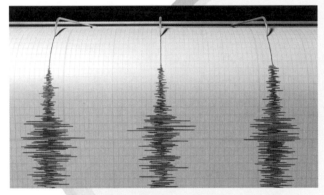

A LIE DETECTOR, OR POLYGRAPH, can detect an individual's responses to questioning and can be effective in supporting the case of an innocent person.

COGNITIVE INTERVIEW TECHNIQUE

Interviews—whether of victims, eyewitnesses, or suspects—are central to criminal investigations and are an area where the expertise of a forensic psychologist is invaluable. The cognitive interview uses a specific method of questioning that in the hands of a skilled psychologist can actually help improve a person's memory of an event. The person needs to feel safe, and the interviewer must be patient, pose the questions in the right way, and allow sufficient time for a response. Some people do not respond to this type of interview, in which case the investigators may need to try a different approach.

> **A safe environment for the witness** is established to ensure a sense of mutual understanding. If the interviewer actively and attentively listens to what the interviewee is saying, even asking them about their general activities and feelings that day, the interviewee will relax and trust the interviewer enough to talk freely.

> **Free-form recollection** is encouraged by posing open-ended questions rather than ones that require yes/no answers. The interviewer must not interrupt the interviewee's response, and allow for plenty of breaks to give them the time to remember events more clearly.

> **A conducive context** is created, for example by describing the background of the event(s) being recalled, which can strengthen an interviewee's memory.

> **Patience is maintained** throughout, especially if the interviewee is uncooperative. It is essential for an interviewer to keep frustration and feelings of coercion in check to avoid the interviewee making a false confession.

At the crime scene

DISTANCE FROM OFFENDER
The greater the distance between the witness and the suspect/event, the less accurate their memory will be.

RACE, GENDER, AND AGE
If a witness is of a different age, gender, or race than the suspect, they are more inclined to misidentify them.

USE OF A WEAPON
If a crime involves a knife or gun, witnesses often remember fewer details as the weapon holds their focus.

OFFENDER'S BEHAVIOR
Witnesses are more likely to remember distinctive aspects of an offender's appearance, speech, or behavior.

STRESS LEVELS OF WITNESS
Experiencing a very stressful crime alters perceptions and memory, and can lead to inaccurate identifications.

FACTORS AFFECTING EYEWITNESS MEMORY
Accounts from eyewitnesses play a key role in police investigations, and a number of factors—both at the crime scene and afterward—affect their accuracy. Erroneous eyewitness evidence and/or identification have often led to false convictions.

AGE OF WITNESS
Children, the frail, and the elderly are vulnerable to the pressure of being interviewed. Older children remember more details than younger ones.

FATIGUE OF WITNESS
Tiredness affects memory. Allowing adequate rest before questioning protects memory from interference and enables more accurate recall.

RETENTION INTERVAL
If a police interview takes place a long time after an event, the witness will recall it in far less detail.

SUSCEPTIBILITY OF WITNESS
When viewing a lineup, law enforcement officers can unintentionally indicate to witnesses who they should choose.

VIEWING A LINEUP
Suspects are displayed in a group or one at a time. The latter requires the witness to compare the suspects with their memory of the offender only.

PROVIDING LINEUP INSTRUCTIONS
Witnesses who are clearly informed that they do not have to choose a suspect from a lineup are less likely to make a false identification.

During questioning

Is there a "criminal type"?

There is no specific set of attributes that conclusively determines criminal behavior, but some are more commonly associated with criminality. These include low intelligence, hyperactivity, difficulty concentrating, a poor education, antisocial behavior, having siblings or friends who are in trouble with the law, and habitual drug or alcohol abuse. In addition, males of any age are significantly more likely to offend than females—especially when it comes to violent crimes. Those who have been convicted are more likely to have had a chaotic or disruptive childhood—but not all such upbringings lead to criminality.

Among the young, the cycle of negative behavior can often be broken by intervention with protective factors, such as positive relationships outside the family, academic achievement, positive attitudes toward authority, and effective use of leisure time.

Offender profiling

This is the process of using evidence and information from both the victim and the crime scene, as well as the characteristics of the crime, to form hypotheses about the type of person who might have committed it. Some crime scenes offer few significant clues, which forces detectives to make imaginative leaps. This is where the developing science of investigative psychology can be utilized. There are two ways of looking at profiling: the top-down method (used mainly in the US) and the bottom-up approach (used in the UK).

> "Psychology often presents individuals as if they are frozen in time and space."

Professor David Canter,
British psychologist

Top-down profiling

> Aims to test reliability of organized/disorganized criminal behavior and motivation, or typologies.
> Matches a general type of criminal to features of a particular crime.
> Aims to detect signature aspects of the crime and patterns of the criminal.
> Relies on the behaviorist perspective (pp.16–17).
> Is best applied to crimes such as rape and murder.

Bottom-up profiling

> Aims to identify a behavior pattern from similarities between offenses.
> Is data-driven and based on clear psychological principles.
> Uses forensic evidence and data to build patterns of behavior piece by piece.
> Produces measured, specific associations between crimes and offenders.
> Makes no initial assumptions about offenders.
> Seeks consistencies in offender behavior, from both crime scene evidence and eyewitness accounts.

Understanding criminality

The search for explanations behind criminal behavior lies at the heart of forensic psychology: is someone inherently "bad," is the behavior created or influenced by circumstance, and are criminals different from noncriminals? Attempts to understand criminality focus on its mental, psychological, social, and biological aspects. These can determine how a suspect is assessed and treated as well as policies for crime reduction.

MENTAL DISORDERS
Convicted offenders commonly suffer from depression (pp.38–39), learning difficulties, personality disorders (pp.102–107), or disorders such as schizophrenia (pp.70–71). Some have psychotic episodes and hallucinate or believe there is a secret force controlling them. However, it is not always clear whether criminal behavior is caused by a disorder or factors such as lifestyle.

PSYCHOPATHIC BEHAVIOR
Many criminals are lucid and fully understand the illegality of their actions. Yet they lie, abuse people, are unpredictably violent, and seem unable to connect with others. This behavior pattern indicates the personality disorder psychopathy (p.104). Psychopaths can be very charming and appear helpful, but they never develop empathy for others and can be vicious.

PSYCHOLOGICAL FACTORS
Criminals generally do not have a strong conscience, do not adhere to social norms, and have not reached an adult stage of moral reasoning. Their behavior reflects a lack of awareness of the consequences of their actions, low self-worth, a belief that offending provides high reward for little effort, an unwillingness to delay gratification, and an inability to control their desires.

PHYSIOLOGICAL FACTORS
Many experts believe that there is a neurological basis for criminal behavior, and that it is the result of a brain disorder or an injury (at birth or from an accident) that affects personality. Others argue that criminals are genetically different—that something in their hormonal balance or nervous system prevents them from learning the concepts of good and bad.

SOCIAL CIRCUMSTANCE
Most crimes are not isolated acts, but the product of social interactions. The roots of criminality may be found in how a criminal interacts with others and the social networks to which they belong. Such people may learn criminality by example. Poor economic status can also be a factor, although poverty itself is never the sole cause of criminal behavior.

The cycle of violence

A violent crime is one in which an offender uses force against a victim. Often, aggression is the result of an inability to control emotions. This may be because a person has grown up in a family or culture where violence was not only accepted, but even encouraged. Sometimes an individual's sole objective is to be violent, but in other situations—such as robbery—it becomes a means to an end. There are individuals who, for example, use physical force as a tool to exert control over their partner, or simply vent their anger, frustration, or jealousy by using force against another person. Such individuals are often caught up in cycles of anger and remorse (right).

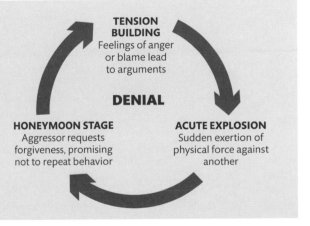

TENSION BUILDING
Feelings of anger or blame lead to arguments

DENIAL

HONEYMOON STAGE
Aggressor requests forgiveness, promising not to repeat behavior

ACUTE EXPLOSION
Sudden exertion of physical force against another

Psychology in the courtroom

Forensic psychologists spend a great deal of time in the courtroom, assessing defendants, assisting lawyers with lines of questioning, delivering expert opinions, and advising on sentencing.

Areas of responsibility

The role of the psychologist has been established in the criminal courts for some time, but it has recently broadened to include advising in family and civil cases, too. When someone is convicted of a crime, or is due to attend civil court, their mental state and their capacity and competence to stand trial is often assessed, especially if they have entered a not-guilty plea. A psychologist will be appointed to evaluate the defendant, searching for evidence of mental disorder or physical illness. The psychologist will also consider external influences and mitigating circumstances. They may testify in court to offer their interpretation of the person's capabilities and how these may have contributed to the outcome of the incident.

The psychological makeup of a jury is also highly relevant to the outcome of a case. Like anyone else, members of a jury are subject to individual biases that may affect their abilities as jurors and so influence the verdict. Some or all of the jury may have difficulty understanding what is expected of them, and they may even be more likely to assume that the defendant is guilty simply because of the complexity of the information being presented. Psychologists can work with the courts to mitigate the effects of these biases.

Assessing a defendant's mental state

If there is any doubt about a person's mental state at the time of a crime, or their ability to understand court proceedings, a lawyer or the police may call on a psychologist to assess their mental capacity. Depending on the results, the person may be considered unable to stand trial. Various potential factors are looked for and assessed.

Insanity

Any person found to be without knowledge of wrongdoing will be acquitted on the grounds of insanity. However, if an offender knew that what they were doing was wrong, they are considered to be legally sane.

Head injury

This can cause personality changes, affect judgment, and result in aggressive and impulsive behaviors.

Incompetence

A defendant may be deemed mentally too damaged or underdeveloped to understand what is happening in court, and so is excluded from prosecution.

Low IQ

Severely low intelligence quotient (IQ) may affect competency to stand trial, and is also considered when deciding the punishment if prosecuted.

Malingering

Some defendants may exaggerate or feign symptoms of short- or long-term physical illness and/or psychological disorder to avoid prosecution.

False confession

People regularly make false confessions to protect someone else, to avoid interrogation or torture, or because they wrongly believe that they are guilty.

Jury decisions

Although the strength of the evidence contributes most powerfully to the outcome of a court case, small differences in jury traits and understanding can make a crucial difference.

❯ **In the US, jury selection consultants** can be called in to identify juror biases. Questionnaires such as the Juror Bias Scale may be used to measure personality traits to predict the likelihood of a juror convicting a particular defendant regardless of the evidence.

❯ **Court language** is often archaic, so psychologists look for clearer ways to present information, using simpler language, forms, and flowcharts to guide jurors and prevent any misunderstanding.

75% of **women** entering **European prisons** are estimated to have a **drug or alcohol problem**

Role of the expert witnesses

Forensic psychologists can be brought into court to assist in the decision-making process in civil, family, and criminal proceedings. As with all witnesses, they must abide by court procedures, but they can go beyond a statement of fact and offer their interpretation of the situation. There are constraints on who can serve as an expert witness.

❯ **Expert opinions** must be limited to the psychologist's specific area of competence. They cannot be asked to state whether they think a person is guilty or not guilty.

❯ **Before a trial,** expert psychologists can work with lawyers to prepare a case, shed light on a defendant, or determine the best method of cross-examination.

Guidance for sentencing

If convicted, an offender will be sentenced to imprisonment, a fine, a community penalty, or probation. In addition to its punitive and reparative goals, the aim of a sentence is to deter similar future crimes, either by the individual in question (the rehabilitative approach) or by another member of the public. A judge may consult a psychologist on the offender's mental state before making the final decision.

❯ **The sentence should be proportionate** to the severity of the offense and the degree of responsibility shown by the defendant.

❯ **Aggravating factors,** such as the vulnerability of the victim, whether the offender was provoked, and whether they show any remorse, must be considered.

❯ **Studies** show that criminals who are jailed for longer are less likely to reoffend after being released than those who serve shorter sentences.

Psychology in prisons

A significant part of a forensic psychologist's role involves working with convicted offenders: assessing inmates; working through preexisting problems; and developing rehabilitation programs.

Challenging environment

A prison is designed to be a place where criminal tendencies can be treated and offending behavior corrected. However, the realities of prison life make it a challenging environment for both inmates and staff, as psychologist Philip Zimbardo demonstrated in his iconic Stanford Prison Experiment of 1971 (p.151). Zimbardo selected a group of ordinary university students to live as inmates and guards in a converted basement "prison" so he could study the effects of prison life. It quickly became an oppressive, hierarchical, and violent environment that altered attitudes and behavior, and the experiment had to be halted after only six days.

Treatment programs

Psychologists can offer guidance to penal institutions and their staff in the planning of treatment and rehabilitation programs. When

PRISONS have their limitations. They are unnatural, harsh places with alien routines, where inmates must interact exclusively with the staff and other offenders.

working with individual inmates, they try to take a holistic view of the person. They look at the problems, such as mental illness or drug addiction, that may have contributed to the criminal behavior. They seek ways to

help each prisoner cope with their current issues and challenges—including their response to being sentenced—and the risks they pose to both themselves and others. A psychologist will also try to identify approaches that might reduce the risk of future offending.

Violent offenders often attend group sessions in which they engage in discussion and role-play to explore the conditions that contributed to their behavior. They can also use this time to work on developing empathy for their victims. Therapeutic communities, in which prisoners join together for discussion, can be beneficial. Programs based around cognitive behavioral therapies (pp.122–129) can enable offenders to change patterns of thought and behavior, and ETS (enhanced thinking skills) can be used to help them develop social skills such as listening and asking for help.

PRISON BEHAVIOR PROBLEMS

The prison regime can have a detrimental effect on inmates as they try to cope with the challenges it presents. This can result in changed behavior patterns that individuals need help to resolve.

❱ **Inmates become reliant on staff** to make decisions for them as they feel isolated and disempowered by the regimented environment.

❱ **Prison breeds suspicion and distrust** among inmates, which sometimes results in a neurotic level of alertness.

❱ **Inmates develop a "mask"** to hide their feelings as a

means of self-protection and self-preservation. This makes it difficult for them to relate to others.

❱ **The dehumanizing and depersonalizing** atmosphere of a prison can erode a prisoner's self-belief. Inmates begin to lose a sense of their own personal significance, uniqueness, and value.

❱ **The harsh and sometimes violent environment** can reactivate memories of traumatic childhood events.

❱ **Despair can lead to suicide,** the rates of which are up to 10 times higher in prisons than in the outside world.

Reducing the risk of reoffending

Reducing the risk of a prisoner reoffending after release is one of the major responsibilities of a forensic psychologist. Various approaches are used to encourage prisoners not to reoffend, the focus being on engendering a sense of personal responsibility and moral self-worth.

PERSONAL RESPONSIBILITY
Prisoners are taught to confront their own destructive thought patterns and offense cycles.

VICTIM EMPATHY
The devastating effects of their crimes are impressed upon offenders to help foster empathy for their victims.

HEALTHY SEX RELATIONS
Healthy sexuality is taught, stressing the connection between dysfunctional sex and offending.

RELAPSE PREVENTION

PERSONAL PREVENTION PLAN
Inmates are asked to identify situations and personal weaknesses that may cause them to relapse.

COGNITIVE BEHAVIORAL THERAPIES
CBT uses imagery and relaxation techniques that are designed to reduce violent impulses and deviant sexual arousal, thereby helping prisoners to learn to curb and ultimately prevent their criminal behaviors. ETS (enhanced thinking skills) addresses the many problems associated with criminal activity and can enable improved social skills, problem-solving, critical reasoning, moral reasoning, self-control, impulse management, and self-efficacy.

EMOTIONAL WELL-BEING
Discussions help prisoners come to terms with any history of abuse or trauma they may have. They also reveal the link between the dysfunction in prisoners' personal and family lives and their offending behavior. Issues of addiction and codependency are also addressed.

ANGER MANAGEMENT
Learning anger management helps prisoners identify their own emotional triggers, and teaches them how to relax when trigger situations arise. Discussions focus on the connection between anger and criminal behavior, and encourage offenders to be assertive rather than aggressive.

10–15%
of people in prison have an ongoing long-term mental illness

WHAT IS VICTIMOLOGY?

This is the study of the relationship between a victim and the perpetrator. Research shows that factors such as proximity to criminals and/or physical or psychological vulnerability mean that some people are more susceptible to victimization than others. Psychologists explore why victims are targeted, and use the patterns they discover to develop strategies for prevention and risk reduction. However, the distinction between victim and criminal is not always clear-cut, as violent environments can turn victims into victimizers.

Psychology in politics

Political psychology applies psychological approaches and models to the world of politics, exploring the minds of citizens and those in power in an attempt to explain their choices and behaviors. It also studies the dynamics of mass political behavior and, at the extreme, seeks to understand why people condone or commit acts of terrorism or genocide and how such behavior could be prevented.

Key theories

People generally base important political decisions on just a few pieces of concrete information, and fill in the rest with assumptions. Attribution and schema theories describe how people arrive at their assumptions.

ATTRIBUTION THEORY

People are problem solvers attempting to understand their own behavior and that of others. They draw on assumptions to come up with theories about why things happen, and try to make sense of the world. There are three ways they may use attribution:

Fundamental attribution error

People attribute (explain) their own behavior as arising from their situation or circumstances, whereas they attribute others' behavior to their disposition or character traits.

Representativeness heuristic

Individuals evaluate or judge other people based on how similar they are to the stereotype of a particular kind of person.

Availability heuristic

People estimate the likelihood of something happening based on how top-of-mind (easy to recall) it is to them, which usually reflects their own recent experience rather than statistical likelihoods.

"What the **human being** is best at **doing** is **interpreting** all new information **so that** their **prior conclusions** remain **intact.**"

Warren Buffett, American business magnate

HOW DO VOTERS DECIDE?

The candidates people choose as their leaders have the power to affect their political, social, cultural, and personal lives. Psychologists have different theories about how people make such momentous decisions:

❯ **Memory-based vs. online evaluation** The memory-based model says that people make political decisions at the moment they must choose, shifting relevant information from long-term to working memory and making a judgment. Conversely, the online model says that voters are constantly updating their views as they receive new information about candidates in real time.

❯ **Counting likes and dislikes** This theory states that people make their decisions in the voting booth by tallying how many things they like and dislike about each candidate, subtracting dislikes from likes, and comparing candidates' net scores.

SCHEMA THEORY
People turn to schemas (preexisting categories, labels, or stereotypes) in order to assimilate new information, rather than treating each new piece of information independently.

KEY THEMES

❯ **Political decision-making** How do citizens interpret political information and make political decisions, and what determines how they vote?

❯ **Opinion and evaluation** What role do emotions, identities, stereotypes, and group dynamics play in evaluating issues and candidates?

❯ **Political violence** Why do discrimination, terrorism, war, and genocide occur?

Voting behavior

People are driven by numerous factors when choosing who to vote for. They have long-term attachments to particular parties, as well as short-term attachments to candidates and issues.

The decision process

During the 1960s people realized that voter choice is not just a case of social or economic status, but that identifying with a party's values can play a key role. Most voters establish a deep emotional attachment to a political party during their early or teenage years, and this often determines their voting behavior for the rest of their lives. The act of voting is often habitual, instinctive, emotional, and based solely on party affiliation. Voters may possess low levels of information, pay sporadic attention to politics, and hold attitudes that are not consistent with any one party—and yet they may still identify strongly as a supporter of a particular party. Party affiliations tend to be stable over time and resistant to change, even when representatives of the chosen party fail, disappoint, or diverge from party ideology. It generally takes a very extreme event such as war or depression to change a voter's party allegiance. Individuals who identify strongly with a party tend

Influences on voting behavior

Many factors affect voting behavior. Some of these are psychological in nature, and are associated with the character traits of voters. Others are sociological, and are influenced by the various social groups to which voters belong. Some factors are stable over the long term, and others—such as the candidates or issues in question—are not.

LONG-TERM FACTORS

These factors, including voters' personal characteristics, are stable over time, and do not change with each election cycle.

Psychological

❯ Psychological attachment to a political party is often formed in childhood or adolescence and built up over the years, influenced by parents or other adults and peer groups. This sort of attachment—the tendency to vote out of habit—is unaffected by changing parties or policies, or by the mass of information available during an election campaign.

SHORT-TERM FACTORS

Variable and changing over time, short-term factors are influenced by each election cycle, as new candidates and new policies enter the spotlight.

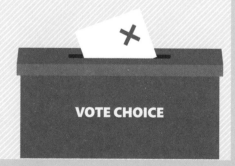

VOTE CHOICE

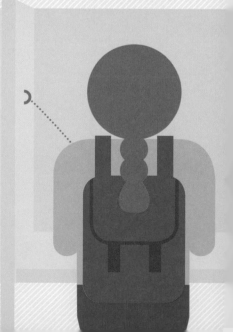

to be selective in their perceptions, exaggerating favorable traits and policies while ignoring unfavorable information or policy positions. Approximately two-thirds of an electorate have stable party loyalties, while the remaining third are only weakly attached to a party, or have more short-term loyalties. These are swing voters, who make their choices based on the issues or candidates at the time. Swing votes therefore often determine election results, but can be difficult to predict.

THE ROLE OF EMOTIONS IN VOTING

Politics are charged with both positive and negative emotions, which are often strong. Happiness, sadness, anger, guilt, disgust, revenge, gratitude, insecurity, joy, anxiety, and fear can all influence political choices and actions. A voter's preferences for political figures and events are rarely, if ever, neutral; they are as much about feelings as about thoughts. Neuroscientists have found that parts of the brain linked with strong feelings like disgust or empathy are also activated by images of politicians. Emotions are valuable and essential to rational decision-making, but they can also lead to highly irrational outcomes and have a harmful effect on politics—extreme nationalism and racism, for instance, often stem from powerful emotion. Furthermore, people's changing moods can affect how they make decisions in ways that have long-term consequences. Depression, for example, can lead to rigid and narrow decision-making.

Sociological

❯ Sociological factors have a strong influence on voting behavior. Issues such as race, ethnicity, gender, sexual orientation, income, occupation, education, age, religion, region of residence, and family all impact voters' choices. People are naturally drawn to candidates who serve the constituencies to which they belong, and who support their groups' causes.

THE MEDIA
Newspapers, television, radio, and social media

❯ Whereas newspapers tend to take an openly political stance, reporting on television often attempts to be neutral. However, televised debates may affect a viewer's opinion of the candidates. Politicians may also use online media to build a positive image and show it to a wider audience.

Fake news

❯ Usually found on social media, articles containing false information can be used to trick voters. Psychologists have found that fake news may be believed as the brain overlooks the falsity of a claim if the information confirms what the individual already believes (confirmation bias). If this bias is in play, fake news is more likely to add to a voter's internal justifications of their choice rather than sway their voting.

Single issue

❯ People who are issue-oriented (they feel strongly about a specific issue that they believe will be affected by an election) may disregard a party's other policies that they do not agree with in order to support the issue that they care about. Issues might include the economy, health care, or civil rights issues like marriage equality.

Leader or candidate image

❯ The personality of a leader or another political candidate can affect the election result, so building a positive candidate image is an important part of an election campaign. Voters may develop preferences based on particularly appealing personal traits, or withdraw their support if a candidate is not compelling.

Obedience and decision-making

The decisions that politicians and civilians make define the laws and future of any state or country. However, decisions are susceptible to the psychological forces of obedience and group dynamics.

The role of obedience

Psychologist Stanley Milgram believed that humans naturally incline toward obedience as a result of interaction with hierarchical social structures. Family, school, university, business, and the military are examples of institutional hierarchies that define people's everyday lives and prime

66%
of participants followed orders in Milgram's obedience study

them for obedience. Milgram famously set up an experiment in which participants administered what they believed to be electric shocks of increasing severity—up to lethal levels—on other humans when ordered to do so by an authority figure. The results of his experiment shed some light on political obedience—why people so readily obey authority figures even when the demands conflict with their own moral and ethical values.

Milgram found that when people obey authority, they often stop feeling responsible for their actions. Without responsibility, they may become capable of violent, even evil, acts. Negating responsibility makes it possible to dehumanize victims and so lose empathy, seen at its most extreme in acts of

genocide, the subject of many case studies (below and right).

The individual also neglects to take responsibility for destructive action in the dynamic named by Irving Janis as Groupthink. Individual decision makers behave more responsibly when they act on their own compared to within a group, when their desire to conform can override realistic appraisal. Groupthink has been the cause of many political disasters, including the Bay of Pigs invasion (below left).

Bad-barrel theory

Psychologist Philip Zimbardo studied the atrocities that took place in Abu Ghraib prison in 2003 during the war in Iraq. He tried to determine whether evil had been carried out by a few evil people ("bad apples"), whether the US soldiers involved were fundamentally good people ruined by a bad situation ("bad barrel"), or whether the system as a whole was toxic and corrupt ("bad barrel makers"). He concluded that if "good people" are put in "bad barrels," they eventually become "bad apples."

 ## CASE STUDY: GROUPTHINK AT THE BAY OF PIGS

In 1973 psychologist Irving Janis used the 1961 Bay of Pigs disaster—in which US-trained soldiers failed to overthrow Fidel Castro's Cuban government after poor decisions made by President Kennedy and his strategists—to study Groupthink. Kennedy's subordinates knew he wanted to overthrow Castro, and they wanted to please their president, which compromised group thinking. They planned less logically, jumped to conclusions, and reacted inflexibly to new information. Their intricate plan relied on every step going right—a military impossibility. In fact, Castro's forces quickly defeated the small US army (air support had been canceled), the hoped-for counterrevolution did not take place, Kennedy looked weak, and the episode heightened tension with Russia.

Bad apples

One notion for unethical behavior is that it is carried out exclusively by unethical people, regardless of the situation. These people are the "bad apples" whose evil acts reflect a fundamentally evil disposition.

SITUATION VS. DISPOSITION

> **Situationism** Philip Zimbardo discovered in his 1971 Stanford prison experiment (p.151) that if you put ordinary people in an extreme situation, the situation can cause them to act against their good dispositions. According to this theory, in alignment with the "bad barrel" idea, everyone is capable of violating their own values and beliefs to obey an authority figure, so evil deeds are not necessarily the work of evil people.

> **Dispositionism** From this perspective, a person's disposition is more powerful than any social situation. If people behave badly, it is because they are basically bad, what Zimbardo called "bad apples." Fundamentally good people are incapable of evil acts.

"Evil is knowing better, but willingly doing worse."

Philip Zimbardo, American psychologist

Bad barrel

This idea holds that people in a bad barrel are not inherently good or bad, but are powerfully influenced by their situation. When ethical people are placed in a bad situation, they become capable of unethical behavior.

Bad barrel makers

Another notion is that evil is a systemic issue, and that unethical behavior is the result of broad forces creating the conditions for evil. These forces may be cultural, legal, political, or economic.

Nationalism

Nationalistic pride can draw people together, but it can also lead to war or even genocide. Understanding how it works can help political leaders to avoid its harmful extremes.

Us and them

Nationalism is a sense of identification among a group of people who share a common history, language, territory, or culture. In its mildest form, it can be a positive force that unites people and creates a sense of patriotism and solidarity. When taken to the extreme, however, it can lead to violence and ethnic conflict.

Psychologically, people like to belong to a group, and social categorization and us-versus-them thinking make it easy to exaggerate differences between in-groups and out-groups. This way of thinking can make an in-group stronger, but it can also worsen out-group discrimination. The in-group may see the out-group as a threat, develop feelings of national and ethnic superiority, and consequently demonize the out-group. Economic and political inequalities often contribute as the different groups struggle to gain or hold onto land and material wealth, or to better their living conditions. Sometimes these grievances may be too strong to be resolved through political negotiation and may escalate into war or even genocide.

An additional factor in nationalistic extremism is authoritarianism, which relies on people's natural tendency to trust and obey a leader. Authoritarians (such as Adolf Hitler) tend to be highly prejudiced against and hostile toward out-groups, and offer a narrative—however fictional—that inflames their followers' sense of grievance.

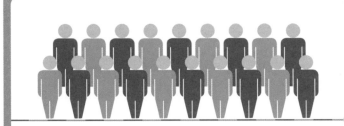

1. Preexisting fault lines Most societies are a mixture of people of different ethnicities and different religious and political beliefs. Periods of economic instability, war, or revolution (situational factors) can bring these differences to light. This can lead to an in-group/out-group mentality among both leaders and civilians.

Nationalistic extremes

Extreme nationalism is the belief that a person's own nation, or ethnic group, is superior and should be advanced above others. This way of thinking can be used as an excuse to commit acts of ethnic displacement or genocide.

"There's nothing quite so psychologically satisfying as the feeling of belonging. Nationalism can be remarkably unifying."

Joshua Searle-White, American author

4. Stereotyping the out-group Once a group has been dehumanized, those people are no longer viewed as complex individuals, but are instead defined by a few fixed and oversimplified attributes such as skin color, for example. They are turned into representatives of everything that the in-group hates and fears.

THEORIES OF NATIONALISM

Realistic Group Conflict Theory

Conflict develops between in-groups and out-groups when one group has a realistic reason to compete or fight with the other. These reasons may include limited land, food, or other resources that are critical—or perceived to be critical—to the group's survival.

Social Identity Theory

Conflict can develop even when the in-group has nothing to gain from competing or fighting with the other. Feeling that their own nation is superior to others serves people's basic need for self-esteem, so they show favoritism toward in-groups and hostility toward out-groups.

Social Dominance Theory

Because people try to maintain a group-based hierarchical structure, group oppression often becomes the norm. In most societies, there is a least one dominant and one subordinate group, which creates inequality with respect to race, gender, ethnicity, nationality, or class.

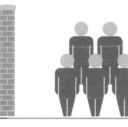

2. A divided society In-group/out-group divisions can form along ethnic, religious, economic, or political lines. As leaders embrace these distinctions, the society can become dangerously divided. Under such circumstances, resentment tends to worsen on both sides.

3. The neighbor as "other" The in-group/out-group mentality causes different groups to view each other as the "other," or as outsiders. This often occurs between people who live close to one another and are similar, such as the Catholics and Protestants of Northern Ireland. This causes distancing and the start of dehumanization of the "other."

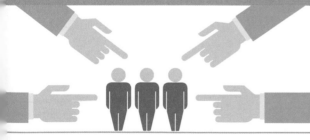

5. Blaming the out-group Because members of the out-group are viewed in stereotyped terms they become easy scapegoats for the in-group's failings and problems. The more problems they are perceived to cause, the angrier the in-group becomes.

6. Eliminating the out-group When people have been marginalized, dehumanized, stereotyped, and scapegoated, they may finally become the victims of atrocities inflicted by the in-group. The Holocaust is an example of how an in-group can seek to destroy and eliminate an out-group.

Discrimination and social hierarchy

Individuals and groups within societies may often discriminate against each other on the basis of attributes such as race, ethnicity, nationality, gender, age, sexual orientation, and class. These attitudes are learned from family, peers, and general social norms and values, and they result in powerful social hierarchies.

People in dominant groups are motivated to maintain the social hierarchy in order to ensure that social and political systems benefit them the most. They may encourage stereotypes, prejudices, xenophobia, and ethnocentrism in order to enhance their power and dominance. Xenophobia often strengthens in-group/out-group thinking, while ethnocentrism often lies at the heart of authoritarian behavior and terrorist acts.

In recent years there has been a great deal of social progress and activism aimed at establishing equality and human rights for all people, regardless of race, sex, or ethnicity. Societies are also becoming more diverse, which tends to increase people's tolerance of those who are different from them. Indeed, the more diverse a society is, the less easy it is to distinguish one group as the "other," and regiment in-group/out-group thinking against it. As a result, discrimination is no longer broadly socially acceptable. However, despite the many advances that have taken place, many diverse societies still struggle with an established social hierarchy, as well as discriminatory beliefs and behaviors.

Allport's scale of prejudice

Psychologist Gordon Allport studied the social, psychological, political, and economic processes that lead a society from prejudice and discriminatory behavior to violence, hate crimes, and even genocide. In his efforts to explain how the Holocaust happened, Allport created a five-stage scale to represent the level and manifestation of prejudice in a society. Progression up the scale shows that prejudice can begin with hateful words, turn into hateful behaviors, and end in violence.

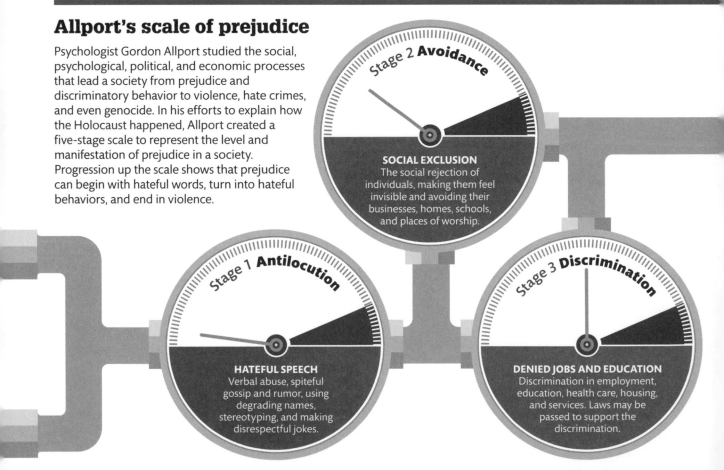

Stage 2 Avoidance

SOCIAL EXCLUSION
The social rejection of individuals, making them feel invisible and avoiding their businesses, homes, schools, and places of worship.

Stage 1 Antilocution

HATEFUL SPEECH
Verbal abuse, spiteful gossip and rumor, using degrading names, stereotyping, and making disrespectful jokes.

Stage 3 Discrimination

DENIED JOBS AND EDUCATION
Discrimination in employment, education, health care, housing, and services. Laws may be passed to support the discrimination.

TERRORISM

Terrorism is the use of force or threats to demoralize, intimidate, and control people—especially as a political weapon. Terrorist acts are violent and dramatic, so as to attract publicity and cause alarm beyond the immediate crime scene. They typically involve an organized group, target civilians, and are carried out by individuals who are outside the government of the target country. One aim of political psychologists is to identify what motivates people who commit such terrible crimes.

❱ **Who is involved?** Terrorist leaders tend to be educated and from a privileged background, but perpetrators are often poor, uneducated, and socially disenfranchised. They therefore may be susceptible to the rewards offered by the terrorist group, such as a feeling of solidarity.

❱ **Justification** Many terrorists feel that they have no choice but to commit their crimes, and that they are acting in self-defense against a political or religious enemy.

❱ **Causes** Various situational factors contribute to terrorism, including weak or corrupt governments, social injustice, and extremist ideologies.

❱ **Effects** Terrorists usually target democracies because they are easier to infiltrate. The public response to an act of terrorism may, in turn, pose a threat to democracy as policies and laws to prevent future attacks run counter to its values. Terrorist attacks often result in an increase in intolerance, prejudice, and xenophobia.

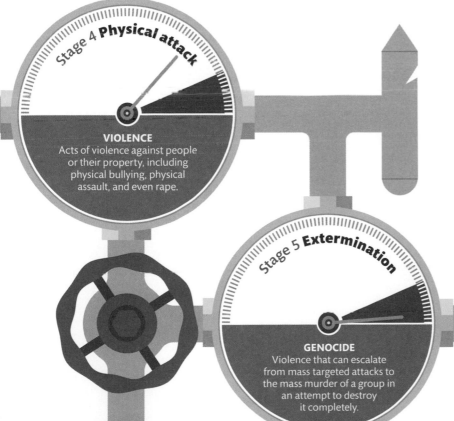

Stage 4 Physical attack

VIOLENCE
Acts of violence against people or their property, including physical bullying, physical assault, and even rape.

Stage 5 Extermination

GENOCIDE
Violence that can escalate from mass targeted attacks to the mass murder of a group in an attempt to destroy it completely.

"... **people** who are **aware of,** and **ashamed of,** their **prejudices** are well on the **road to eliminating them.**"

Gordon Allport, American psychologist

Psychology in the community

The communities—and, more broadly, the societies and cultures—in which people live have a profound impact on their psychological development. The people and places that surround an individual form the context in which they think, believe, and behave, and also construct the unspoken and spoken norms that govern their daily lives. But just as individuals are influenced by their surroundings, so, too, do individuals create and shape their cultures and communities.

Fields of study

The ways in which people both influence, and are influenced by, the world around them is a vast topic that can be broken down into a number of fields of psychological study. All of these fields of study aim to improve the quality of people's lives, interactions, and institutions.

Community

This forms the intersection between the individual, social, cultural, environmental, economic, and political aspects of people's lives. Psychologists in this field can improve the health and quality of life of entire communities by working to empower and solve the issues of marginalized individuals.

Culture

The sum of a group of people's attitudes, behavior, and customs passes from one generation to the next through language, religion, cuisine, social habits, and the arts. Cultural psychologists believe that different cultures engender different psychological responses in individuals.

Community center

"Sense of community is ... a shared faith that members' needs will be met through their commitment to be together."

Seymour B. Sarason, American principal leader in community psychology

KELLY'S ECOLOGICAL PERSPECTIVE

Psychologist James Kelly likens communities to an ecological system built on four principles:

> **Adaptation** Individuals continually adapt to the needs and constraints of their environment and vice versa.

> **Succession** The history of a community informs the current attitudes, norms, structures, and policies.

> **Cycling of resources** Individual talents, shared values, and the tangible products resulting from these resources need to be identified, developed, and nurtured.

> **Interdependence** Changes to one aspect of a setting, such as a school, affect the whole, since all systems are complex.

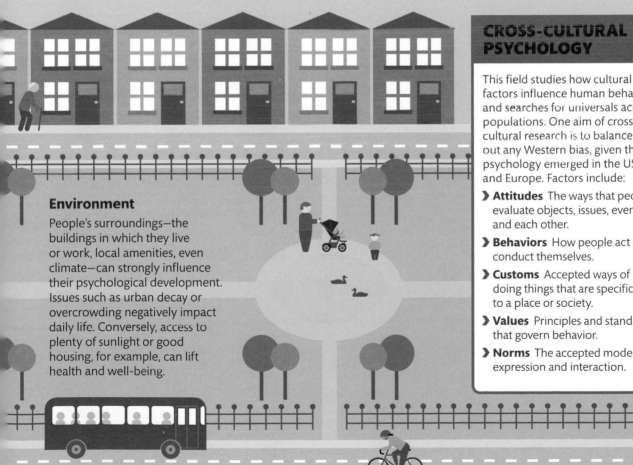

Environment

People's surroundings—the buildings in which they live or work, local amenities, even climate—can strongly influence their psychological development. Issues such as urban decay or overcrowding negatively impact daily life. Conversely, access to plenty of sunlight or good housing, for example, can lift health and well-being.

CROSS-CULTURAL PSYCHOLOGY

This field studies how cultural factors influence human behavior and searches for universals across populations. One aim of cross-cultural research is to balance out any Western bias, given that psychology emerged in the US and Europe. Factors include:

> **Attitudes** The ways that people evaluate objects, issues, events, and each other.

> **Behaviors** How people act or conduct themselves.

> **Customs** Accepted ways of doing things that are specific to a place or society.

> **Values** Principles and standards that govern behavior.

> **Norms** The accepted modes of expression and interaction.

How community works

Communities are continually evolving ecosystems of individuals who share something in common, and both feed into and reflect the broader culture.

What is it?

Communities form around a variety of commonalities, such as living in close proximity, or shared interests, values, occupations, religious practices, ethnic origin, sexual orientation, or hobbies. Communities support individual identities while also giving everyone the opportunity to be a part of something larger and more integrated. This involvement contributes to a person's psychological sense of community—feeling similar to others, acknowledging interdependence, belonging, and being part of a stable structure.

Community psychologists McMillan and Chavis list and define the four elements that contribute to a psychological sense of community as membership, influence, integration, and emotional connection. Membership gives a sense of safety, belonging, and personal investment. Influence refers to the reciprocal relationship between a group and each of its members. Integration and fulfillment of a community member occurs when they are rewarded for their participation in the community. Shared emotional connection, including a shared history, is arguably the most defining element of a true sense of community.

INTERACTION EFFECT
The ways that individuals interact form the basis of community.

The individual
This is the smallest unit in the culture cycle. How the individuals think and behave collectively shapes the wider culture in which they live.

Interactions
Guided by implicit behavioral norms, people's daily interactions with other people and products continually reflect and reinforce the culture cycle.

INSTITUTIONAL INFLUENCE
Institutions create and uphold the norms that govern interactions within the community.

"A community is like a ship; everyone ought to be prepared to take the helm."

Henrik Ibsen, Norwegian playwright

The culture cycle

In this reciprocal process, the thoughts and behavior of individuals shape the broader culture, while culture simultaneously molds individuals' thoughts and behaviors—perpetuating the culture. The cycle involves four planes: individual selves, interactions between people, institutions, and ideas.

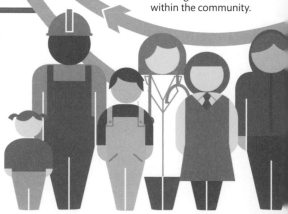

INDIVIDUAL EFFECT
Individuals are the building blocks of interactions, institutions, and ideas.

Institutions

Everyday interactions take place within institutions that both establish and uphold cultural norms. They may be economic, legal, governmental, scientific, or religious.

Ideas

Cultures are held together by ideas. They inform practices and patterns, as well as people's sense of self, their interaction with others, and societal institutions.

INFLUENCE OF IDEAS
Ideas are the foundation of all individual and collective behavior.

What do community psychologists do?

Community psychologists seek to understand how individuals function within groups, organizations, and institutions, and use this understanding to enhance the quality of lives and communities. They study people within the various contexts and environments of their day-to-day lives, including their home, work, school, places of worship, and recreational centers.

The aim of community psychologists is to help people take greater control of their environment. They develop systems and programs that promote individual growth, prevent social and mental health problems, and help everyone to live dignified lives as contributing members of their community. This involves teaching community members to identify and correct problems, and implementing effective ways for marginalized or institutionalized people to reenter mainstream society.

IMPORTANCE OF DIVERSITY

Diversity, whether of race, gender, religion, sexual orientation, socioeconomic background, culture, or age, is an essential part of a healthy and progressive community. Inclusive communities have been shown to be more productive, because diversity spurs people to question their assumptions and consider alternatives, encouraging hard work and creativity. Diversity also provides everyone in the community with a richer life experience and a broader frame of reference, increasing the psychological well-being of the group.

PEOPLE FROM DIFFERENT BACKGROUNDS offer varying perspectives, generating a range of ideas that fuel ingenuity.

Empowerment

The active process that enables people to make positive social changes and gain control over issues at both an individual and a wider level is known as empowerment.

What is it?

One of the goals of community psychology is to empower both individuals and communities, particularly those that have been marginalized by mainstream society. Empowerment helps people and groups pushed to the edges of society to access resources previously denied to them.

Marginalized people may include racial, ethnic, or religious minorities; the homeless; or people who have deviated from societal norms—for example, as a result of substance use disorder (pp.80–81). One of the consequences of marginalization is a downward spiral—an individual is unable to find a job; because they have no job, they are not self-supporting and lack a sense of professional pride and achievement; their self-confidence suffers as a result; and eventually their social and

psychological health suffers, increasing dependence on charity and social welfare programs. Empowerment involves putting measures in place to give such individuals autonomy and self-sufficiency. Social justice, an action-oriented approach to research, and an effort to influence public policy are its building blocks.

Community psychologists can help people to find employment, encourage them to develop useful skills, and work with them to eliminate their dependence on charitable support. They carry out their tasks with great respect and reflection about what is best for individuals and their communities and how to deliver this positive change. At its heart, empowerment celebrates all cultures, supports community strengths, and reduces oppression by honoring human rights and respecting diversity.

ZIMMERMAN'S THEORY

Community psychologist Marc Zimmerman defines empowerment as "a psychological process in which individuals think positively about their ability to make change, and gain mastery over issues at individual and social levels."

Zimmerman has highlighted the difference between empowerment in practice and empowerment in theory. Although people often

consider the practical manifestation of empowerment—the actions taken to bring about positive social change—it also exists as a theoretical model, giving it broader and more long-term relevance. The theory of empowerment is a useful tool for understanding the process of exerting influence over decisions across all levels of a society, from the individual to the community as a whole.

Three-tiered system

Empowerment theory can apply to three distinct but interrelated levels in society: the individual, organizations, and the community. Each level links to the others as both a cause and a consequence of empowerment. The degree of empowerment at each level directly affects empowerment across the whole of society.

Empowerment of the community

Improves the quality of people's collective access to government and community resources.

Empowerment of organizations

Improves the health and functioning of organizations, which is crucial to the health of communities and societies overall.

Empowerment of the individual

Supports individuals in their interactions with organizations and their community.

80%
of homeless people in the UK report mental health issues

Mental Health Foundation

How does it work?

Psychologists empower across two levels. First-order change tackles social issues at the microscopic level— helping individual lives as a way of fixing a larger problem (such as making it easier for people who have suffered discrimination to file a complaint).

Second-order change deals on a macroscopic level—addressing the systems, structures, and power relationships that contribute to the problem (for example, instituting anti-bullying laws). This type of change takes longer to implement and disrupts the status quo, often to wide-reaching positive effect.

TAKING ACTION FOR WELL-BEING

Community-based organizations can use four strength-oriented principles (known as SPEC) to guide their actions and decisions, and to promote positive change in the community:

❯ **Strength** Acknowledging the strengths of individuals and of communities helps people to thrive, whereas focusing on weaknesses strips them of dignity.

❯ **Prevention** Preventing health-related, social, and psychological problems is more effective than solving established problems.

❯ **Empowering** Giving people power, control, influence, and choices helps them to achieve individual and community well-being.

❯ **Community change** Improving the conditions that initially created the problems brings about real change; it is not enough to change each individual problem.

Urban communities

Environmental psychology looks at people's behavior in relation to their surroundings, including open spaces, public and private buildings, and social settings.

Why place affects people

Psychologist Harold Proshansky was among the first to hypothesize that people are fundamentally shaped by their environment. He believed that understanding the direct and predictable effects of surroundings would allow people to seek out, design, and build physical environments that could promote success and well-being.

Research in environmental psychology has indeed shown that environment plays a critical role in a person's psychology, that people identify strongly with the notion of place, and that their behavior changes to match the setting.

For instance, children tend to behave differently at home, at school, and on the playground, adjusting their level of energy to match the environment. Research has also shown that people can concentrate better indoors when they can see the world outdoors, and that they are more comfortable

INTIMATE SPACE
1½ FT (0.45 M)
Reserved for people's closest relationships, such tight proximity allows for whispering and embracing.

PERSONAL SPACE
4 FT (1.2 M)
Reserved for good friends and family, this close space must feel comfortable and allows for quiet talking.

SOCIAL SPACE
12 FT (3.6 M)
Used with acquaintances and coworkers, this level of proximity allows for interaction but no intimacy.

PUBLIC SPACE
25 FT (7.6 M)
The distance used for public speaking, this space allows for communication but not interaction.

70%

of people in the world will live in urban communities by 2050

World Health Organization

Space

Cross-cultural anthropologist Edward T. Hall developed the theory of "proxemics," which describes how people use space, and the effects of population density on behavior, communication, and social interaction. He identified four interpersonal zones, which may vary among individuals according to their culture and age—spaces that are intimate, personal, social, and public.

if they maintain some degree of personal space (below, left).

People's mental, physical, and social health can suffer when their environment is blighted by issues such as crowding, noise, lack of natural light, decrepit housing, or urban decay. This is why the design of buildings and public spaces is so important to the overall health and well-being of individuals and societies. Architects, city planners, geographers, landscape architects, sociologists, and product designers all use environmental psychology to inform their vision of how people can improve their lives.

Crowding and density

Environmental psychologists make a distinction between the physical measurement of density (how many people are in a particular space) and crowding (the psychological feeling of not having enough space). Usually, high density is needed for the phenomenon of crowding, which makes people experience sensory overload, a lack of control, and rising stress and anxiety.

However, some psychologists see crowding as neutral rather than invariably negative, and believe that people's moods and behaviors intensify as density increases. So if

an individual is looking forward to a concert, say, the feeling of crowding enhances their enjoyment of the performance. But if they are dreading an event, crowding will make the person's experience of it even worse.

Put into a community setting, crowding may accentuate the dominant behavior—an aggressive group may turn violent as density rises. Conversely, creating positive social spaces such as parks and pedestrian areas in high-density urban environments may help to lift the general mood and defuse tension.

MODERN URBAN LIVING makes it difficult to maintain a comfortable level of personal space. High population densities lead to overcrowding on the streets, on public transport, and in offices and other buildings. One solution is careful environmental design.

Safety in the community

Communities have many systems in place to keep their members physically and psychologically safe in the face of threats, both in the real world and online.

Dealing with danger

In order for communities to flourish, individuals need to have an overall sense of physical and psychological safety. As well as causing physical damage and practical consequences, crime (such as burglaries, murders, and cybercrime) can have a long-term psychological impact. People exposed to crime directly or indirectly may experience stress, fear, anxiety, sleep problems, a sense of vulnerability and helplessness, or extreme conditions like PTSD (p.62) and amnesia (p.89).

Bystander effect

People witnessing a crime are less likely to help victims if other witnesses are present. The more bystanders there are, the less likely it is that anyone will offer assistance. This inaction stems from the ways in which onlookers see or interpret the situation.

Level of emergency

A victim is less likely to be offered help when bystanders interpret the situation as an everyday matter rather than a serious one.

Ambiguity

In high-ambiguity situations, where people are unsure if a person requires help, they are slower to act than where the need for assistance is clear.

Environment

When bystanders are unfamiliar with the environment where a crisis occurs, they are less likely to offer help than if they are familiar.

How to prevent it

The bystander effect can be reversed by cues that raise public self-awareness and remind people of their social reputation. Placing security cameras in public spaces can create these cues.

Communities implement many strategies to maintain order and to keep people safe. In cities, these measures may involve a focus on first responders (emergency medical teams, police, and firefighters), streamlining emergency communication and collaboration, clear road signage, and adequate street and park lighting.

A high priority within communities is protecting children, so there is often an emphasis on school safety. A safe environment is essential for learning, because prolonged stress impairs children's cognitive ability. School safety can be increased by installing locking doors, adequate hallway lighting, and check in systems for visitors and guests. However, extreme

measures, such as security cameras, metal detectors, and security guards, may actually increase fear, constantly reminding children of possible danger.

There is a growing trend for video surveillance in public places in an attempt to reduce crime. Although CCTV (closed-circuit television) cameras can help law enforcement officials to prevent crimes and quickly solve criminal cases, questions have been raised about the ethics and effectiveness of these cameras. Some criminologists have argued that cameras do not prevent most crimes and may provide a false sense of security, causing people to take fewer precautions, thereby increasing their risk of becoming a victim.

Social cues

People look to each other for cues about how to behave in a situation. Inaction by some bystanders will most likely lead to inaction by others.

Diffusion of responsibility

When several people witness a crime, they are less likely to help the victim because they expect someone else will take responsibility.

CASE STUDY: GENOVESE MURDER

Shortly after 3:00 a.m. on March 13, 1964, 28-year-old Kitty Genovese was murdered outside her apartment building in New York City. She was returning home from her bar shift when Winston Moseley attacked, stabbed, and raped her. The initial news reports stated that there were 38 witnesses to the attack—neighbors who stood by and did nothing to help Genovese. In the light of those reports of witness inaction, psychologists coined the term "Genovese syndrome" and began to study this social-psychological phenomenon, which has since become known as the "bystander effect" (left).

ONLINE COMMUNITIES

In the digital age, online communities and social networks are primary places where people fulfill their psychological needs for companionship, self-esteem, acceptance, and belonging. However, virtual connection can also present dangers. The sense of anonymity and invisibility can encourage people to say and do things online that they would not do in person. This is known as the "disinhibition effect," which can result in hate speech, cyberbullying, trolling, and grooming. Learning how to stay safe online is therefore essential, especially for vulnerable populations such as children.

Consumer psychology

The study of customers and how they behave—what they want, what they need, and the factors that influence their buying habits and choices—is called consumer psychology. From the essentials of food, shelter, and clothing to common luxuries such as smartphones and cars, people are constantly making decisions about what products and services to buy and from whom.

What drives consumer behavior

There are numerous factors that influence consumer choice: cost, brand, accessibility, shipping times, a product's shelf life, the shopper's mood, packaging, and endorsement. Businesses strive to understand their customers' needs and motivations so that they present their products and services in a way that appeals to them directly. Manipulating even tiny details can sway attitudes and persuade people to purchase a company's products.

ADVERTISING POWER

Consumer psychology plays a large role in making advertising memorable as people today are bombarded with advertisements both offline and online.

> **Traditional approach** Bright colors and catchy jingles are still effective and popular in TV advertising.

> **Shared knowledge** Drawing on shared representations of society, such as referring to a popular television show, involves the audience.

> **Graphic design** In newspaper and magazine ads, the layout, use of contrast, and style of lettering are critical.

> **Humor** Making people laugh avoids viewer boredom and helps to fix the name of a product in the mind, making all the difference to which brand is chosen.

> **Consumer input** Ironically, not mentioning the name can be effective, as cognitive psychology shows that people remember things better if they have to work them out rather than passively absorbing.

Personal recommendations
People like to buy products that their friends and role models are using.

Reviews
Consumers read customer reviews to help decide what to buy.

"**Knowing** who your **customers** are **is great,
but knowing how they behave** is even **better.**"

Jon Miller, American marketing entrepreneur

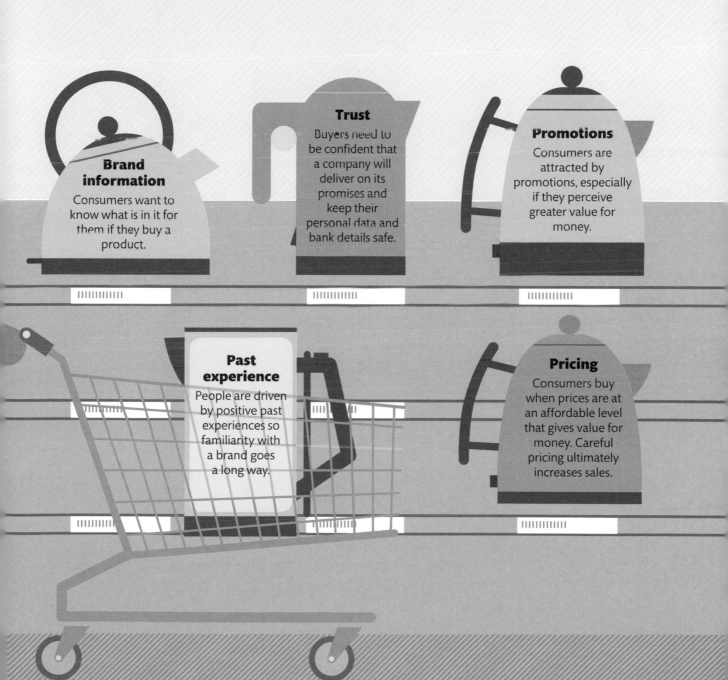

Brand information

Consumers want to know what is in it for them if they buy a product.

Trust

Buyers need to be confident that a company will deliver on its promises and keep their personal data and bank details safe.

Promotions

Consumers are attracted by promotions, especially if they perceive greater value for money.

Past experience

People are driven by positive past experiences so familiarity with a brand goes a long way.

Pricing

Consumers buy when prices are at an affordable level that gives value for money. Careful pricing ultimately increases sales.

Understanding consumer behavior

Understanding how people make decisions about what they want, need, and buy is essential to successful marketing because it helps companies to predict how consumers will respond to new products.

Deciding what to buy

Consumer behavior is affected by psychological factors, such as a person's perception of what they need, their attitude, and their ability to learn; personal characteristics—someone's habits, interests, opinions, and style of decision-making—and social considerations, including family, work colleagues or school friends, and group affiliations.

Companies collect and analyze data on such behavior from focus groups and online sources such as customer reviews, question-and-answer websites, surveys, keyword research, search engine analysis and trends, blog comments, social media, and government statistics.

How people decide which options will bring them the greatest

present and future satisfaction is called consumer prediction. It has two dimensions: the utility of a future event (how much pleasure or pain a person will get, for example, from a trip to Paris rather than a break in New York, or whether they would get more pleasure from eating chocolate or celery) and how likely that event is to occur.

Emotional response

Emotions are a huge factor in consumer behavior and decisions. They affect what consumers focus on, what they remember, how they process information, and how they predict they will feel after making a decision. Feelings override reason when evaluating advertisements, and produce faster and more

"Once you understand customer behavior, everything else falls into place."

Thomas G. Stemberg, American philanthropist and businessman

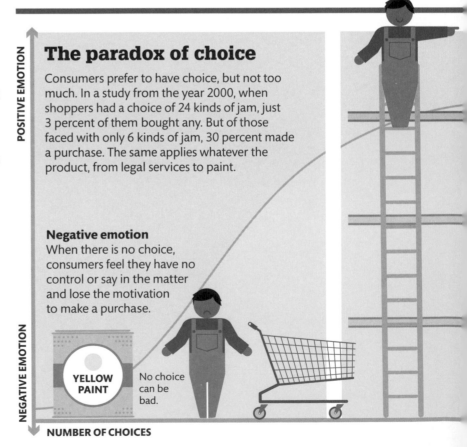

POSITIVE EMOTION

NEGATIVE EMOTION

The paradox of choice

Consumers prefer to have choice, but not too much. In a study from the year 2000, when shoppers had a choice of 24 kinds of jam, just 3 percent of them bought any. But of those faced with only 6 kinds of jam, 30 percent made a purchase. The same applies whatever the product, from legal services to paint.

Negative emotion
When there is no choice, consumers feel they have no control or say in the matter and lose the motivation to make a purchase.

YELLOW PAINT

No choice can be bad.

NUMBER OF CHOICES

consistent judgments. Companies constantly try to glean emotional reactions to their products from prospective consumers, as positive and negative emotions are present at every step of the buying process, from searching to evaluating to choosing to consuming and, finally, to disposing of a product.

Companies evaluate valence (how positive or negative the emotion is) and arousal (how worked up the consumer is) in as much detail as possible. Cognitive appraisal analyzes what and how consumers think about their feelings. All contribute to how ready a consumer is to take action.

CUSTOMER PROFILING

Marketers create detailed portraits of their customers' buying habits, preferences, and lifestyles from their own data and use external sources to help predict future consumer behavior and promote effectively. They use a number of variables to build up a detailed profile of their target market.

❭ **Psychographic** Personality; positive or negative attitude toward life; ethic—whether someone works hard or gives to charity, for example

❭ **Behavioral** Preferred shopping location, online and offline;

frequency of purchases; typical expenditure; credit-card usage; degree of loyalty to a brand

❭ **Sociographic** Use of social media; level of activity in community; political views; membership in groups and clubs

❭ **Geographic** Continent lived in; city or countryside; zip code; associated work and social opportunities; climate

❭ **Demographic** Age group; partner status; number of children, if any; nationality; ethnic background; religion; occupation; salary

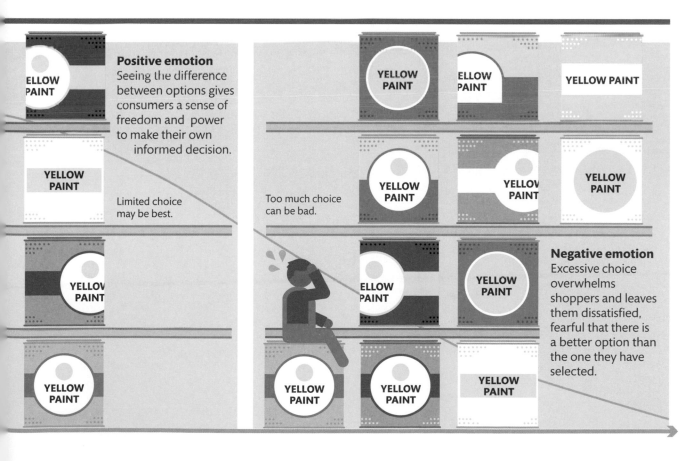

Positive emotion
Seeing the difference between options gives consumers a sense of freedom and power to make their own informed decision.

Limited choice may be best.

Too much choice can be bad.

Negative emotion
Excessive choice overwhelms shoppers and leaves them dissatisfied, fearful that there is a better option than the one they have selected.

Changing consumer behavior

A company's success depends on how well it sells its products to consumers, and that requires persuasion. At the heart of effective persuasion is the ability to change people's attitudes.

Attitudes and persuasion

In order to persuade the public to buy their products, companies need to influence attitudes—the evaluations people form about ideas, objects, and other people. Consumer psychologists are interested in how attitudes can be shaped, and in how potential customers respond to persuasion.

Attitudes can be a core driver of consumer behavior. They affect whether a consumer makes a purchase now or later, spends more or less money, or chooses one product over another. How much consumers like or dislike a product, brand, or company reflects their attitudes—positive, neutral, or negative. The longer an attitude has lasted and the stronger it is, the more

THE GOLDEN RULES OF MARKETING

The Internet has revitalized marketing, providing advertisers with a new and expanding reach. But the heart of good marketing remains the same: product, price, promotion, and place.

❯ **Product** Whether tangible goods or an intangible service, the product must fulfill a customer's wants or needs and benefit them.

❯ **Price** Supply, demand, profit margins, and marketing strategy all rest on price. Even minor tweaks affect returns.

❯ **Promotion** Communicating relevant product information well to customers is known to promote sales.

❯ **Place** Finding the ideal selling place converts potential clients into real clients. SEO (search engine optimization) is a way of improving search engine rankings and so helps online business.

The power of persuasion

There are six principles of persuasive marketing that retailers and other businesses make full use of. Even if people resist persuasion initially, their attitude and behavior may be more open to change over time.

Commitment

People feel they are part of a community when companies give them a say in the product or service—for example, issuing a membership card that offers discounts—and are more likely to buy.

Authority

Customers want to believe in leaders and salespeople. They look for credentials and experience, and prefer to buy from someone who evidently knows their product, and can sell them the most suitable type.

Liking

People are more inclined to buy from those who like, compliment, or appreciate them. Expressing approval ("That dress looks great on you!") encourages a potential buyer to spend money with that company.

resistant it is to change. The underlying base may be a feeling ("This sofa looks beautiful"), a belief ("It is made of environmentally friendly materials"), or a behavior ("My family has always bought this brand"). Persuasion that matches the consumer's base works best—an appeal about the look of the sofa will get the best response from a feelings-based attitude.

Persuasion—who, what, and to whom

Who (the persuader), what (the message), and to whom (the recipient) all factor into persuasion. The persuader needs to have credibility and it helps if they share

similarities with their audience. The message comes across as more positive if it contains two sides, covering the pros and cons of a product, rather than a one-sided list. Messages are strongest when they highlight consequences that are highly desirable, highly likely, and important. They should give as much detail as possible. The message can be repeated but not to the point of overexposure. Those with high intelligence are harder to persuade because they are better at evaluating the message. It is easier to persuade people who are already feeling happy because they link their mood to the product.

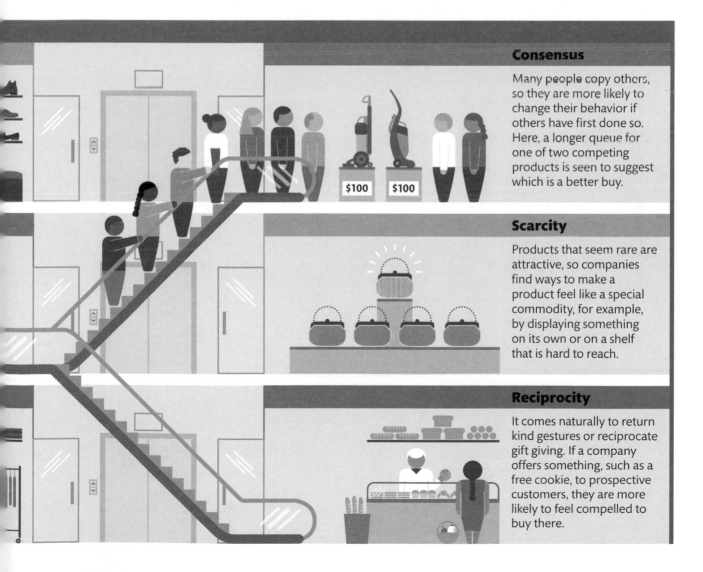

Consensus
Many people copy others, so they are more likely to change their behavior if others have first done so. Here, a longer queue for one of two competing products is seen to suggest which is a better buy.

$100 $100

Scarcity
Products that seem rare are attractive, so companies find ways to make a product feel like a special commodity, for example, by displaying something on its own or on a shelf that is hard to reach.

Reciprocity
It comes naturally to return kind gestures or reciprocate gift giving. If a company offers something, such as a free cookie, to prospective customers, they are more likely to feel compelled to buy there.

Consumer neuroscience

For companies, neuroscience—imaging the brain—adds another layer to understanding how consumers behave.

Neuromarketing

Neuroscientists study the structure and function of the brain and its impact on a person's thought processes and behavior. Applying their methods to company-specific market research is known as "neuromarketing." Large companies such as Google and Estée Lauder employ neuromarketing research companies, and many advertising agencies have neuromarketing divisions or partnerships.

Rather than relying on what consumers tell them—and many individuals either cannot or choose not to express their preferences—neuromarketers see how the brain activity of volunteers is stimulated by emotions, the key to deciding whether to buy something. The use of fMRI—functional magnetic resonance imaging, a technique for measuring brain activity—answers questions such as how specific brain circuits contribute to decision-making, and which areas of the brain encode preferences for certain products over others or for product features like brand labels. Research has shown, for instance, that activity increases in the mesolimbic (reward-linked) brain area when participants are shown cars they find attractive, and that people's decisions change when they are more hungry, stressed, or tired than usual.

Price psychology

Because fMRI scans produce a sequence of images, they show that people respond to a product before making a conscious or subconscious decision. So the order in which potential consumers receive information is important. Consumers respond differently depending on whether they learn what the price is before or after seeing the product. It shifts the focus of the decision from "Do I like it?" to "Is it worth it?" The first question is an emotional, intuitive feeling, whereas the second is rational, and so different areas of the brain are called into play.

Infographics

Condensing data or information into a chart or diagram helps it lodge in the consumer's mind. It is said that a good infographic is worth a thousand words.

Fonts

How appealing the letters look and how easy they are to read affect whether the consumer wants to read the message they contain.

Dorsolateral prefrontal cortex
This is linked to memory and has a role in recalling cultural associations that modify consumer behavior.

Ventromedial prefrontal cortex
Preferred brands activate this part of the brain more than other brands in the same category of goods.

Videos

Moving images can tell a story well and appeal to consumers who are used to getting their information from television and video clips on the Internet and social media.

Visual responses

Most people are highly visual, so the images and graphics used in marketing have a deep neurological impact. High-quality visuals draw consumers' attention and increase their engagement.

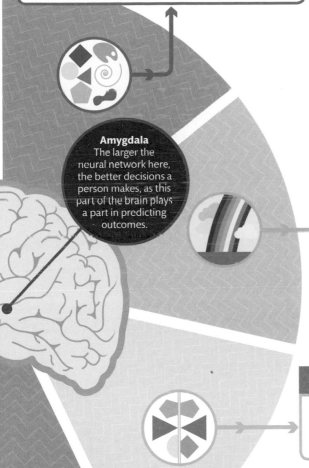

Shapes

Geometric shapes make a product look dependable and familiar, whereas organic forms suit a creative idea. Straight edges and corners seem more severe than curves and flowing lines.

Amygdala
The larger the neural network here, the better decisions a person makes, as this part of the brain plays a part in predicting outcomes.

The psychology of color

Colors, above all, communicate mood and emotion and provoke a reaction. Designers and marketers choose color to fuse the nonverbal mood with the message the company or brand wants to get across.

❯ **Green** Foliage and bright greens look restful and suggest a product is natural, healthy, restorative, reassuring, a new beginning, environmentally aware, and fresh. Darker, emerald green speaks of wealth.

❯ **Red** Bright red gets a fiery response: exciting, sexy, passionate, urgent, dramatic, dynamic, stimulating, adventurous, and motivating. In a dangerous context, it can give an aggressive, violent, or bloody impression.

❯ **Blue** Sky blue seems cool, dependable, serene, and suggestive of infinity, whereas bright blue crackles with energy. Dark blue has authority and is associated with professionals, uniforms, banks, and tradition.

❯ **Pink** While light pink comes across as innocent, delicate, romantic, and sweet—sometimes verging on the sentimental—bright pink, like red, is a hot, sensual, attention-seeking, energetic, and celebratory color.

❯ **Purple** Linked to intuition and imagination, purple is a contemplative, spiritual, and enigmatic color, especially on the bluer side. Red-purples imply something more thrilling—creative, witty, and exciting.

Symmetry and proportion

Symmetrical, well-proportioned images convey a sense of harmony, while asymmetry and distortion suggest dynamism or discord.

Memes

Wittily captioned photos, often ridiculing human behavior, are spread rapidly via social media. The combination of image and humor lodges an idea or a cultural symbol in the brain.

A signature color can increase brand recognition by

80%

The power of branding

A brand distinguishes a company, or its goods or services, from the competition. Its values may be expressed in images, color, logo, slogan, and jingle. The brand creates a bond between the supplier and the customer.

Identifying with a brand

Most people engage in identity-signaling behavior, such as driving a sports car, posting political articles on social media, or reading a Shakespeare play on a train. In today's market, brands are as important to the consumers who buy into them as they are to the companies making money from them, because consumers see their possessions as a part of themselves. Their buying behavior can be motivated by a need to belong, a need for self-expression, or a need for self-enhancement.

Iconic brands allow consumers to live out desires about their identity. They deliver on the promise of "what could be," rather than being limited by "what is." Consumers can be who they want just by changing what they buy, projecting their chosen self-image

Brand personalities

Companies try to project a distinct character through the personality of their brand. Most brands can be grouped into one of five broad personality types. Merchandise reflects the brand personality and so do its users—you are what you buy.

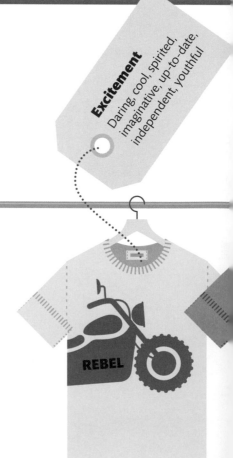

Excitement
Daring, cool, spirited, imaginative, up-to-date, independent, youthful

REBEL

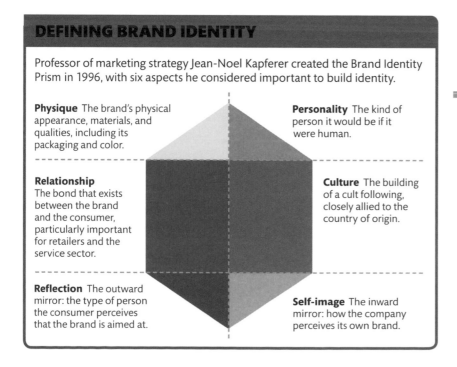

DEFINING BRAND IDENTITY

Professor of marketing strategy Jean-Noel Kapferer created the Brand Identity Prism in 1996, with six aspects he considered important to build identity.

Physique The brand's physical appearance, materials, and qualities, including its packaging and color.

Personality The kind of person it would be if it were human.

Relationship The bond that exists between the brand and the consumer, particularly important for retailers and the service sector.

Culture The building of a cult following, closely allied to the country of origin.

Reflection The outward mirror: the type of person the consumer perceives that the brand is aimed at.

Self-image The inward mirror: how the company perceives its own brand.

via the brands they select or identify with. Word of mouth influences brand loyalty, particularly with the rise of social media. For example, 29 percent of Facebook users follow a brand and 58 percent are reported to have "liked" a brand.

Engagement marketing

In traditional marketing, a brand is presented to the customer as fixed, to be either accepted or rejected. Engagement marketing encourages customer input as a brand is developed to help build long-term loyalty. The aim is to lure potential customers to the company's website or outlet, and then work hard to keep them there.

77%
of consumers make **purchases** based on **a brand** name

Sincerity
Down-to-earth, honest, family-oriented, wholesome, cheerful

Ruggedness
Tough, strong, outdoorsy, masculine

Competence
Reliable, hardworking, intelligent, corporate, successful, confident

Sophistication
Glamorous, good-looking, charming, smooth, feminine

CAREGIVER

EXPLORER

LEADER

SEDUCER

The power of celebrity

Companies often use celebrities as spokespeople. Someone famous can strengthen the bond between consumers and the brand.

In the media spotlight

How human behavior interacts with media and information technology comes under the heading of media psychology. This branch of psychology arose in the 1950s with the advent of the television. Today, it is increasingly relevant. The selling power of celebrities is of great interest to media psychologists—and to companies that want a figurehead for their brand.

People who are constantly in the public eye are seen as opinion formers, and can connect with potential and existing customers in a way that the brand alone cannot. Consumers, particularly in younger age groups, are increasingly obsessed with celebrity status.

For celebrities to endorse a brand effectively, they need to match both it and the target audience. And if there is a gap between brand and consumer, the celebrity must bridge it. The celebrity needs to have credibility, so they should share the values of the brand. This can mean working in the same profession or a linked one, for instance, a football player endorsing a make of football,

or someone who relies on their looks such as a model, actor, or pop singer promoting a shampoo brand. The company also needs to look at the celebrity's image, selecting someone known for their healthy lifestyle to back a new brand of organic fruit drink, for example. The ideal celebrity is already a brand user.

Physical attractiveness is linked to positive attitude, so the better looking the celebrity is, the more successful their endorsement will be. However, some media psychologists think that a highly attractive noncelebrity could be just as effective a spokesperson, thus saving the company a large amount of money.

Celebrity endorsements

The advantages of a famous spokesperson outweigh the disadvantages, as long as the match is right. Success breeds success, and the arrangement is usually of mutual advantage to company and celebrity.

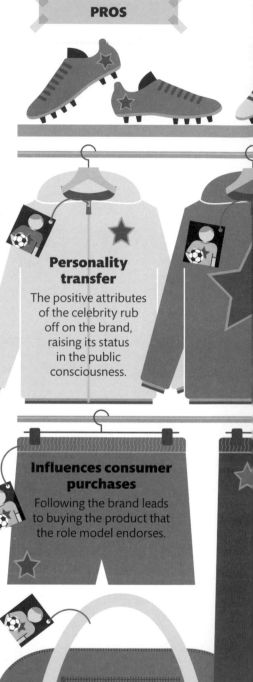

PROS

Personality transfer

The positive attributes of the celebrity rub off on the brand, raising its status in the public consciousness.

Influences consumer purchases

Following the brand leads to buying the product that the role model endorses.

45% of Americans believe celebrities help promotion

Instant brand awareness

As more people link the celebrity to the brand, it becomes more recognizable, widely known, and desirable.

Define brand image

The celebrity makes the brand clearer and better defined, and can even help refresh and rebrand a tired image.

New consumers

The celebrity's followers start to follow the brand so that they can be more like their idol.

Brand positioning

The positioning of the brand strengthens it over competing products.

Lasting publicity

The association with the celebrity lasts even after the endorsement deal ends.

CELEBRITY STALKING

Most stalkers of noncelebrities know their victims personally. Stalkers of celebrities, however, do not generally know the person that they target—they just think they do. Whether they are endorsing a brand or promoting themselves, the most successful stars give the impression that they are speaking personally to each member of their target audience. A mentally unstable individual can take this at face value. Dr. Sheridan, a forensic psychologist, says: "One of the most typical types of celebrity stalker is someone who genuinely believes that they have some kind of relationship with their target .... For them it's the real deal."

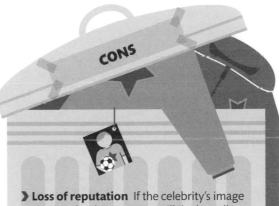

CONS

> **Loss of reputation** If the celebrity's image changes for the worse, so will the brand's reputation.

> **Loss of popularity** If the celebrity's star wanes, the brand will lose the loyalty of its followers as well.

> **Overexposure** If celebrities have multiple endorsements, consumers may follow their other brands rather than this one.

> **Overshadowing** Consumers focus on the celebrity rather than making a connection with the brand.

The psychology of sports

While coaches mainly focus on physical technique, sports and exercise psychologists are concerned with the behaviors, thought processes, and mental well-being of athletes. Sports psychologists work with individuals, helping them to manage the demands of their sport and improve their performance. Exercise psychologists have a broader role, promoting a healthy lifestyle and advising people on the psychological, social, and physical benefits of regular exercise.

Different aspects

Sports psychologists use various techniques to help performance, tailored to the individual's sport as well as their personality, motivation, stress, anxiety, and arousal. In team sports, the overall environment and group dynamics can also have an impact on athletic success.

Developing routines

The sports psychologist can help a player plan mental pregame and preshot routines and improve practice efficiency. This partly comes down to time management—using a planner, setting realistic goals, and maximizing practice time.

Self-talk

What the player says or thinks to themselves affects how they feel and act. Changing negative thoughts to positive ones improves performance.

I CAN SAVE THIS!

Visualization

Creating a picture of successful play in the mind is useful for mental preparation, anxiety control, attention, building self-confidence, learning new skills, and injury recovery. Visualization works best in a relaxed, quiet setting where the athlete can practice creating vivid and controllable images.

Goal setting

Setting goals helps motivation, focusing attention on the aspects of performance that are most in need of improvement.

WHAT DO SPORTS AND EXERCISE PSYCHOLOGISTS DO?

The approaches that sports psychologists take can help athletes and team players before, during, and after performance, on and off the playing field. Exercise psychologists motivate the general public.

❯ Performance fears
Teach techniques to improve focus under stress and cope with anger and anxiety.

❯ Mental skills
Help players improve confidence, composure, focus, trust in ability to perform; communication with teammates; and motivation levels.

❯ Recovery from injury
Psychological help tolerating pain, getting used to being on the sidelines, and maintaining a physical therapy regime to help players cope with the pressure of returning to their skill level of pre-injury performance.

❯ Motivating the young
Exercise psychologists go into schools to help PE teachers and coaches encourage children to take up sports and make it fun. Can also help motivate older groups to lead more active lifestyles.

"**Champions** are made from **something** ... deep inside them—a **desire**, a **dream**, a **vision**."

Muhammad Ali, world heavyweight champion boxer

Team building
Particularly useful at the start of a season, team building helps a group work cohesively and sets out group objectives, trust, and respect. A free and open environment, active communication, and assertiveness training all contribute to success.

Managing anxiety
When arousal is too high or too low for optimal performance, a sports psychologist can help an athlete to manage anxiety, stress, and anger using techniques such as breathing exercises and meditation.

Improving skills

An understanding of the psychology behind learning skills helps an athlete hone their technique during practice sessions so that they perform at their highest level in competitive play.

Learning a new skill

All sports are based on skills and techniques that require training and practice. There are different ways of learning and developing skills, depending on their complexity. Some skills are best learned by breaking them down into individual components and practicing each part separately.

Called part learning, this technique is good for complex skills such as a tennis serve that can be split into component parts. Once the athlete has worked on each element individually, they can put the whole skill back together and practice it all at once. Other skills are best learned and practiced in their entirety, from start to finish.

This method, known as whole learning, is good for skills such as a cartwheel that cannot easily be separated into subparts.

Learning plateau

Learning a new skill starts out slowly because everything is unfamiliar. Learners then enter a phase of steep acceleration as the

Continuum of skills

Open and closed skills exist along a continuum, with most actions falling between the two extremes. Tennis players have to master both open and closed skills, because they initiate some actions but also have to respond to their opponent's shots.

CLOSED SKILLS
Serving in tennis is a closed skill. It is carried out in a stable and predictable environment, and the player knows exactly what to do and when to do it. The action of serving the ball has a clear beginning and end.

Turning the parts into a whole

Serving a tennis ball involves a complex series of six moves that the player can part learn on their own. Once the player has established the skill for the first four components, they can practice serving using the whole method, enabling them to get a feel for the technique in its entirety.

1. Grip the ball loosely with your fingertips.

2. Bounce the ball 2–4 times.

3. Toss the ball up in the air, slightly in front of you.

"The sky has no limits. Neither do I."

Usain Bolt, Olympic sprint champion

physical movements become more familiar, rehearsed, and automatic. Finally, there is a plateau in the learning curve, when the learner stops progressing because they are bored or because the next stage seems too complex. To move on and up from the plateau, the learner or their coach needs to reset the goal, ensure physical readiness for the next step,

shorten practice times to avoid fatigue, or break down the skill into parts.

Some skills are totally within the learner's control (closed) and others require the player to react (open), for instance, by returning a ball (below). Different types of practice are suited to each type of skill, but the more enjoyable the training is, the faster the learner moves on.

PHASES OF LEARNING

Athletes pass through three stages of learning when they are trying to master a new skill.

❭ **Cognitive or understanding phase** Performing the skill requires all of the athlete's attention. It is a process of trial and error, with a low success rate.

❭ **Associative or verbal motor phase** Performance is more consistent in this stage as motor programs (ways in which the brain controls movements) form. Simpler elements of the skill now look fluent, but more complex elements require attention. The athlete is also more aware of what is going wrong.

❭ **Autonomous or motor phase** Performance is now consistent and fluid, motor programs are stored in the long-term memory, and the skill is automatic, requiring little or no conscious effort. Spare attention can be focused on opponents and tactics.

OPEN SKILLS
Receiving the ball in tennis is an open skill, so the player must cope with a changing and unpredictable environment. Weather, terrain, and opponents are all variables to which an athlete might need to adapt.

FIXED OR VARIABLE PRACTICE

Sometimes known as drills, fixed practice involves repeatedly practicing a whole skill in order to strengthen muscle memory, making the skill more natural and automatic. This type of practice works best with closed skills.

Best used for open skills, variable practice involves performing a skill in varying situations. This helps an athlete to build up a set of responses for multiple scenarios to use in competitive play.

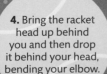

4. Bring the racket head up behind you and then drop it behind your head, bending your elbow.

5. Hit the ball at its highest point with the center of the racket head.

6. Follow through by bringing your racket down near your opposite foot.

Keeping motivated

Athletes have to keep motivated. Without the continuous desire and drive to improve their performance, physical preparation and psychological factors such as focus and confidence fall apart.

How it works

Athletic training, conditioning, and competition require self-discipline and can be stressful. To set themselves realistic goals, athletes must maintain high levels of motivation, particularly when confronted with fatigue or failure. This motivation can be intrinsic (internal and personal) or extrinsic (based on external rewards).

When people participate in sports or exercise for the love of the activity or a sense of personal fulfillment, they are intrinsically motivated. Since this motivation reflects deeply held attitudes, it tends to be consistent and leads to better focus and enhanced performance. Making mistakes is less stressful for athletes who are intrinsically motivated because they focus on improving their skills rather than simply winning.

People who participate in sports or exercise in order to gain tangible rewards or praise or to avoid negative consequences are extrinsically motivated. They focus on the outcomes of competitions rather than the rewards of training and preparation. Although extrinsic motivation is less consistent than intrinsic, it can be a powerful driver of competitive performance.

SMART goals

However a player is motivated, their goals are achievable only if they are SMART—specific, measurable, achievable, realistic, and time-bound. One such goal might be to run 3 miles (5 km) in 30 minutes after six weeks of timed practice runs.

> "... you need to **find something** to hold on to, something **to motivate you** ... to **inspire you.**"
>
> Tony Dorsett, former running back

Intrinsic motivation

Intrinsically motivated athletes take part in sports for personal reasons, such as enjoyment, the challenge of competition, the desire to perform well and succeed, and skill improvement. In this case, the sheer thrill of diving is the motivation.

Staying motivated

Motivation is crucial to make athletes practice regularly, develop their skills, and perform to the best of their ability. Both internal and external factors drive motivation and setting regular goals maintains it.

REPUTATION

POINTS

PRIZES

AROUSAL THEORY OF MOTIVATION

Arousal means the intensity of motivation, from boredom to anxiety or excitement. Outgoing people need high arousal to feel excited about sports, while shyer athletes perform better at lower arousal levels.

> **Hull's Drive Theory** Performance improves with arousal levels. Top athletes perform better under pressure due to their superior skills and ability to manage stress.

> **Inverted U Law** Arousal improves performance, but only up to a point.

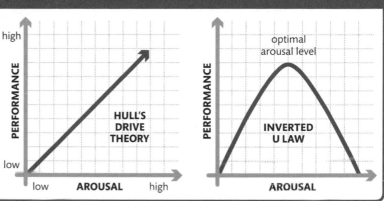

TEAM MOTIVATION AND SOCIAL LOAFING

Team performance does not necessarily improve as team size increases because of a concept called social loafing. Participants tend to contribute less to the group's goal when there are many people involved than they would if they were doing the same task on their own. This can create conflict and have a negative impact on the team dynamic.

For example, if motivated team members repeatedly feel others are relying on them to do most of the work, they may deliberately reduce their workload or even stop collaborating so less productive members do not exploit them.

To overcome this problem, a coach may use performance evaluation to define each player's role, strengths, and weaknesses, and how they can individually benefit the team. This helps to ensure that everyone on the team is working toward a common goal.

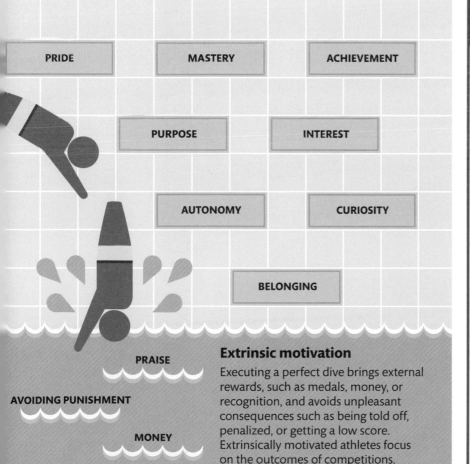

Extrinsic motivation

Executing a perfect dive brings external rewards, such as medals, money, or recognition, and avoids unpleasant consequences such as being told off, penalized, or getting a low score. Extrinsically motivated athletes focus on the outcomes of competitions.

Getting in the zone

An optimal psychological state occurs when there is a balance between the level of challenge posed by an activity and a person's ability to meet that challenge. It is called flow.

What is flow?

Hungarian psychologist Mihaly Csikszentmihalyi identified a state "in which people are so involved in an activity that nothing else seems to matter; the experience is so enjoyable that people will continue to do it even at great cost, for the sheer sake of doing it." He defined this elusive state as "flow."

Flow is one of the richest and most performance-enhancing experiences for an athlete. Sometimes described as being "in the zone," this state of mind occurs when athletes feel fully engaged in their performance, lose their perception of time, are able to concentrate on the moment without any distraction, feel challenged but not overwhelmed, and have a sense of being connected to something that is greater than themselves. In a state of flow, performance becomes consistent, automatic, and exceptional.

Achieving flow

Whatever their level, athletes can find flow. Coaches can create an environment that is conducive to flow by encouraging commitment and achievement, setting teams and individuals clear goals, presenting athletes with activities that challenge them but are within their capacity to perform, and offering consistent and nonjudgmental feedback.

Prefrontal cortex switches off

Higher thought processes such as problem-solving and self-criticism are temporarily deactivated.

Brain in flow

The brain experiences various changes in the flow state, enabling a person to be completely absorbed in the task and perform exceptionally well without conscious thought.

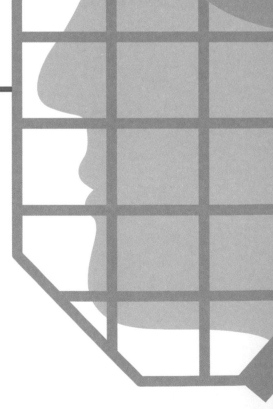

ACHIEVING FLOW

> **Choose an activity you love** If you look forward to a task, you will find it easier to lose yourself in it.

> **Make sure it is challenging, but not too hard** The task should be challenging enough to require your full concentration, but it should not be beyond your capabilities.

> **Find your peak time** You can enter flow more easily during a time of peak energy.

> **Eliminate distractions** Clearing away distractions allows you to focus completely on the task.

Neurochemicals are released

The brain releases a series of performance-enhancing neurochemicals.

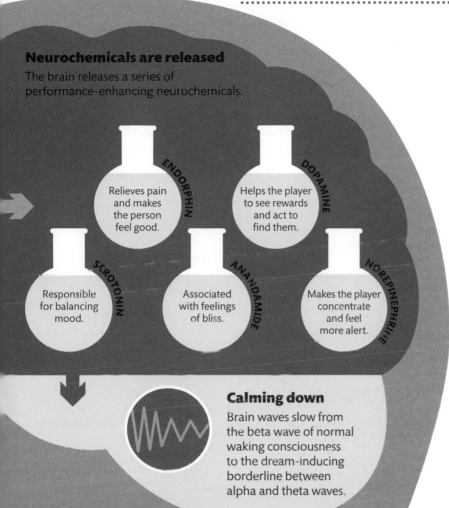

ENDORPHIN
Relieves pain and makes the person feel good.

DOPAMINE
Helps the player to see rewards and act to find them.

SEROTONIN
Responsible for balancing mood.

ANANDAMIDE
Associated with feelings of bliss.

NOREPINEPHRINE
Makes the player concentrate and feel more alert.

Calming down

Brain waves slow from the beta wave of normal waking consciousness to the dream-inducing borderline between alpha and theta waves.

Brain waves

Synchronized electrical pulses from neurons communicating with each other produce brain waves. They are divided into speed bands (Hz). The faster the speed, the more alert the person is.

GAMMA
31–100 Hz

BETA
16–30 Hz

ALPHA
8–15 Hz

THETA
4–7 Hz

DELTA
0.1–3 Hz

TEAMWORK AND FLOW

Sometimes, strong group members can help to bring about a flow state for the whole team. Flow is also critical in sports partnerships, such as doubles tennis, where the two must work as a unit, and even more so in figure skating, for example, where a mistake by one partner could make the other fall.

❯ **Unity** and emotional connection between teammates provides the positive feedback that helps lift them to high performance levels.

❯ **Harmony** between team members means they communicate more successfully than normal.

❯ **The successful interaction** between all members of a team is essential in sports such as rowing, in which if one teammate is out of rhythm or failing to keep up, the whole team suffers. Regular group practice is key.

JOINT EFFORT in sports such as synchronized swimming, where the parts form a greater visual whole, is vital as team members rely utterly on each other to reach the zone where perfection seems effortless.

Performance anxiety

Nerves afflict many athletes, causing them to tense up and perform below their optimal level. There are psychological techniques to help manage such anxiety.

What is it?

A certain level of anxiety is normal and healthy before a match or contest, and actually improves performance. However, intense anxiety that continues during the contest itself can cause the athlete to underperform or even "freeze," damaging self-esteem and ultimately hindering a career. Sometimes called "choking" or "stage fright"—performance anxiety can affect actors and musicians, too—physical symptoms include a racing heartbeat, dry mouth, tight throat, trembling, and nausea. This is the fight-or-flight response—a flooding of adrenaline that puts the body in a state of high arousal. Psychological symptoms include a sudden, uncharacteristic reluctance to compete or loss of interest in the sport, fatigue, sleep disturbance, and even depression.

Performance anxiety can be triggered by self-consciousness and overthinking the physical moves. Many actions are best performed outside conscious awareness—instead relying on muscle memory—such as running, swinging a bat, or playing the violin. To achieve optimal performance, parts of the brain should be on automatic pilot rather than consciously monitoring the action.

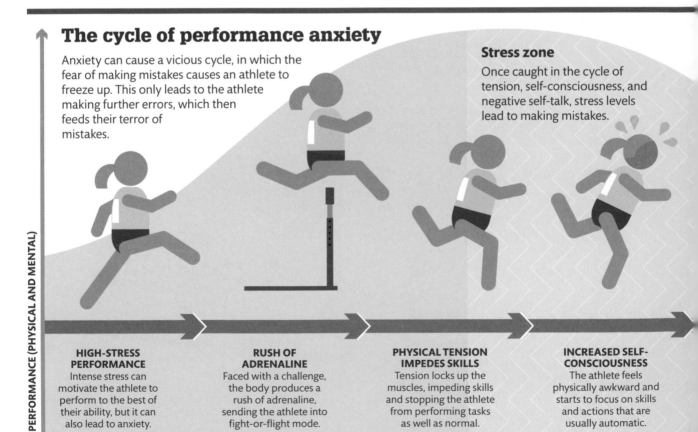

The cycle of performance anxiety

Anxiety can cause a vicious cycle, in which the fear of making mistakes causes an athlete to freeze up. This only leads to the athlete making further errors, which then feeds their terror of mistakes.

Stress zone

Once caught in the cycle of tension, self-consciousness, and negative self-talk, stress levels lead to making mistakes.

PERFORMANCE (PHYSICAL AND MENTAL)

AROUSAL LEVEL

HIGH-STRESS PERFORMANCE
Intense stress can motivate the athlete to perform to the best of their ability, but it can also lead to anxiety.

RUSH OF ADRENALINE
Faced with a challenge, the body produces a rush of adrenaline, sending the athlete into fight-or-flight mode.

PHYSICAL TENSION IMPEDES SKILLS
Tension locks up the muscles, impeding skills and stopping the athlete from performing tasks as well as normal.

INCREASED SELF-CONSCIOUSNESS
The athlete feels physically awkward and starts to focus on skills and actions that are usually automatic.

Who can help?

Working with a coach or sports psychologist can help a player to control the tendency to "choke" when performing. One important factor in overcoming the anxiety is the person's level of confidence in their skills and abilities. By highlighting successes and celebrating efforts—and by avoiding adding too much performance pressure—a coach or sports psychologist can help build self-confidence and self-belief. Over time this approach can help to prevent, minimize, and counteract performance anxiety.

MANAGING PERFORMANCE ANXIETY

While coaches and psychologists can help manage performance anxiety, there are also many techniques and practices that athletes can do on their own to reduce anxiety.

⟩ **Normalize the nervousness** Everyone feels some performance anxiety—it is normal.

⟩ **Prepare and rehearse** Hone muscle memory and so build up confidence.

⟩ **Visualize a successful performance** Mentally walk through every step and imagine an experience free of pain and anxiety.

⟩ **Positive self-talk** Challenge negative thoughts, and replace them with positive ones.

⟩ **Take care of yourself** Exercise, eat healthily, and allow time for plenty of sleep before performance day.

⟩ **Remember you are there to have fun** Shift the focus from your performance to your pure enjoyment of the sport.

"Never let the fear of striking out get in your way."

George Herman "Babe" Ruth, American baseball legend

FREEZING AND INCREASED ERRORS
As anxiety and tension mount, the athlete freezes up and cannot carry out their activity, leading to more errors.

NEGATIVE INNER MONOLOGUE
Self-talk becomes more negative and critical, focusing on mistakes and perceived weaknesses.

MORE ERRORS
The negative inner monologue increases both anxiety and distraction from the task at hand, causing even more errors.

Arousal levels

Up to a point, increased arousal can fuel good performance. However, if anxiety rises above that zone of optimal arousal, it causes self-doubt, freezing up, and errors.

Psychometric tests

First developed for use in educational psychology at the start of the 20th century, psychometric tests are popular today with employers who use them to analyze the suitability of new recruits.

What are they?

French psychologist Alfred Binet devised the first modern intelligence test in 1905 in response to a law that made it compulsory for children in France to attend school from the age of 6 to 14. Some children with learning difficulties were struggling to cope with the demands of the curriculum. The education system needed a way of measuring the extent of these difficulties so they could determine which children needed to receive special schooling. Binet set out to formulate tests that assessed innate ability and not scholastic achievement. He tested his methods on his two daughters, as he was intrigued by the different ways in which they explored and responded to the world.

Helped by his colleague Théodore Simon, Binet developed 30 tests, some for each age group, to be given under controlled conditions. They ranged in difficulty from, for example, counting the number of petals on a picture of a flower to drawing an image from memory. The aim was for the child to pass as many tests within their age group as possible, and reach a standard level of competence for their age.

Psychologist Lewis Terman at Stanford University adapted the tests, publishing the Stanford-Binet Intelligence Scales in 1916. These measures formed the basis of IQ tests for much of the 20th century. Psychometric tests today still owe much to the French–American work, although their scope has broadened, and they are more widely used to aid adult recruitment and career choice than to test children's intelligence. Employers use psychometric tests to screen out unsuitable candidates and to match individuals to the most appropriate occupations. Therefore it is important that they have confidence in the accuracy of the tests.

MAKING THE TESTS FAIR

As psychometric test results can directly affect whether someone gets the job they want, they have to conform to rigorous standards. Tests should be:

> **Objective** There must be no scope for the marker's subjective views to affect the score.

> **Standardized** Test conditions must be the same for all participants. There is a strict time limit for aptitude tests, usually a minute per question. However, personality questionnaires may not have a time limit, as accuracy and honesty are more important than speed.

> **Reliable** There should not be any factors that could skew the results of the tests.

> **Predictive** The tests must make an accurate prediction of how the participant will perform in real life.

> **Nondiscriminatory** The tests must not put any participant at a disadvantage on the basis of, for example, their gender or ethnicity.

Types of test

Most employers who use psychometric tests include a personality questionnaire to assess a candidate's motivation, enthusiasm, and fitness for a particular working environment. As more jobs are now customer focused and there are generally fewer tiers of management, "soft skills" of communication and getting along with people, which personality tests can reveal, are increasingly important. The employer may also use aptitude tests to measure specific intellectual abilities against a standard score.

80%

of the top companies in the UK and US use psychometric testing when recruiting staff

Aptitude tests

The participant answers multiple-choice questions (often online) under exam conditions on a range of subjects or on an area specific to the job they have applied for. Verbal, numeric, and abstract reasoning questions appear in most general aptitude tests to assess communication skills, numeracy, and ability to learn new skills, whereas other tests are more specialized.

 Verbal ability Spelling; grammar; working by analogy; ability to follow instructions and evaluate arguments—for most jobs.

 Numeric ability Arithmetic; number sequences; basic mathematics—for most jobs. Interpretation of charts, graphs, data, or statistics—for managerial posts.

 Abstract reasoning Identifying the logic of a pattern to complete the sequence (the patterns are usually pictorial)—for most jobs.

 Spatial ability Manipulating 2-D shapes; visualizing 3-D shapes in 2-D images—for jobs requiring good spatial skills.

 Mechanical reasoning Assessing understanding of physical and mechanical principles—for jobs in the military, emergency services, crafts, technical areas, and engineering.

 Fault diagnosis Assessing logical ability to find faults and repair them in electronic and mechanical systems—for technical jobs.

 Data checking Assessing speed and accuracy of error detection—for clerical and data-input jobs.

 Work sample Real-world simulation exercise; participating in a group meeting; giving a presentation—specific to the job.

> # "Psychometrics provides something that we as humans are not very good at—objective, unbiased, reliable, and valid measures of people's traits and characteristics."

David Hughes, lecturer in organizational psychology at Manchester Business School

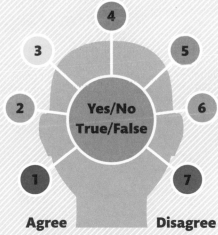

Agree   **Disagree**

Personality questionnaires

The participant responds to a series of statements such as "I enjoy parties and other social occasions" with Yes/No or True/False, or on a five- or seven-point scale of Agree/Disagree. There is not a right or wrong answer and it is best to reply genuinely. Someone who does not enjoy parties but states that they do may find themselves in a client-facing role, for example, for which they are wholly unsuited.

Index

Page numbers in **bold** refer to main entries.

12-step program 117

A

absence, moments of 86
Abu Ghraib prison 208
acceptance and commitment therapy *see* ACT
accidents, prevention of **192–193**
acetylcholine 28
achievement-oriented leadership 184
ACT (acceptance and commitment therapy) **126**
actions, responsibility for 133
active listening 164
acute confusional state *see* delirium
acute stress reaction *see* ASR
adaptation 215
adaptations, psychological 22
addictions 36, **82**, 117
ADHD (attention deficit hyperactivity disorder) 8, **66–67**, 100
adjustment disorder **64**
Adler, Alfred 15
adolescents *see* teenagers
adrenaline 29, 46, 62, 159, 244
advertising **224**
age, and identity 147
aggression 70, 78, 80, 85, 102, 156, 199
agitation 73
agoraphobia **50**
agreeableness 151
Ainsworth, Mary 154, 157
airline safety 188, 189, 192–193
alcohol abuse 38, 62, 75, **80–81**, 115
alerts, visual and audible 190
Allport, Gordon 13, 212–213
alternative therapies 115
alters 86
Alzheimer's disease 76
amnesia, dissociative **89**
Amok syndrome **108–109**
amygdala 26, 32, 33, 62, 135, 231
anandamide 243
anemia 60, 95
anger 33, 44, 62, 94, 105, 127, 133, 199, 237
anger management 85, 137, 203
animal phobias 49
animal-assisted therapy **137**
anorexia nervosa **90–91**, 92

anthropometry **189**
anti-anxiety drugs 142–143
antidepressants 142–143
antilocution 212
antipsychotics 142–143
antisocial PD **104**, 105
anxiety 46–47, 51, 56–57, 189
  managing 237
  performance **244–245**
anxiety disorders **46–55**
appearance, excessive concern about 59
appraisals, workplace 176, **181**
aptitude tests 247
Aristotle 24
arousal 82, 98, 227, 245
  theory of motivation **241**
arts-based therapies **137**
AS *see* Asperger's syndrome
ASD (autism spectrum disorder) 66, **68–69**, 96, 97
Asperger's syndrome (AS) **69**
ASR (acute stress reaction) **63**, 64
assault 63, 213
assertiveness training 123
assessment centers 179
athletes **236–245**
attachment
  psychology of **156–157**
  science of love **158–159**
  styles **156**
  theories of 65, **154**
attention
  and engineering display 190, 191
  and memory 30
attention deficit hyperactivity disorder *see* ADHD
attitudes
  changing consumer 228–229
  and culture 215
attraction
  body language 160
  chemical **159**
attribution theory 204
authoritarianism 210, 212
authority
  and consumer behavior 228
  obedience to 208, 210
autism spectrum disorder *see* ASD
autonomy 218
availability heuristic 204
aversion therapy 128
avoidant PD **106**, 107

B

babies, attachment 156–157
baby blues 42–43
Baddeley, Alan 31
Bandura, Albert 169, 172
basal ganglia 101
Bay of Pigs invasion **208**
BDD (body dysmorphic disorder) **59**
Beck, Aaron 13, 124
behavior
  and brain activity **24–25**
  consumer **226–227**
  and cultural factors 215
  and emotions **32–33**
  and irrational thoughts **122–123**
  learned **16–17**
  and unconscious mind 14
  unethical **208–209**
behavior cycles 125
behavioral assessments 37
behavioral problems 175
behavioral psychology 13, **16–17**, 150
behavioral strategies 123
behavioral therapy 122, **124**, 125
behaviorism 13, **16–17**
behaviorist theory 150, 151
"being"/growth needs 153
belonging, sense of 152–153, 210
bereavement 38, 46, 62, 63, 64
beta blockers 63
biases
  cognitive **21**
  juries 200, 201
  performance ratings 18
Binet, Alfred 246
binge-eating disorder 90, **94**
binge-purge cycle 92
biographical information 179
biological factors 16, 17, 18, 150
biological psychology 13, **22–23**
biopsychosocial model **114–115**
biotherapies **142–143**
bipolar disorder **40–41**, 72, 75, 142
birth complications 70
birth order 139
birthweight, low 66
blame, of out-group 211
blood-injection-injury phobias 49
body
  disconnection from 88
  mind-body dualism 25
  somatic therapies **135**
  and stress **115**

body awareness, mindful 129
body image, eating disorders 90–95
body language, and attraction 159, 160
bonding, with primary caregiver 65
borderline PD **105**
bottom-up profiling 198
boundaries, setting clear 67
Bowen, Murray 139
Bowlby, John 154, 156
brain
    biotherapies **142–143**
    consumer neuroscience **230–231**
    in flow state 242–243
    functioning of **24–29**
    information processing 20–21
    learning 168–169
    and love 155, 159
    mapping **26–27**
    survival reactions 62
    teenage 22
brain stem 27
brain tumors 75
brain waves **243**
brainstorming 18
brand 163, 225, **232–233**
    celebrity endorsements **234–235**
Brand Identity Prism **232**
breathing
    difficulties 48
    mindful 129
    techniques 134, 135
Broca's area 25, 27
bulimia nervosa 90, **92–93**
bullying 38, 90
business 167
Byrne, Donn 161
bystander effect 222–223

C

cancer 80, 112, 115
carbohydrates 45
cardiovascular system 115
catalepsy 73
cataplexy 99
catatonia **73**
catatonic schizophrenia 70
CBT (cognitive behavioral therapy) 13, **125**
    in prisons 202, 203
    third wave **126**
CCTV 223
celebrity endorsements **234–235**
cerebellum 27
cerebral cortex 24, 26, 31, 33
cerebral hemispheres **24**, 25, 26
cerebral palsy 68, 96, 100
change
    consumer behavior **228–229**
    and empowerment 218, 219

guidelines to facilitating **187**
    workplace 177, **186–187**
Charcot, Jean-Martin 119
Chavis, David M. 216
checking, continual 56, 57
chemical imbalance 23
childbirth 38, 42
childhood fluency disorder 96, **97**
children
    ADHD **66–67**
    adjustment disorder **64**
    ASD **68–69**
    Asperger's syndrome **69**
    attachment 154, **156–157**
    communications disorders **96–97**
    development 17, 21
    DMDD **44**
    high functioning autism **69**
    identity formation **148–149**
    learning 168–169
    neglected/abused 141
    protection of 223
    pyromania **85**
    reactive attachment disorder 65
    selective mutism **55**
    separation anxiety disorder **54**
    see also families
choice
    honest 153
    paradox of **226–227**
"choking" 244, 245
chronic traumatic encephalopathy see CTE
class, and identity 147
classical conditioning **16**, 124
classroom
    disruption in 175
    educational theories 168
    structure 167
    teacher effectiveness in 172
claustrophobia **51**
cleft lip/palate 96
clinical interviews 37
clinical psychologists **113**
Clore, Gerald 161
closed skills 239
CLT see Cognitive Learning Theory
clumsiness 67
cognitive appraisal 227
cognitive and behavioral therapies 116,
    122–129
    methods used in **128**
cognitive behavioral therapy see CBT
cognitive bias **21**
cognitive defusion 126
cognitive interview technique **196**
Cognitive Learning Theory (CLT) 168–169
cognitive processing therapy see CPT
cognitive psychology 13, **20–21**
cognitive therapy 122, **124**, 125
cognitive training 17

collaborative therapy **123**
collective unconscious 120
collectivism 19
color, psychology of 190, 231
commitment
    consumers 228
    and love 158
    in relationships 162, 163
communication
    and change 187
    problems with 68, 71
    in relationships 154, **164**
communication disorders **96–97**
community psychologists 217, 218
community psychology 13, **214–223**
    empowerment **218–219**
    how community works 216–217
    safety in the community **222–223**
    urban communities **220–221**
compartmentalization 118
compulsions 56–57, 82, 84, 90, 107, 117, 125,
    128
computer science 20–21
computer/internet addiction 82
concentration 38, 52, 62, 63, 66, 67, 71, 76,
    77, 79
conditioning **16–17**
confabulation 30
confessions, false 200
conflict, in relationships 154
confusion 42, 76, 77, 78, 79, 80, 98, 99, 148,
    149
conscientiousness 151
conscious mind **14–15**
    emotional response 32–33
consensus 229
consumer prediction 226
consumer psychology 13, **224–235**
    and brand 163, 225, **232–233**
    changing consumer behavior **228–229**
    consumer neuroscience **230–231**
    power of celebrity **234–235**
    understanding consumer behavior **226–227**
consumer relationships 163
contamination, fear of 56
contempt 165
contextual therapy **141**
control
    eating disorders 90
    impaired 81
    sense of being controlled 70
coping mechanisms 128
copralalia 101
cosmetic surgery 59
counseling psychologists **113**
counselor 112
couples therapy **154**
courtrooms 194, **200–201**
CPT (cognitive processing therapy) **127**
crime, and community safety 222–223

criminal activity 80
criminal behavior **198–199**, 202
criminal investigation 194, **196–199**
criticism 165
    constructive 181
cross-cultural psychology **215**
crowding 221
Csikszentmihalyi, Mihalyi 242
CT scans 13, 26
CTE (chronic traumatic encephalopathy) **78**
cultural psychology 13, **214–215**
culture
    and community 214, 215
    cycle 216–217
    and identity 147
customer profiling **227**
customs 215
cyberbullying 223
cybercrime **195**
cyclothymia 40

D

danger
    anticipation of 52
    poor sense of 66
Darwin, Charles 22
dating 155, **160–161**
dating coaches **161**
Davis, Keith 161
DBT (dialectical behavior therapy) **126**
death, inevitability of 133
decision-making 20, 52, 62, 73, 77, 183, 189
    political 205, **208–209**
defense mechanisms **15**, 86, 118, 153
defendants 194, 200, 201
defensiveness 165
"deficit" needs 153
dehumanization 202, 208, 211
delirium (acute confusional state) **79**
delusional disorder **74–75**
delusions 40, 42, 70, 72, 74–75, 76, 79, 103,
    108
dementia **76–77**, 78, 79
    drugs for 142–143
denial 15, 80, 118, 199
dependent PD **106**, 107
depersonalization **88**, 202
depression 18, 22, **38–39**, 40–41, 42–43, 45
    as symptom of disorders 48, 53, 58, 59, 63,
        65, 66, 68, 73, 75, 76, 80, 83, 84, 90, 92,
        94, 102, 105, 108–109
derealization **88**
Descartes, René 12, 24, 25
desensitization, systematic 128
detachment 65
developmental psychology 13, **146–153**
diagnosis **36–37**
dialectical behavior therapy see DBT

DID (dissociative identity disorder) **86–87**
dieting, excessive 59, 90–91, 92
differences, individual 22
directive leadership 185
discrimination 210–213
disgust 33, 73, 94, 108, 207
disinhibited social engagement disorder 65
disinhibition effect 223
disorders, psychological **34–109**
    diagnosing **36–37**
disorganized schizophrenia 70
disorientation 42, 98, 99
display, design and perception **190–191**
dispositional theory 150
dispositionism 209
disruptive mood dysregulation disorder see
    DMDD
dissociative amnesia **89**
dissociative behavior 63
dissociative disorders 86–89
dissociative identity disorder see DID
distress tolerance 126
diversity **217**
DMDD (disruptive mood dysregulation
    disorder) **44**
DNA 22, 23
dopamine 29, 40, 66, 70, 143, 159, 168, 243
dorsolateral prefrontal cortex 27, 230
Down syndrome 68, 96, **108–109**
dreams 14, 98
    analysis 118, 119, 120
    recurrent 63
drug abuse 22, 38, 62, 65, 75, **80–81**, 115
drug therapy 13, **142–143**
dualism 24, 25
Duck, Steve 164
dyadic developmental therapy **141**
dyscalculia 174
dysgraphia 174
dyslexia 174
dyspraxia 108, 174

E

eating disorders **90–95**
eating, mindful 129
echolalia 73, 101
echopraxia 73
ecosystems 215, 216
ECT (electroconvulsive therapy) 13, 142, 143
education
    cognitive psychology 21
    and identity 146
educational psychology 12, **166–175**
    assessing problems **174–175**
    educational theories **168–171**
    psychology of teaching **172–173**
    psychometric tests 246
EFT see emotional freedom technique

ego 14–15
    states 121
elections 200–207
electroconvulsive therapy see ECT
elimination disorders in children **108–109**
EMDR (eye movement desensitization and
    reprocessing) **136**
emergencies 222, 223
emotion-focused therapy **134**
emotional freedom technique (EFT) **135**
emotional regulation 126
emotionally focused therapy **134**
emotions **32–33**
    and consumer behavior 226–227
    flattened 71
    inability to control or express 76
    and memory 30
    and voting **207**
empathy
    difficulty with 77, 104, 199
    loss of 208
    therapists 121, 131, 132
    with victims 202, 203
employment see workplace
empowerment **218–219**
empty chair technique 133
endorphins 29, 243
enhanced thinking skills see ETS
environment
    and community 215, **220–221**
    disconnection from 88
environmental factors 22, 23, 38, 46, 48, 65,
        70, 80, 82, 88, 142, 148, 150, 151, 154
environmental psychology 221
environmental stimuli 20, 169
equipment design 188, **190–191**
ergonomics **189**
Erikson, Erik 15, 148, 149, 150
erotomanic delusions 74
error see human error
esteem 152–153
estrogen 159
ethnic conflict 210
ethnocentrism 212
ETS (enhanced thinking skills) 202
evil, disposition for 208–209
evolutionary psychology **22**
evolutionary theory 150
excoriation **60**
exercise 39, 168
    excessive 59, 82, 92
    psychology of 236–237
exercise addiction 82
existence, givens of **133**
existential therapy **133**
expert witnesses 195, **201**
exposure therapy 128
extermination 211, 213
extrinsic motivation 240, 241
extroversion 151

extroverts 120, 178
eye contact 55, 68, 71, 179, 181
eye movement desensitization and
       reprocessing see EMDR
Eysenck, Hans 150

F

facial expressions
   conscious and reflex 33
   frozen 55
fake news 207
families
   conflicts 64
   dynamics 138, 139, **141**
   and identity 147
   imbalances 141
   systemic therapies **138–141**
family systems therapy **130**
fantasy 133
fatigue 42, 43, 45, 71, 99, 108, 197, 239, 240,
       244
fear 33
feedback 181
fetal alcohol syndrome 68
fight-or-flight response 32, 46, 63, 135, 244
fires, pyromania **85**
Fisher, Helen 159
flashbacks 62, 63
flow (state) 242
fMRI 26, 230
fonts 230
food, eating disorders 90–95
forensic psychology 13, **194–203**
   courtrooms **200–201**
   criminal investigation **196–199**
   prisons **202–203**
forgetfulness 67, 86
Four Horsemen of the Apocalypse 164, **165**
free association 118, 119
free will 16, 18, 133
freedom, and responsibility 133
"freezing" 244, 245
Freud, Sigmund 13, **14–15**, 16, 23, 118, 119,
       150, 156
frontal lobe 26, 27, 33
fronto-temporal dementia 76
fugues, dissociative 89
fulfillment 152–153
fundamental attribution error 204

G

GABA 29
GAD (generalized anxiety disorder) **52**, 59
Gagne, Robert 168
gambling disorder **83**
gastrointestinal system 115

gender
   discrimination 212
   and identity 147
gender dysphoria **108–109**
general medical practitioners 112
generalized anxiety disorder see GAD
generational patterns 139
genetics 22, 23
   and personality 150
   and relationships 154, 159
genocide 208, 210, 211, 212, 213
Genovese, Kitty 223
gestalt psychology 13, **18**
gestalt therapy **133**
glutamate 28
goals
   achievable 134
   self-actualization 152–153
   setting 100–181, 236
   SMART 240
   workplace 177, 180–181
Gottman, John 154, 164
government 167
GPs 112, 113
grandiose delusions 74
Greeks, ancient 12
grimacing 73
groaning, sleep-related 98
grooming 223
group dynamics 138, 139, 182, 184, 208
group identity 146
group therapies **117**
Groupthink **183**, **208**
growth, personal 130, 132
   barriers to 153
guilt 38, 45, 60, 82, 84, 92, 94, 109, 127, 132,
       133, 148
   lack of 104

H

hackers 195
hair-pulling disorders **60**
Hall, Edward T. 220
hallucinations 42, 70, 72, 74, 78, 99
Harlow, Harry 154
harm, fear of causing 56, 58
Hatfield, Elaine 161
head injuries 78, 200
headaches 52, 54, 63, 78, 83, 143
health
   physical and psychological **114–115**
   preoccupation with 52, 61, 108–109
   and therapy **112–113**
health psychologists 13, **112**, 114–115
heart rate, increased 29, 32, 46, 47, 48, 63
hemispheres, cerebral **24**, 25, 26
HFA see high functioning autism
HFE psychology 13, **188–193**

engineering displays **190–191**
   human error and prevention **192–193**
hierarchies 208, 212
high functioning autism (HFA) 69
hippocampus 26, 31, 32, 62
history of psychology **12–13**
histrionic PD **105**
Hitler, Adolf 210
HIV 75
hoarding disorder **58**
hobbies 146
holistic therapy 135
Holocaust 211, 212
homelessness 218, 219
hormones 16, 18, 23, 28, 159
hospitals 188, 192
House, Robert 184
Hull's Drive Theory 241
human error 189, 190, **192–193**
human factors and engineering see HFE
       psychology
humanism 13, **18–19**, 130
humanistic theory 151
humanistic therapies 117, **130–137**
humanitarian work psychology movement
       177
Huntington's disease 100
hyperactive delirium 79
hyperactivity 66
hypersomnolence 98–99
hyperventilation 46
hypnotherapy **136**
hypoactive delirium 79
hypochondria **61**
hypomania 40, 44
hypothalamus 26, 32, 62

I

id 14–15
ideal self 18–19
ideas, and culture 217
identity
   alteration 86–87
   formation of **148–149**
   individual **146–147**
   personality **150–151**
identity status theory 149
illness anxiety disorder **61**
immune system 80, 159
improvements, suggesting 187
impulse-control disorders 60, **82**, 83, 84,
       85
impulsivity 64, 65, 66, 67
in-group/out-group mentality 210–211, 212
inattentiveness 66, 67
incentive schemes 67
incoherence 79
incompetence 200

individual
  and community 216–217
  empowerment 218–219
individualism 19
industrial psychology 12, 166, **177**
inferiority complex 15
infertility 90
infographics 230
information processing **20–21**, 22
insanity 200
insomnia 98–99
institutions, interactions with 217
instructions, clear 67
interaction 216–217
interdependence 215
interests, obsessive 69
intermittent explosive disorder 82
interpersonal effectiveness 126
interviews
  criminal investigations **196–197**
  workplace 176, **179**
intimacy, and love 158
intimate space 220
intrinsic motivation 240
introverts 120, 178
intrusive thoughts 56, 57, 84
IQ 200, 246
irrational thoughts and behavior
      122–123
irritability 44
Islamic scholars 12
isolation 52, 53, 58, 92, 97, 137
  existential and attendant 133

J

Janis, Irving 208
jealous delusions 75
job analysis 178
judgment 20
  impaired 77, 78
Jung, Carl 13, 15, 120, 178
Jungian therapy **120**
juries 200, 201

K

kaizen 187
Kapferer, Jean-Noel 232
Kelly, James 215
Kennedy, John F. 208
Kerckhoff, Alan 161
King, Martin Luther, Jr. 185
kleptomania **84**
Knapp, Mark 162–163
knowledge, acquisition of 168–169
Kolb, David 168
Koro (genital retraction syndrome) **108–109**

L

language
  development 17
  problems with 25, 68, 76
language disorder 96, **97**
language therapy 55
leadership
  and change 187
  political 207
  qualities of great **184**
  transformational **185**
  in workplace 177, 183, **184–185**
learning 20
  difficulties 65, 97, **174–175**
  educational theory **166–169**
  goals 172
  phases of 239
  plateau 238–239
  pyramid 172
  strategies to improve 166–167
legal system
  cognitive psychology 21
  forensic psychology 194
lethargy 43, 71, 79, 80, 93
Levinson, Anne 163
Lewy bodies, dementia with 76
lie detectors 196
life experiences, and personality 150
lifestyle management 41, 42, 44, 45, 50, 58
limbic system 26, 32–33, 143
listening, active and reactive 164
Locke, Edwin 180
logic 20, 24, 128, 168, 247
loneliness 38, 137
long-term memory 30, 31
love **155**
  and dating **160–161**
  needs 152–153
  romantic attachments **157**
  science of **158–159**
lupus 75
lust 159

M

machines, effective **190–191**
McMillan, David W. 216
malaria 75
malingering 200
mania 40–41, 44, 72
mannerism 73
Marcia, James 149
marginalization 211, 214, 218
marketing
  customer profiling **227**
  engagement 233
  golden rules of **228**

neuromarketing **230**
masks 202
Maslow, Abraham 13, 18, 150, 153
massage 135
mastery goals 172
meaninglessness 133
media
  and consumer behavior 226, 227, 230, 231,
      232, 233, 234
  social media 147, 207
  and voting behavior **207**
medication 117, **142–143**
melatonin 45, 99
memes 231
memory 20, 21, **30–31**
  buried memories 118
  dissociative amnesia **89**
  and engineering display 190, 191
  fallibility 196
  lapses 192
  problems 71, 77, 78, 79, 86
mental health
  and criminal behavior 199
  and physical health **114–115**
  rating **115**
mental model 190, 191
Mere Exposure Effect 158
meridians 135
mesolimbic brain area 230
methodological behaviorism 16
Milgram, Stanley 208
military combat 62, 78
mindfulness 48, 126, **129**
mistakes 192–193
mixed dementia 76
moment, living in the 153
money worries 38, 41, 52, 83
monoism 25
mood
  disorders **38–45**
  low 38, 42, 59, 94
  neurotransmitters and 29
  swings 40–41, 42, 63, 72, 79
mood stabilizers 41, 142–143
motivation
  education 166, 168, 169, 172, 173, 175
  lack of 71
  self-actualization **152–153**
  sports **240–241**
  workplace 176, **180**
motor cortex 27
motor disorders **100–101**
motor responses, bizarre 68
motor skills 69, 76
motor tics 100, 101
multiple personality disorder
      see DID
multiple sclerosis 75
Munchausen's syndrome **108–109**
muscles, tics 100, 102

muscular dystrophy 68
musculoskeletal system 115
music, as therapy 137
mutism
  catatonia 73
  selective **55**
myelin 169
Myers-Briggs Type Indicator (MBTI) 178

N

N-REM (Non-Rapid Eye Movement) sleep 98
narcissistic PD **105**
narcolepsy 98–99
National Training Laboratories Institute
  172
nationalism 207, **210–213**
natural environment phobias 49
natural selection 22, 150
nature versus nurture 22, 151
needs
  five basic 132
  need hierarchy theories 152–153, 180
negative thoughts 50, 51, 52, 53, 59, 64, 115,
  122, 123, 124, 125, 126, 127, 133, 135,
  236
negativism 73
neighbor, as "other" 211
Neo-Freudians 15
nervous system 23, 115
neural pathways 28, 30, 137
neurochemicals, performance-enhancing
  243
neurocognitive disorders **76–79**
neurodevelopmental disorders **56–71**
neurons 28, 30, 168, 169
neuropsychology 24
neuroscience 24, 168–169
  consumer **230–231**
neuroticism 151
neurotransmitters **28–29**, 40, 143, 159
neutral stimuli 16, 124
night terrors 98, 99
night-eating disorder 95
nightmares 62, 98
norepinephrine 29, 40, 66, 143, 243
norms 147, 214, 215
nuclear power 188, 192
nurses, psychiatric 112
nutrient deficiency 95

O

obedience 208
object relations **121**
obsessive compulsive disorder *see* OCD
obsessive compulsive PD 106, **107**
occipital lobe 26, 27

OCD (obsessive compulsive disorder) 48,
  56–57, 58, 59, 60, 100, 107, 124
offenders
  assessment of 195
  in prisons 202–203
  profiling 198
  trials 200–201
olfactory bulb 26
online communities **223**
open skills 238
open-ended questions 131, 196
openness 151
operant conditioning **17**, 125
orbital frontal cortex 27
organizational psychology 12, 166, **177**
organizational skills, poor 67
organizations
  culture of **186**
  empowerment 218–219
  see also workplace
out-group discrimination 210–212
oxytocin 137, 159

P

PACE (playful, accepting, curious,
  empathetic) 141
palilalia 101
palpitations 52
panic attacks 46, 48, 50, 51, 54, 62, 63, 86
panic disorder **46–47**
paranoia 42, 70
paranoid PD 102, **103**
paranoid schizophrenia 70
paraphilic disorders **108–109**
parasomnia 98–99
parents
  bonding 65
  and child development 17
  overprotective 54
  training and support 54
parietal lobe 26, 27
Parkinson's disease 22, 75, 76, 78, 109
participative leadership 185
party affiliations 206–207
passion 158
path-goal theory 184–185
Pavlov's dogs 16
PD (personality disorders) 80, **102–107**
  cluster A: odd/eccentric **102–103**
  cluster B: dramatic/emotional/erratic
    104–105
  cluster C: anxious/fearful **106–107**
peak experience 153
peer group 146
perception 18–19
  engineering displays 190–191
  impaired sensory and visual 69
perfectionism 52, 69, 107

performance anxiety **244–245**
performance appraisal **181**
performance goals 172
perinatal mental illness **42–43**
PERMA model 129
persecutory delusions 75
person-centered therapy 18, **132**
personal prevention plans 203
personal space 220, 221
personality **150–151**
  brand 232–233
  changes 40, 86
  development of 14–15
  disorders *see* PD
  and job suitability 170
  questionnaires 246, **247**
persuasion 228–229
phishers 195
phobias **48–51**
physical examination 37
physiological factors, criminal behavior 199
physiological needs 152–153
Piaget, Joan 13, 166, 168–169
pica 95
Pick's disease 76
pleasure principle 15
police force 194, **196–199**
political identity 147
political psychology 13, **204–213**
  nationalism **210–213**
  obedience and decision-making **208–209**
  voting behavior **206–207**
polygraphs 196
population density 220, 221
positive affirmations 134, 135
positive psychology **129**
post-concussion syndrome *see* CTE
post-traumatic stress disorder *see* PTSD
postpartum depression (PPD) (postnatal
  depression) 42–43
postpartum psychosis 42
posturing 73
potential, realizing 131, 152–153
poverty 177
PPD *see* postpartum depression
practice
  and learning 168, 169, 170, 171, 172
  and sports 238, 239
preconscious mind 14–15
prefrontal cortex 62, 242
pregnancy 38, 42, 70
  anorexia and 90
  nutrition in 96
  pica 95
prejudice 212
premature birth 66, 68
prices, consumers and 225, 228, 230
primary visual cortex 27
prisons 151, 195, **202–203**, 208
problem-solving 76, 125, 132, 168

process loss 182
promotions 225, 228
proportion 231
Proshansky, Harold 220
proxemics 220
psychiatrists 112
psychoanalysis 13, 14, 15, 116, **119**, 130
psychoanalytical theory **14–15**
psychodynamic theory 150
psychodynamic therapies 39, 116, **118–121**
psychoeducation 55, **113**, 127
psychological behaviorism 17
psychological tests 37, 179
psychology/psychologists
    community **214–223**
    consumer **224–235**
    educational **166–175**
    forensic **194–203**
    HFE **188–193**
    industrial/organizational **176–187**
    political **204–213**
    relationship **154–165**
    roles and types **112–113**
    and self-identity **146–153**
    sports **236–247**
psychometric tests 13, **246–247**
psychomotor functioning 73
psychopathic behavior 199
psychopathy **104**
psychosexual stages 14–15
psychosurgery 143
psychotherapies **116–117**
psychotic disorders 58, **70–75**, 85
psychotic symptoms 39, 70, 71, 72, 103, 199
PTSD (post-traumatic stress disorder) 48,
    62, 63, 127, 136, 222
public opinion 205
public space 220, 222
punishment 17
purging disorder 95
purpose, sense of 153
pyromania **85**

Q

questionnaires 115

R

Race, Phil 168
racism 207, 210, 212
radical behaviorism 17
rational emotive behavior therapy see REBT
rationalization 118
reaction formation 118
reactive attachment disorder **65**
reactive listening 164
realistic group conflict theory 211

reality orientation therapy 70
reality therapy **132**
reasoning 20
reassurance, asking for 57
REBT (rational emotive behavior therapy)
    127
receptors 27, 32, 143
reciprocity 229
recommendations, personal 224
recruitment 176, **178–179**
rehabilitation 115
    of offenders 195, 202–203
reinforcement 17
reinforcement theory 180
relational ethics 141
relationships
    balancing 138
    building/breakdown 155, **162–165**
    dating **160–161**
    issues 38, 41, 65, 78, 132
    psychology of attachment **156–157**
    psychology of **154–165**
    science of love **158–159**
    stages of **162–165**
religion
    and discrimination 212
    and identity 146
REM (Rapid Eye Movement) sleep 98, 99,
    136
repetitive behavior 60, 68, 97
representativeness heuristic 204
repression 15, 118, 119
reproductive system 115
resistance analysis 118, 119
resources, shared 215
respect 137, 152, 153, 165
respiratory system 115
responsibility
    accepting 133
    diffusion of 223
    and freedom 133
    mutual 141
    personal 203
restless leg syndrome 98, 99
restlessness 52, 66, 73, 79, 99
reviews, consumer 224
risky behavior 81
rituals 56, 57
    tidying or ordering 68
road traffic 192, 193
    accidents 63
Rogers, Carl 13, 18, 131
role play 133
roles, and identity 147
romantic attachments 157, 158–159
routines
    developing 236
    setting predictable 67
Rubin Vase illusion 18

rule-breaking 193
rumination disorder 95
Rusbult, Caryl 158–159, 161

S

SAD (seasonal affective disorder) **45**
sadness 33, 38, 41, 64, 73, 94, 133
safety 152–153, 188, 189, **192–193**
    in the community **222–223**
scapegoats 211
scarcity 229
SCD see social communication disorder
schema theory 205
schizoaffective disorder **72**
schizoid PD 102, **103**
schizophrenia 22, **70–71**, 72, 75, 80, 102, 142
schizotypal PD 102, **103**
school 167
    problems at 64
    see also education
Schrenck-Notzing, Albert von 195
Search Engine Optimization (SEO) 228
seasonal affective disorder see SAD
security, sense of 154, 156
security cameras 222, 223
selective mutism **55**
self, differentiation of 139
self-acceptance 130–131, 132, 137
self-actualization 19, 131, 132, 146, **152–153**
self-awareness 123, 130–131, 133, 134
    private and public 147
self-belief 132, 245
self-confidence 245
self-consciousness 53, 244
self-disclosure 161, 164
self-efficacy 172
self-efficacy theory 180
self-esteem 132, 137, 147
    low 38, 42, 65, 94
self-fulfillment 130–131
self-harm 38, 42
self-help 53
self-help groups 50, **117**
self-identity, psychology of **146–153**
self-image 18–19, 232
    negative 59, 92
self-improvement 131
self psychology **121**
self-realization 18
self-talk 236, 245
self-worth 18–19
Seligman, Martin 129
sensations
    feeling 70, 74
    and memory 30
senses 20
sensory cortex 27, 32
sensory skills 69

sentencing 201
sentimental items 58
separation anxiety disorder **54**
serotonin 29, 40, 45, 70, 143, 159, 243
sex
   addiction 82
   healthy 203
sexual attraction 159
sexual dysfunction **108–109**
sexual selection 150
sexuality, Freud's theories of 14–15
shapes, geometric 231
shopping
   shopping addiction 82
   see also consumer psychology
short-term memory 30, 31
side effects, drugs 143
Simon, Théodore 246
SIT (stress inoculation therapy) **128**
situation awareness 189
situational phobias 49
situationism 209
skills, improving sports **238–239**
skin-picking disorders **60**
Skinner, B.F. 17
skull, blows to 78
sleep
   disorders **98–99**
   disturbance 42, 54, 63, 64, 66, 68, 79
   excess 45
   insomnia 52, 54, 62
   and learning 169
sleep aggression 98
sleep apnea 98
sleep paralysis 98, 99
sleeping drugs 142–143
sleepwalking 98, 99
SMART goals 240
smell, sense of 159
social anxiety disorder **53**, 59
social circumstance, and criminal behavior
   199
social communication disorder (SCD) 96, **97**
social cues 223
social division 211
social dominance theory 211
social exclusions 212
social fears 52
social hierarchy 212
social identity 146
social identity theory 211
social impairment 81
social interaction 220
   difficulties with 65, 68, 69, 77
social justice 218
social learning 150
Social Learning Theory **169**
social loafing **241**
social media 147, 207, 226, 227, 230, 231,
   233

social organization 188
social space 220, 221
social workers 112
solution-focused brief therapy **134**
somatic delusions 74
somatic symptom disorder 61, **108–109**
somatic therapies **135**
sound
   psychology of 190
   sensitivity to 69
space 220
speech
   difficulties 68, 77, 96–97
   selective mutism 55
speech therapy 55, 96
speech-sound disorder 96, **97**
Sperry, Roger 25
sports
   CTE 78
   getting in the zone **242–243**
   improving skills **238–239**
   keeping motivated **240–241**
   performance anxiety **244–245**
   psychology of **236–245**
Spreng, Nathan 168
SSRIs (selective serotonin reuptake
   inhibitors) 46, 69, 74, 84, 142
Staats, Arthur W. 17
"stage fright" 244
stalkers, celebrity **235**
Stanford prison experiment **151**, 202, 209
status 146
stealing 84
stereotyping 210
stereotypy 73
Sternberg, Robert 158
stimulants 142–143
stimulus-response 16
stonewalling 165
strategic family therapy **140**
streptococcal bacteria 101
stress 38, 41, 55, 189
   adjustment disorder **64**
   affect on body **115**
   ASR **63**
   dissociative disorders 88, 89
   performance anxiety 244
   PTSD **62**
stress inoculation therapy see SIT
students, teaching methods 172–173
stupor 73
stuttering 96, 97
subconscious 14, 15, 118
subculture 146
substance use disorder **80–81**, 102
suicide
   in prison 202
   suicidal thoughts 38, 73, 86
sunlight levels 45
superego 14–15

supplementary motor cortex 27
support groups 46
supportive leadership 185
surprise 33
survival reactions 62
sustainability 177
symmetry
   consumer neuroscience 231
   fear related to 56
synaptic transmission 28
syphilis 75
systemic therapies 13, 117, **138–141**
systems theory 138

T

Tai Chi 135
Taijin Kyofusho **108–109**
tapping points 135
teaching
   education psychology 166–167
   psychology of **172–173**
   see also education
team building
   sport 237
   workplace 182–183
team development 177, **182–183**
team motivation **241**
teamwork
   and flow **243**
   workplace 189
technology, psychology and **188–193**
teenagers 22, 148–149
temper tantrums 44
tempo-parietal junction 27
temporal lobe 26, 27
tension
   muscle 100, 244
   release of negative 135
Terman, Lewis 13, 246
terrorism 212, **213**
testosterone 159
thalamus 26, 30, 32
therapy
   and health **112–113**
   role of **116–117**
third wave CBT **126**
threat, perceived 56
thyroid, overactive 46
tic disorders 66, **100–101**
TMS (transcranial magnetic stimulation)
   142, 143
top-down profiling 198
Tourette's syndrome 66, **101**
traffic psychology **193**
training 188
trait theory 150, 151
traits, human 188
transactional analysis **121**

transcranial magnetic stimulation *see* TMS
trauma 46, 62, 78, 86, 88, 89, 127, 136
  and physiological problems 135
trauma- and stress-related disorders **62–65**
trials 200–201
trichotillomania **60**
trolling 223
Tuckman, Bruce 182
Tulving, Endel 30
twins 22, 23, 151

U

unconscious mind 14–15, 150
  emotional response 32–33
  psychodynamic therapies 118–121
unemployment 38, 177
unethical behavior 208–209
unresponsiveness 73
urban communities **220–221**

V

valence 227
values 147, 215
vascular dementia 76
vasopressin 159
ventromedial prefrontal cortex 230
verbal abuse 212
verbal tics 100, 101
victimology **203**
victims, empathy for 202, 203
video surveillance 223
videos 230

violence
  cycle of **199**
  political 205, 210, 213
visual responses
  consumers 230–231
  displays 190–191
visualization 129, 133, 134, 169, 236
voices, hearing 70, 86
volume control, lack of 66
vomiting 92, 95
voting behavior 205, **206–207**

W

walking, mindful 129
war, nationalism and 210
war zones 192
Watson, John 13, 16
waxy flexibility 73
weight
  eating disorders **90–94**
  gain 80
well-being
  community 215, 217, **219**
  emotional 203
Wernicke's area 25, 27
willpower, lack of 71
winter depression 45
withdrawal 71
witnesses
  of crime 222–223
  in criminal investigations 194, 196, 197
  expert 195, **201**
word association 120
work issues 38, 41

work samples 179, 247
workload 189
workplace, psychology in **176–187**
  identity 147
  leadership **184–185**
  managing talent **180–181**
  organizational culture and change **186–187**
  psychometric tests **246–247**
  recruitment **178–179**
  safety 188
  team development **182–183**
World Health Organization 39
worries 38, 50, 52, 53, 54, 55, 59, 61, 90, 99, 106

X

xenophobia 212

Y

yoga 135

Z

Zajonc, Robert 158
Zimbardo, Philip 202, 208, 209
Zimmerman, Marc 218

Acknowledgments

Dorling Kindersley would like to thank Kathryn Hill, Natasha Khan, and Andy Szudek for editorial assistance; Alexandra Beeden for proofreading; and Helen Peters for indexing.

The publisher would like to thank the following for their kind permission to reproduce their photographs:

(Key: a-above; b-below/bottom; c-centre; f-far; l-left; r-right; t-top)

33 Alamy Stock Photo: David Wall (bc). **39 Alamy Stock Photo:** Anna Berkut (r). **48 Alamy Stock Photo:** RooM the Agency (cra). **51 Alamy Stock Photo:** Chris Putnam (b). **57**

Getty Images: Mike Kemp (br). **63 iStockphoto.com:** PeopleImages (crb). **77 Getty Images:** danm (crb). **93 Alamy Stock Photo:** dpa picture alliance (r). **103 Alamy Stock Photo:** StockPhotosArt - Emotions (crb). **117 Alamy Stock Photo:** BSIP SA (cra). **121 iStockphoto.com:** Antonio Carlos Bezerra (cra). **136 Alamy Stock Photo:** Phanie (cl). **143 iStockphoto.com:** artisteer (tr). **154 iStockphoto.com:** Ales-A (crb). **159 iStockphoto.com:** ANZAV (crb). **180 Alamy Stock Photo:** Drepicter (ca). **189 iStockphoto.com:** Eraxion (cr). **193 iStockphoto.com:** DKart (cra). **196 Alamy Stock Photo:** Allan Swart (cr). **202 iStockphoto.com:** PattieS (ca). **217 Getty**

Images: Plume Creative (br). **221 iStockphoto.com:** LanceB (b). **243 Alamy Stock Photo:** moodboard (br)

Cover images: Front: 123RF.com: anthonycz cla, Chi Chiu Tse ca/ (Bottle), kotoffei cla/ (Capsules), Vadym Malyshevskyi cb/ (Brain), nad1992 cl, nikolae c, Supanut Piyakanont cra, cb, Igor Serdiuk cla/ (Spider), Marina Zlochin bc; **Dreamstime.com:** Amornme ca, Furtaev bl, Surachat Khongkhut crb, Dmitrii Starkov tr/ (cloud), Vectortatu tr

All other images © Dorling Kindersley
For further information see:
www.dkimages.com